# FINDING SELF

*Healing the Past to Unveil
Your Inner Strength*

TRAUMA. RECOVERY. FORGIVENESS.

**GAYNELLE GOOCH**

ISBN: 979-8-9892746-7-3 (Paperback)

Written by Gaynelle Gooch
Cover design by Jody Colvard
Cover art by Stan Sours
stansours53@gmail.com
First printing edition 2025

FMG Press
FMGPress.com

# Dedication

This book is dedicated to my sons,
Abram and Noel, and to my husband, Jerry.
I treasure their unconditional love and support.

*One of the most important things human beings need in life is to know that they are not alone. Early childhood trauma can isolate an individual which only fosters a sense of aloneness and pain. Gaynelle presents her life story in this book because she has learned how to make meaning of the events of her life and because she desires that others would not feel alone in their life journeys. Through faith, psychology, and positive relationships, Gaynelle is more than an overcomer—she is an inspiration!*

— The Reverend Shannon Coon, Pastor of Adult Ministries, St. Andrew's Presbyterian Church, Newport Beach, California

# Contents

# Introduction

To merely survive is a conglomerate of tragedy. Finding meaning, and a path toward vigorous flourishing, is a journey through a labyrinth of emotional mysteries. I survived sexual, emotional, and mental damage that infiltrated my being and radically shaped my personality. A life of love and joy was passing me by, but I was determined not to let that happen. I was desperate to find a way to trust myself, to lessen my anxiety, and to establish and enjoy relationships. I longed to have healthy feelings, clear thinking, and to love and be loved. I longed to *thrive*. Was there a door to open where I might find peace and harmony in my mind and soul? I tethered myself to a faint hope and held on.

My goal is to share my traumatic experiences and relate my story of healing, relapse, and the recalibration of my emotional responses. I found a way through my torment by training my over-stimulated arousal system and reprogramming my body and mind into a calmer state, using psychology and brain science. Both are significant tools in explaining the effects of trauma and illuminating a path to healing. I hope that this book will inspire you to find your path out of the shadows and experience the joy of living a positive and meaningful life.

## CHAPTER 1

# Setting the Scene

*An unlearned carpenter of my acquaintance once said in my hearing: "There is very little difference between one man and another, but what there is, is very important."*

WILLIAM JAMES

My grandfather locked my tiny wrist in his giant hand and dragged me into the bathroom. I saw my three goldfish swimming in the toilet bowl. "You didn't change your pajamas when I told you to!" My fish swirled and disappeared. Frantic, helpless to save them, I shrieked and jumped up and down. I tried to imagine what happened to them, but had no idea where the fish went, only that they were gone forever. When I screamed, Granny came running. She looked into my pleading eyes, but she froze, knowing it was impossible to cross her husband. My Mom and Dad were gone for a week, and my dad's parents were in charge of my two sisters and me.

Many years later, as an adult, I visited my older sister, Peggy, at her home in Northern California. By this time, our father, at eighty-six, had driven over five hundred miles to join us there. One morning Peggy placed bowls of blueberries and cereal at each place setting. My father stepped over, eyed the breakfast table, and before he could utter a word, in perfect unison, Peggy and I piped up, "Do you want a big spoon or a little spoon?" We turned toward each other and hooted with laughter.

"What's so funny? Let me in on the secret," Dad said. We couldn't tell him, of course. Why did we need to ask such a ridiculous question? Well, if a little spoon had been on the table, my father would have asked for a big one. If a soup spoon was placed beside the bowl, he would have demanded a teaspoon. To avoid conflict and the extra steps to comply with his wishes, we learned to ask him for exactly what he wanted. In our growing up years, being alert and specific in our house was critical to self-preservation. The good news is that we chuckled.

The next day the three of us piled into dad's Volkswagen Jetta, Peggy next to him up front. She placed her purse on the floor against the console, and Dad said, "That's no place for your purse! Put it in the back." My sister, the ever-dutiful daughter, tossed it on the back seat beside me. The next day, we three popped into his car and Peggy put her purse in the back seat. Seemingly dismayed, Dad barked, "That's no place for your purse. It should be in the front with you!"

What was right yesterday is wrong today. This is what I call 'make-wrong.' Our dad was an authority figure, and it seemed he was out to dismantle our confidence and undermine our ability to make decisions, even simple ones. Daily choices, such as what kind of spoon should be on the table, or where to place a purse, kept us hypervigilant.

Dad's eyes were in constant surveillance, looking for the opportunity to remind us that he was the master and we were subservient. This daily vigilance in our home became a habit, and these habits became ingrained and played out in our adult lives.

Making another person wrong, identifying another's shortcomings, and indulging in put-down humor are shortcuts to self-aggrandizement. This kind of behavior is always at the expense of the other. It's not difficult to make another person feel small or doubt oneself; it's manipulation. This was the daily reality with our father.

When Peggy was two years old, she and my mom moved in with my father's parents while my dad served in Japan during WWII. Dad was gone for two years, and those two years were traumatic and injurious for her.

She related this story to me: "When I was four, I was excited about Dad's homecoming, because I was hoping to be rescued from our grandfather." As she recounted this story, her voice softened, and tears welled in her eyes. "Every morning, I would look forward to picking a flower for Dad's lapel. When I handed him a carnation, he was pleased. But one time he scolded me about the flower I had chosen. He bellowed and pointed to a different flower."

"But Daddy, I thought you meant this one!"

"Don't you defy me!"

Peggy's voice intensified with anguish and disbelief, "I didn't even know the word 'defy,' but somehow I knew exactly what it meant. Dad whipped off his belt, pulled my underwear down, and spanked me. He grabbed hold of my ear and dragged me to my room. I was grounded for a week. That was when I knew he was going to be just like Grandpa."

Later, as an adult, Peggy told me that she and her therapist counted the weeks she was grounded while living with dad's parents. Between the ages of two and four, she was grounded, alone in her bedroom, for a total of nine months. During those years, she missed language development, social stimulation, and attention and affirmation from the significant adults in her life.

When I was three, I played ball on the front lawn with my dad. One day, from the corner of my eye, I saw Peggy hurrying home from her friend's house down the street.

Dad ran to her as if it were an emergency, yelling, "You're late! You are supposed to be home by the time the streetlights come on." Clamping down on her ear, he pulled her across the lawn toward the house.

"But Daddy, I was inside playing and couldn't see the streetlights," Peggy protested. "I came home as soon as I saw it was getting dark. I glanced at the streetlights and noticed that they were on."

Dad marched her into the house, towing her by the ear. He dragged her up the front porch steps, saying gruffly, "You're grounded for a week." I shudder, remembering these experiences, but they were normal for me to watch, and for Peggy to endure. I feared my father and became hypervigilant about meeting his expectations so I would not get punished. Peggy told me more stories about Dad. "He marked a line on the sidewalk to show me how far I was allowed to ride my tricycle. I rode over the line to turn around, and Dad yanked me off my trike and took off his belt." She demonstrated the action of unbuckling his belt and pulling it outward. "He pulled my panties down and spanked me outside in front of the neighborhood! I was sent to my room."

Peggy seemed relieved to share her terrifying childhood experiences with me. She continued, "And then one day I was turning the jump rope with friends in the front yard and accidentally hit the jumper's leg with the rope." I didn't want to hear what happened next, but it was predictable: she was admonished and quarantined in her room. The slightest mistake was serious and punishable.

Her stories reminded me of things that happened to me. When I was three, Dad spanked me at dinner several nights because he assumed I spilled my milk on purpose. I developed performance anxiety and stopped drinking milk, which to this day upsets my stomach. I crept on tiptoe to the bathroom at night, terrified I'd wake my father. I remember wishing he wouldn't come home at night.

When I was six, I got up one morning and noticed Peggy wasn't in her bed. I was scared something had happened to her in the night and ran to find Mom. "She is okay. She's staying at a friend's house for a few days."

My mind jumped back to Dad's anger toward Peggy the night before, "You get out of this house and never come back!"

Peggy told me years later that when these episodes occurred, Mom called her friends and arranged a place for her to stay for a few days. I lived in fear that I would be kicked out of the house too. When Dad was around, I pretended to like him, though I didn't trust him. I knew I needed him, and I sought his love.

Mom dutifully tended to the needs of the household—children, meals, laundry, cleaning, and sewing—but she was obsessive-compulsive. We had to keep everything in the house in perfect order: no lint on the carpets, an immaculate kitchen with sparkling linoleum, and bathrooms scrubbed twice a week. Perhaps because of the helplessness Mom experienced in her childhood, the perfection of the house gave her a feeling of worth and allowed for something she could control. However, in the interest of maintaining her standards, she controlled me. Accomplishments mattered more than developing our sense of self. "We don't want you children to be selfish or boastful!" The need to be good enough plagued everyone in our family.

As sisters, we each had a different relationship with our mother. Peggy felt that Mom saved her when they lived with dad's parents, and though she spent a lot of time alone, Mom came into her room for an hour each night before bed. Diane was three years younger than me and ten years younger than Peggy. By the time Diane was six years old, my parents were too busy with the social life of golf and bridge to care for her. Inevitably, she was neglected, and this resulted in long-term damaging effects.

When I was young, my parents gave me chores, but my efforts seemed not good enough. One chore was to sweep a long corner-lot sidewalk after Peggy mowed the lawn. Whenever I missed any grass, Dad rushed over, pointing at the sidewalk, "You can't even sweep the sidewalk right! Sweep that grass off now!" I was four years old! Once I missed a single weed in a small garden, "Do you see that weed? You missed it. That won't do. Go to your room while we eat lunch."

For my sixth birthday, I was given a blue bike. I was so happy and rode it all over the neighborhood. "Now be careful with that bike, Gaynelle, because if you leave it on the front porch, it could get stolen," my dad warned. One day I went into the house to get a drink of water and something to eat. When I came out, my bike was gone. Guilty and devastated, my dad told me, "I warned you. There are thieves, and you must take care of your things!" So my bike was gone. A few days later I was playing in the backyard, and my dad disappeared into the bushes. He walked out with my bike on his shoulders. "I wanted to teach you a lesson!" Yes, I learned a lesson, all right: never trust this man, he is a liar.

My sisters were quieter than I was. I was rambunctious, always on the move. I loved to climb trees, hide in the bushes at the park, play on the monkey bars, and swing as high as I could, while my sisters quietly read books or played in their rooms. I noticed that Mom tussled their hair and felt close to them, but she seemed estranged from me. Usually, she spoke to me only to tell me to do something. No hugs, stories, or words like "I love you." I can't recall an embrace or show of affection other than on one occasion when my cousin and I refused to go to sleep, and she rubbed my back to calm me. It felt unfamiliar but oh, so good. I wished she'd done that more than once in my life. She often seemed frustrated with me, glared at me, and used an impatient voice.

For a short while she read bedtime stories to me, and I enjoyed her rare attention, staying awake to listen. But then she scolded me, "Why aren't you asleep yet? I read to you, so you'd fall asleep!" Soon she stopped reading to me altogether. She had no idea that I stayed awake because I enjoyed the stories and her presence. She made me feel that I was a nuisance and that being with me was a waste of time.

My childhood memories are laced with fear, guilt, and self-condemnation. My parents perceived me as disobedient, anti-social, non-responsive, and generally difficult. My dad thought I intentionally refused to do what I was told, and my mother was ashamed of me. My perception of myself, stemming from the feedback I got, was distinctly negative. I believed there was something wrong with me; obviously I was different, but in a negative way. Yet somewhere in the depths of my soul, I didn't believe I was bad. I was trying so very hard, trying to do it right, whatever it was. My interpretation of their input was that I was never *'good enough.'*

Sometimes when my parents criticized me, I told them, "I'm doing the best I can." "Well, your best isn't good enough," Dad retorted. "Do it right. Do it right the first time or you're just wasting your time."

I didn't give up trying to please them. *I can do it. I'll show them. I'll get better.* Then an inner voice, the one that mimicked my dad's, shouted back at me, "Who do you think you are, anyway?" I vacillated between pep talks to myself and harsh self-condemnation. This constant rehash of conflicting thoughts and feelings plagued me for years and wore me out.

I became an overachiever, ensuring that I was always busy, focusing on doing more and giving more. Later in life, after I started teaching, I tutored children even when I had little time and was already weary from full-time work. My tendency to volunteer too often meant I did more than I could manage, at the cost of losing sleep. I had no healthy sense of boundaries and spent hours helping casual acquaintances while ignoring my own well-being. I wanted to prove to myself and others that I was valuable, that I was *enough*.

Stress from overdoing intensified my stress and anxiety because I neglected my own needs. This affected my ability to think clearly and make good decisions. I felt vulnerable, and I struggled to make sense of an array of unmanageable emotions. As a child, my strategies were limited.

When I was thirteen, I was inspired by the theme of love triumphing over selfishness. I watched *Beauty and the Beast*, and I surmised that a woman's sacrificial love has the power to change a negative, ego-centered man. Love could transform a beast.

The gift of love is a common theme across cultures. I followed Belle's beautiful example, believing my love and sacrifice would bring me a reward like hers, that is, the love of a 'prince,' or perhaps my father.

If the beast would not respond to my love, then it had to be me who was not loving enough. This reasoning bolstered my already well-defined script of trying, failing, blaming myself, and then trying harder. Yet how powerful and good I would feel about myself if my love was responsible for the desired change in the beast! *Keep giving and loving more*. I waited for the reward that Belle earned by her sacrifice, not realizing that my ideal came from a fairy tale.

I didn't recognize the fallacy of my strategy until I was fifty-three and had come to understand something of the nature of God. With the help of counseling and introspection, I accepted that love cannot be earned. It is not my responsibility to change anyone, and it never has been. That is God's job. God's love. It takes a willing person to be open to receiving this divine love. It is His love and grace that produces change, not mine. God's plan for me was to learn my value, and with strength from within, learn that I am *good enough*.

In a poem called *Two Sisters*, Max Lucado personifies pride and shame. "They appear so different. Pride puffs out her chest. Shame hangs her head." These emotions have the same origin and impact, and they hinder a person from having a healthy connection with God.[1] We lose touch with our core being and seek something to fill in the gap. In my case, it was a swing between pride and shame.

I believed the lie that love might ricochet back to me through giving and sacrificing. The tiniest indication of rejection left me feeling ashamed, striving harder to earn acceptance. This was a cover-up because secretly, I feared that my shame would be visible. Living between the twin sisters of pride and shame daily resulted in turbulence and ambiguity. I found myself in tears often, crying at night to God. It seemed my love didn't change my father, and I was ashamed that I was even trying. *Dear God, please help my life to change. I need help.*

*Even if no one loves me, I think God will.* If I could love my dad more, if I could satisfy my mom and be a better daughter, would they acknowledge me? *Is it possible for them to see my worth? Could my parents ever see how hard I tried to please them?*

*Maybe I should just die.*

Something had to change. I needed to find love somewhere. There had to be a way to freedom from this terrible conflict. *It doesn't make sense to be on this gift-giving earth, filled with the beauty of nature, and at the same time doubt that I should be alive on the planet. I need a change.*

Somehow, I knew God would help me and show me my value. I knew I was worth loving because *something bigger,* beyond myself, was at work.

*The LORD will guide you always; he will satisfy your needs in a sun-scorched land and will strengthen your frame. You will be like a well-watered garden, like a spring whose waters never fail."* Isaiah 58:11

## CHAPTER 2

# The Man Who Split Time

*A rather absentminded professor used to come up*
*from Winston-Salem to Washington frequently.*
*He was known by the train people, but he couldn't ever find his ticket.*
*One time, the conductor said, "That's all right, doctor; surely*
*you'll find it and you can turn it in on the next ride."*
*But the professor said, "Mr. Conductor, it isn't alright.*
*I've got to find that ticket because I don't know where I'm going."*

EVERETT MCKINLEY DIRKSEN

Peering into our large Southern California home in the early 1950s, things looked normal for an affluent young family. All the amenities portrayed success: newly invented Formica countertops, a dishwasher, a front-loading washer and dryer, and a gas jet fireplace, with an attached indoor barbecue. We moved in on my fourth birthday, so my gift was my new room.

My Dad was determined to give his children a better childhood than he'd had. He was thirteen in 1929 when the Depression ravaged the country. He understood hunger, and the result was that he worked long hours to provide more than enough for us. We could afford luxuries due to my dad's entrepreneurial success. Over the years our family vacationed at many national parks, camping in our small travel trailer.

We went on fishing expeditions to the ocean nearly every weekend during the summer. Unfortunately, our unhealthy family dynamics invariably interfered with our attempts at happiness during these vacations.

We visited Yellowstone National Park when I was eight years old. Our family stood on a platform overlooking the canyon walls of Lower Yellowstone Falls. (That platform is no longer there.) Looking at the raging falls, a sense of terror came over me as I checked the whereabouts of my father. I was worried he might push me over the ledge, but was cognizant enough to ask myself: *Where did I get an idea like that?* Several times Dad had snapped at me, "If I tell you to jump over a cliff, I expect you to do it!" It was no doubt an effort to ensure we minded him in every situation, but I distrusted him. It was obvious what the result would be if I followed those orders to jump off a cliff. My fear of him tainted my experiences with our family.

We often camped at Joshua Tree National Park in our trailer. One time my parents quarreled, standing a foot apart, snarling at each other with their arms flinging about. It was clear that Dad was in a fury over something having to do with church and God. I had never heard any mention of church or religion before, but Dad was irrational, and his outbreak left me bewildered. I hid on the trailer bed, which was three feet away from them, and curled up while I waited for them to stop. *I guess church is something to shut up about.*

Not all my childhood memories were traumatic. While camping in Yellowstone, a black bear came into the bathroom and rummaged through the trash can while I braced myself against the wall, frozen. The bears would run through our campsite, climb in nearby trees, and wrestle with each other in the meadow where we camped. I loved watching them play. I learned that black bears rarely attack people, and they are not as scary as they look.

Every morning at 5:00 a.m. our family went out in two small rowboats to catch fish on Lake Yellowstone. Dad taught Peggy and me how to clean trout, and Mom cooked them for dinner. Over the years our family shared our recollections of this memorable trip.

One day my father carried a large box into the house, his face flushed with excitement. He was eager to share some modern technology with us. He untangled the packaging and unveiled a three-foot-high, two-foot-wide, polished wooden box. The front was covered with silver-gold woven cloth. "This is a Hi-Fi!" Dad announced.

Our Hi-Fi played record after record: melodies, romance, jazz, Italian and French music, symphonies, Rodgers and Hammerstein, and Christmas music. Music became my savior. I memorized verses and melodies and sang along. In fifth grade I asked my parents if I could learn to play a musical instrument, but Dad nixed the idea immediately, saying, "You are not capable of learning to play an instrument, or to keep up the discipline needed to succeed." (I later discovered that this was an excuse. Dad was irritated by the years he had to listen to Peggy practice her clarinet. He wasn't going through that again.)

When I was eleven, my life veered in a new direction. Our family moved to Riverside where Dad opened a savings and loan business. Four months later, my older sister, Peggy, who was like my surrogate mom, went away to college. I didn't get to see much of her for the next twenty-five years. I understood that she wanted out as badly as I did, and it was her turn to leave and start a new life. I missed her terribly, and my loneliness intensified.

My parents began playing golf four times a week, so gone were the PTA meetings and my Girl Scout troop that Mother helped lead. It seemed as if my parents thought it was their turn to have fun, and they figured their two younger daughters would turn out fine without them. They didn't seem to notice Diane, and it became my job to watch out for her and complete the chores. Golf shots and bridge hands became the topics of conversation between my parents. They had nothing to talk about with Diane and me, and the natural consequence was that we were lonely and felt abandoned. We missed our friends in Brownies and Girl Scouts, and we knew no one in our new neighborhood. Our preoccupied parents were ignorant about children needing love and emotional support, they must have figured that food and a bed to sleep in were sufficient. Maybe it was more than what they had during those Depression years.

I always cared deeply for Diane and tried to be the big sister to her that Peggy had been to me. When Diane was a baby, I lay by her crib while she slept. When she peered over the side of her playpen, I was in awe of her cuteness. As she got older, I played dolls with her endlessly. We made sandcastles on the beach, searched for seashells together, and played card games. I made every effort to make her feel secure, and I never excluded her. When my parents fought, I closed the bedroom door and tried to entertain her. Sometimes I waited for hours before their shouting stopped, hoping that Diane was distracted and unaware of the chaos.

I was eleven and Diane was eight when we moved into our new house in Riverside. The second night there, my parents decided to return to the old house to pick up some things they had left. The sun had set, and I begged them not to leave us alone. "Mom, can't you at least stay home? I don't want to be here alone." The windows did not have curtains or drapes yet, and I felt exposed and scared. Mom's solution was to ignore my fears and tell me to watch Diane.

I continued to plead, "Can't you go another time? It's almost dark!" I was ignored. Invisible. *Why even say anything about what I need? I don't matter.* My parents didn't return for several hours, and my terror morphed into a deep rage. I knew we were vulnerable in a lit house without curtains—like little goldfish swimming in a giant glass bowl. I knew about scary men, and I feared if one saw us alone in the house, he might break in and do... well, I wasn't sure what he might do to us, but I knew it would be bad. I played with Diane in the hallway and bathrooms, the only places where we could not be seen from the outside. It was a long wait for two hungry little girls.

Being left alone that night was proof of my worst fears: my parents didn't love me, nor did they care what happened to me or Diane. They simply wanted me to be her caretaker. Something in me snapped. Hurt and angry, I refused to oblige, and soon I became a recluse in my room under the guise of having to study. My childhood thoughts and perceptions of myself were already on shaky ground, but after our move, my dysfunctions deepened, as did my depression. Weekends with my family and friends vaporized, leaving me adrift at sea. I was entering a new school in seventh grade, a time well known to be challenging for most kids. My hormones were changing, boys and girls were all over the map at different maturity levels. I felt like a social misfit. There was no longer one teacher to trust, but six teachers, who seemed to care more about their subject matter than their students.

To make things worse, something was happening behind the scenes that undermined our family's tenuous unity and resulted in my mother's frequent tears. My parents were fighting often, and Dad snarled at me regularly, blaming me for my mother's unhappiness. "I come home from work and see your mother crying," he'd say. "What did you do?" *I don't know!* I internalized this responsibility for her sorrow. Years later I learned that Dad was having an affair with one of the women in his office. I remembered he invited his 'friend' home for dinner. Yes, dinners my mother prepared and served. The tension in our house splintered our family's fragile cohesiveness.

My adolescence cornered me unaware. I ended up in emotional chaos without support. With no friends, no social community, no family who cared about me, and no big sister, I was incapable of handling and adapting to the barrage of loss I was experiencing. My body was changing, and no one acknowledged or explained it to me, though Dad stared at my developing breasts. We were taught in school about menstrual cycles, but when my first period came, I didn't understand what was happening, and my parents were out of town. I was enveloped in grief that left me lonely beyond comprehension and unsure of the reasons for it.

I lapsed into a shell of shyness and the inability to speak up. I was ashamed and surmised that anyone who looked at me would instantly perceive my shame. With so much conflict, isolation was inevitable. Some of the boys at school sensed my inability to stand up for myself and began feeling me up in the crowded hallways. They laughed when they touched me; my only defense was to try to stay away from the abusive ones. It never occurred to me to bring the situation to the attention of a teacher. *Why would an adult be concerned about my problems?*

Wherever I was, confusion, fear, and anger were my companions. No place felt safe.

The two most common responses to churning emotions are to blame others or blame oneself. I wanted to lash out, but being angry with Mom or Dad was too dangerous, so I took the only path available to me, which was an inward, lonely one. I furiously berated myself for my shortcomings, but eventually this self-blame tactic would overwhelm me. Unexpectedly, I'd explode in anger, kicking doors and breaking picture frames, which alarmed everyone as well as me. This unintentionally strengthened my belief that I was an out-of-control 'nobody,' unseen and unwanted. During the next four years my depression intensified, and I frequently found myself crying uncontrollably.

I had entered an altered state of reality, which I labeled as 'shut down,' because what I experienced was the onset of numbness to life. This period in my life still baffles me, yet now I understand I had no sense of balance, no one to trust, and had lost hope. I had no identity. I felt invisible and ashamed.

The first Christmas in our new house I was twelve. I lit the gas fireplace and stacked Christmas records on the Hi-Fi. I loved music, and listening to the traditional Christmas music was cherished in Christmases past in our old house. I assumed my family loved our Christmas tradition as much as I did, so I was excited as I gathered Mom, Dad, and Diane into the living room. It was a big deal to me, a time for simple pleasures. It was a rare opportunity to create warm feelings that came from deep inside me. I especially needed to cuddle on the couch and listen to the music while enjoying the crackling fire and the sparkly, flocked Christmas tree nearby. It might have been that the music softened my parents' hearts—it was a rare time for family bonding.

But alas, before the first song finished, my dad jumped up and announced, "I'm going to watch TV." Mom followed him out, sat down in the dining room to read the newspaper as she did every night, and Diane went to her room. I sank into the couch, dazed. The little bit of rapport we had developed completely disappeared that night. Each found a hideaway that kept us separate, unable to know or support one another. We remained as far apart and unfriendly as cacti in the desert.

With no one joining me, I laid on the living room floor and began listening to Christmas music. The twinkling lights on the tree and the bright flames from the fireplace brightened my spirits. Music was a balm for my troubled soul, and as I listened, I felt an inner strength and hope.

At the end of Christmas vacation, Mom said she was going to take down the Christmas tree the next day. "Mom, please don't take the tree down yet!" She decided to give me one more day. As I gazed at the tree, I heard Perry Como's soothing voice singing a familiar Christmas song:

*I heard the bells on Christmas day, Their old familiar carols play. And loud and sweet the words repeat Of Peace on Earth good will to men.*

*Then on that day I bowed my head, "There is no peace on earth," I said. For hate is strong and mocks the song of Peace on Earth good will to men.*

In despair, my throat tightened, and my heart sank. Yes, hate is strong. Peace is a mockery. No peace in my life. Not in Mom or Dad's life either. *What is peace, anyway?* In my family emotional chaos ruled. No goodwill toward one another. Or on earth....

Then this last verse calmed my aching heart:

*Then pealed the bells more loud and deep. God is not dead, nor does he sleep. The wrong shall fail, the right prevail, With peace on Earth, goodwill to men.*[2]

*God isn't sleeping! The right will prevail.* I replayed the song and sang along. A glimmer of hope arose within me. *The wrong shall fail.* More hope! A sense of something deeper than what meets the eye. *Something beyond me!* I wanted to believe that there was a loving God in the world. I repeated these phrases to myself: *God is not dead, nor does he sleep.* Gradually, these thoughts became part of my thinking and gave me courage. Someday, all the wrongs will be righted.

The next song continued...Como's voice penetrated my being, but I suddenly realized I didn't understand the words.

*God rest ye merry gentlemen, let nothing you dismay.*
*Remember Christ your Savior was born on Christmas Day,*
*To save us all from Satan's power when we had gone astray.*
*Oh, Tidings of comfort and joy, comfort and joy,*
*Oh, Tidings of comfort and joy.*[3]

Later that day while helping Mom empty the dishwasher, I asked her, "What are tidings of comfort and joy about?"

"Well, comfort and joy come from Jesus," she answered matter-of-factly. Her brows crumpled and her brown eyes narrowed as she looked at me as if I were missing my marbles. Her face clouded as she recognized my ignorance. I persisted, "Well, who is Jesus?"

"Well.... Jesus is Christ," Mom said.

"Well, who is Christ?"

She paused. She was at a loss. "He's the Man who split time."

My blank face stared back at her, "What does that mean? How can you split time?"

"He is the man who changed... you know, B.C. and A.D." She assumed I knew what B.C. and A.D. meant; I didn't, but I was longing to know.

"What does B.C. and A.D. mean?"

"B.C. means Before Christ's birth and his life here on earth. A.D. stands for after Christ's Death. He changed time."

"What does it mean, 'Saved us all from Satan's power?'"

"Jesus protects us," she briefly replied.

"Who is Satan? What power?" No answer.

The dishes were now put away, and Mom was off to do other household duties. That was the extent of our conversation. I didn't know anything about the narratives of Jesus' birth or death, or even that the songs I was singing were about a man called Jesus. We never again discussed protection from evil, or anything else about Jesus.

In post-modern times the acronym for B.C. is BCE meaning Before the Common Era, and A.D. refers to the Latin, *anno domini,* meaning "in the year of our Lord."

Jesus' teachings ushered in a new era of thinking. The common era, one might say, is a meridian, meaning an intersection, a crest, or a culmination of something supremely excellent entering the Cosmos.[4] A new system of time was developed and accepted, and, as Mom noted, Jesus was the Man who split time. Even though the Chinese and Jewish calendars are still acknowledged, the Man who split time, the meridian, is generally accepted worldwide. It would be two more decades before I would fully grasp these concepts.

I stood in our kitchen bewildered. Apparently, the life of Jesus was something that I should have known about. *If this was common knowledge, why didn't I know about it?*

Mom grew up in a home where the entire family went to church. She understood, but somehow did not teach me. She assumed that I knew what she knew without any teaching or discussion. I guess she thought learning happened by osmosis!

How long I stood in the kitchen thinking, I don't know, but I would reflect on this sentence and this Jesus guy for a long while. *The Man who split time. The Man who split time… hmm… Who is this Man?* The intrigue drove me to greater questioning. *A Man who changed time, and the entire world followed?* I did not know what Mom meant, but I did know this: I wanted to learn who this person was. My search began.

I still didn't get that the Christmas carols were a celebration and thanksgiving of Jesus' birth, or that Jesus is recognized by millions as the Messiah or Christ. If I had heard the word 'Messiah,' it would have been Hebrew to me. Nor did I gain any other knowledge about Jesus' identity or what Easter meant. The word 'resurrection' was above my vocabulary. I knew where I wanted to go, but I had no idea how to get there. Still, I had my ticket.

*O Lord, you have searched me and you know me. You know when I sit and when I rise; you perceive my thoughts from afar. You discern my going out and my lying down; you are familiar with all my ways. Before a word is on my tongue you know it completely, O Lord…. You have laid your hand upon me. Psalm 139: 1-5.*

*Let us walk undisturbed, Through each transitory illusion, and respond to change with a grateful heart, bend gracefully with the flow of time, with patience.*
*With endurance.*

Sarah Robbins

## CHAPTER 3

# The Ever-Present One

*Faith is not a shelter against difficulties,*
*but belief in the face of all contradictions.*

PAUL TOURNIER

Finding out the identity of this man named Jesus wasn't as easy as one might assume in a supposedly Christian nation. My father's mother, Granny, read her Bible when she visited us, and upon learning of my interest in knowing more about Jesus, she gave me a *King James Bible*. She instructed me in how to read it, which I eagerly embarked upon, beginning with Genesis. I vaguely understood some of the stories as I deciphered the archaic use of thee, thou instead of you and yours, and "th" at the end of verbs, such as doth instead of does. Dutifully I went on to Exodus, but there my journey of Bible reading ended. Confused and clueless, my old feelings of inadequacy reared up.

I shared my frustrations with Granny, but she stayed tight-lipped and unresponsive. I implored her for clues because I knew she knew. It didn't make sense to me that she wouldn't talk to me. Since she read *The Ugly Duckling* and *Cinderella* to me repeatedly, I couldn't understand why she had nothing to say. Her husband, my dad's father, the grandfather Peggy and I hated, died of Parkinson's when I was seven. When Granny came to visit or babysit, I wanted her to stay and live with us—even if I had to give up my bed. I knew she loved me; she was the only person in my family who ever nestled close to me. *Why would Granny deny me an explanation when I am so eager for it? Did she no longer care?*

I knew absolutely nothing, not even that Jesus was thought to be the Son of God. I could not comprehend what being a Christian meant. *But the Man who split time must know things, something more than the rest of us.* I yearned for answers.

Forty years later I inadvertently learned why my grandmother was silent. With a disgruntled air, my father quipped, "It is my mother's fault that you became a Christian. I told her not to speak to you about anything religious." Granny's fear was that if she breached my father's wishes, she might be rejected or admonished and find herself without a family. It was too big a risk to answer my questions, and today I can sympathize. My false assumption at sixteen was that I was rejected.

Time marched on. In tenth grade I decided to attend a Young Life meeting. I was bereft of understanding and clueless about what they were talking about, but I figured I could learn. More devastating to my psyche, however, was that no one acknowledged my presence. Most of the kids went to my school, and yet no one offered a greeting, not even a hello. I was too shy and insecure to initiate talking to anyone, and no one ventured to dent my shield.

*It's me. Something is wrong with me.* My perception of the Young Life chapter in our town was that it was for the 'in crowd.' After two meetings, I gave up. I was seeking something, but did not know what or where to find that something. Others seemed to know but I did not. I searched while God, the Ever-Present, watched.

Headaches, stress in school to perform with good grades, and intense menstrual cycles began. I cried more and experienced chronic depression. This may be why people didn't talk to me at school, why I felt alone. Unknowingly, I had developed a negative belief system that was sapping my life dry and empty.

I endured criticism and anxiety. Pain and depression overwhelmed me, and I thought about killing myself. Alone at night, I cried out to God. Then I decided that if I could endure the pain, I'd grow up and leave home. *When I leave, no one will have to put up with me any longer. I will get out of their way and stop making them so unhappy.* I wasn't lashing back, vindictive, or seeking to cause them feelings of rejection. I honestly believed they would be happier without me, and that the nicest thing I could do was to get out of their lives.

My mother and I didn't share thoughts or hugs, nor did we respect one another. It took me years to uncover the reasons for our estrangement. Part of my lifetime grief was suffering the loss of what our relationship was supposed to be; that is, what I noticed my girlfriends had with their mothers, and the attention Peggy and Diane got from Mom. The lack of a loving relationship with my mother ate away at my value and affected my personhood.

In eleventh grade, I turned sixteen and began driving. On Sunday mornings, I assumed my mother's duty of picking up Granny and dropping her off at church. My father sternly reminded me that he did not want me to attend church with her. This was a further indication of my father's vendetta against Christianity and Jesus. But Dad was playing golf and wouldn't know, so I began to attend church occasionally with my grandmother. It was our closely guarded secret. We went to a Baptist church, and I listened to sermons addressed to knowledgeable Christians who related to the *King James Bible*. I am not an auditory learner, and this was all new to me, so I remained clueless. *All these people go here for some reason, but it is beyond me.*

My mother's words to me, "Jesus was the Man who split time," became one of her unknowing contributions and legacies for the direction of my life. Words from my mother's mouth directed my life and kept me searching.

I refer to the traditional words used to refer to Christian concepts as 'Christianese,' or Christian lingo. Even though I am now familiar with its language, I still believe that we who profess to 'know the way' alienate those who are searching by using meaningless clichés. Words like redemption, salvation, reconciliation, sin, sanctification, justification, and grace, are conceptual words needing context, and newly interested persons are left out of the loop. At sixteen, Christianese made as much sense to me as if I were hearing an engineer explain the blueprints of the Golden Gate Bridge. My confusion and inability to understand Christian concepts confirmed what I believed to be true, *I must be stupid and inadequate.* It didn't occur to me that I didn't know because no one taught me. Still, I had hope. *There has to be something more. I just haven't found it yet.*

To give me some "Christian education," Mom put me in Job's Daughters, an organization she enjoyed before she married my dad. She told me stories about princesses and queens, as though I knew what she meant without any context. Before she married my dad, she was ready to be the "queen" of her Job's Daughters chapter in Omaha. This says something positive about my Mom before she married. However, Job's Daughters is a hierarchical organization, which has never been my style. When I attended these meetings, I still didn't know what the church kids my age knew, so I was unable to join in the conversations. The only thing I learned was a few new hymns, and these led me forward in my search for "the Man."

My first boyfriend in high school invited me to the junior prom in the spring. I was excited and drove to the shop where my prom dress had been altered. The floor-length, powder blue dress was wrapped in a plastic dress bag, and I held it high above the ground and began walking back to my car. A young man walked by and flipped up his middle finger in my face, startling me. I immediately felt ashamed because I felt a strange flush throughout my sexual organs. The language 'turned on' wasn't in my vocabulary, and I had no idea why my body responded this way. Weird. My confusion about this followed me until adulthood, when I learned more about the root cause of my strange response.

By the second semester of my senior year in high school, I knew that I wanted to attend a small, private Methodist school on Point Loma in San Diego. The minute I walked on the campus of Cal Western, I knew this was the place for me. Everything drew me in: the big date palm trees that waved their majestic branches in the breeze, the open grass beneath their graceful trunks, the salty sea air and the exquisite sunsets. I'm drawn to nature, and I hoped that this beauty would help me heal. I was accepted to Cal Western, and my spirits lifted. I looked forward to getting away from home and making new friends. I would learn to think for myself and, maybe, fall in love. I experienced a new restlessness and a severe case of senioritis.

I believed I would move on with my life, and with these thoughts my tears began to subside. Hope was in my heart.

Off to college I went, grieving only the loss of seeing Diane every day. Mom drove me to San Diego and helped move me into the dorm room, and when it was time for her to leave, I was surprised to see tears in her eyes. We looked at each other almost as if we were strangers. Since we'd never hugged, it didn't occur to either of us to offer one. When I said goodbye to her, she didn't say a word, turned, walked out the door, and drove away. I watched her Cadillac go up the hill and out of sight. *Goodbye, Mom!* I chose to believe that perhaps she loved me but had no way to express it, and even in my loss, I'd learned to accept our relationship.

*I am surrounded by an unparalleled landscape overlooking the vast Pacific Ocean.* I had so many hopes and dreams. *Maybe I can find whoever that elusive man is who is somehow linked to Christianity. I am so fortunate that my father can afford the luxury of such a privileged setting and education for me. Maybe my emotional pain will go away.* I never took it for granted. I worked hard, made friends, and even had a boyfriend. I wasn't crying myself to sleep, though I still had bouts of severe depression. I didn't feel so alone and that made a big difference. The healing was happening slowly, and I kept learning.

My mind expanded, as I absorbed and deeply enjoyed what I was taught. Later I would learn that one of my dominant strengths is learning anything new.

I coped as best I could with my depression. A memory from when I was sixteen popped up: I asked my mother to help me. I told her about the nagging pain that stabbed my core. Mom inquired about it, and as I tried to describe it, she nodded as though she understood. "Well, everyone feels like that. It's just part of life." Then she walked down the hallway to take care of the urgent household responsibilities, and my need to visit or make a connection with her was dismissed.

*Oh, so it's just part of life, and this pain is normal?* I thought. *I guess there is no other choice but to accept my life as it is.* Thirteen years later I discovered that this was not reality for everyone, and there were some answers to resolve my pain.

Overcoming my feelings and discouragement taxed my energy, and the voice in my head echoed that of my parents: *"Look happy, smile because no one wants to be with an unhappy person."* And tagged to that mantra were more one-liners: *"What are you so happy about?"*, *"You think you deserve to feel good after* (going to a dance," or fill in the blank), and again, *"Why are you so glum? Put a smile on your face!"*

Always double messages. Trying to juggle these daily opposing demands was demoralizing and confusing, and to little avail. Being at college didn't erase the voices in my head that began in childhood.

I met Christian friends at college who were genuinely friendly and good for my soul. One of the requirements at this Methodist school was to attend church service each Friday at 10:00 a.m. in the gym. I didn't resent this as many students did because my intention was to puzzle out this Christianity thing. I cherished the opportunity to learn more! So, when a group of Christian friends asked me to attend a Kathryn Kuhlman meeting, I agreed to go without knowing who she was or what she did. I surmised that Ms. Kuhlman knew and spoke about Jesus. *Okay then, I'm in.*

Sixteen of us piled into three different cars and traveled four hours to arrive at the Shriners Auditorium in Los Angeles. From our seats in the balcony, I could see that the crowd was exceptionally excited when Ms. Kuhlman arrived on the stage. It reminded me of a concert, not a speaking engagement. The momentum grew and within an hour I found myself among a mob of seemingly crazy-like people. When she spoke, everyone cheered. People around me were crying out, "I've been healed!" One man threw his cane in the aisle, "It's a miracle, I can walk!" My friends stood up, cheered and waved their hands like we were at a football game. Some people seemed to be speaking gibberish. I sat there, taking it all in, but, once again, I was totally bereft of understanding. *What is happening here?* I kept still, observing the mayhem. As people went up on stage, Ms.

Kuhlman touched them, and they immediately proclaimed healing.

Someone in our aisle fainted. These exhibitions seemed weird to me, almost scary. Seeking to become invisible, I cowered lower in my chair. When the frenzy was over, I was relieved. *Now we can get out of here and go home.*

Alas, not my little group of Christians. They wanted to go downstairs and meet Ms. Kuhlman. *Meet her?* I was a tag-along with no voice. I felt compelled to stay with my group, my only security in an auditorium of, well, who knows what? I doubted the sanity of my friends because they had participated in this lunacy. As the auditorium emptied out, I thought, *I suppose it will be ok.*

Three large men, likely her assistants, escorted our group up some side stairs and onto the stage. My inclination was to stay by the foot of the stairs, but I didn't know how to tell them *I'll wait here!* Voiceless and vulnerable, I found myself standing alongside my friends in a circle on the stage of the auditorium. I wore a dress and high heels (pants for women were not yet accepted attire). I assumed Ms. Kuhlman was praying, because her hands were lifted, and her eyes closed. Afterwards, she walked to the inside of our circle and faced everyone individually before putting her hands on the shoulders of each person. She said something I couldn't understand, and suddenly one of my friends fell backward onto the floor. Behind each of us was one of her assistants whose duty was to catch the falling person and gently lower them to the floor. When a burly, defensive lineman from our football team had his turn, I thought, *No one's going to be able to take him down!* But when Katherine faced him, placing her hands on his shoulders as she spoke, to my dismay he fell backward. When their turn came, each of my girlfriends, the ones who had invited me, and whom I trusted, fell to the floor. I began to panic, wondering: *What's wrong with them? I'm not falling just because someone touches my shoulders. When she touches me, I'm just going to stay standing.* I stiffened my legs and my resolve, balancing in my three-inch heels.

When my turn came Kathryn Kuhlman faced me squarely, and with outstretched arms, put her hands on my shoulders and spoke words I could not comprehend. I held my ground as she deepened her grip on my shoulders a second time, again muttering something, and gave me a slight push. At that same moment, the man behind me shoved his knees into the back of mine. I lost my balance, was caught, and found myself on the floor. I felt like I'd been hit by a stun gun. I turned my head and watched three more people fall, or were they forced, onto the floor. *Now she has us!* It seemed she had unnatural, witch-like control over people. I was slightly terrified, caught in a realm of eerie nonsense.

On our way home, sitting in the back seat, I was filled with fury. I was silent but my thoughts raced. *How dare they do that to me! I trusted my friends and saw what happened!* I was devastated. *This can't be about Jesus!* A flood of terror engulfed me and wiped out my ability to think. I sobbed uncontrollably for hours as we drove back to San Diego. My friends could not console me, and they continued to converse and laugh. *Why are they so happy?* So once again I was out of the norm. Exhausted emotionally and physically, I returned to my dorm room at 2:00 a.m. and collapsed onto bed, bewildered, embarrassed and ashamed.

I woke up confused but had this thought: *Surely the pastor at the school chapel can explain what happened to me.* When I spoke to him about my experience, he had a blank look and offered no explanation. *If he doesn't know, who does?* Another dead end. Later I would learn that Ms. Kuhlman was a faith healer. I'm sure that my friends had a valid experience, but it was confusing for me.

God, the Ever-Present-One, watched.

*For he will command his angels concerning you, to guard you in all your ways; they will lift you up in their hands, so that you will not strike your foot against a stone.* Psalm 91:12.

*By looking into our past, we can begin to understand and transform that which seems difficult or at times impossible.*

Gaynelle

CHAPTER 4

# The Gift of a Lifetime—1966

*Every experience God gives us, every person he puts in our path, is the perfect preparation for the future only he can see.*

ANONYMOUS

I resumed my daily routine: attending classes, studying at the library, enjoying friends, and dating on Friday and Saturday nights. I treasured my daily afternoon walks overlooking the spectacular, moody Pacific Ocean. My love for its mysteries grew as I trekked back and forth between classrooms and the dorm. *I live on Point Loma!*

*Something beyond me must be at work.* What an incredible gift it was to live there for four years. As a young schoolgirl, my dad had steered our little outboard boat into and out of San Diego Bay along the eastern shore of Point Loma. I gazed up, enamored, and softly expressed my dreams, "Someday I'm going to live on Point Loma," I announced.

Dad said with a big laugh, "You won't be able to afford to live on Point Loma!" Even though his response hurt me, I was not surprised that he didn't understand. He thought it best that I not get my hopes up, and thus avoid disappointment. Secretly I held out hope for my dream.

It turned out that we were both right! I couldn't afford to live on Point Loma, but when he offered to pay for my college education, there I was living on Point Loma, just as I had dreamed. This was only one of many childhood dreams that came true. *Was I given some kind of foreknowledge when I made that statement so many years ago? Or had God seen me and my desires, and turned them into reality?* Somehow, I knew: God was watching and acting too. It was my first recognition of an answered prayer. This glorious Pacific paradise created for me an ever-changing canvas of ocean and sky. Being there with the vastness and beauty of nature contributed immensely to my healing.

I kept a lookout for information about Jesus; I tried going to church again, but it was still Christianese. I asked my friends questions—*more nonsensical language. A man paying the price for my sins! What sins? The God of the universe needs to be appeased? That doesn't make sense.*

No one offered me a Bible or invited me to a study group. I didn't consider trying to read the Bible on my own again. However, I was learning and studying other things—logic, history, liberal arts. I kept thinking the 'answers' would come from somewhere, and I knew that my education and living at Cal Western were gifts from heaven, which I equated with God.

In my junior and senior years, I started taking child psychology classes and fulfilling the requirements of an elementary teaching credential. My psychology professor was a retired Methodist minister. I trusted him and made a concerted effort to study. Insights about childhood experiences and resulting behaviors brought me some personal validation. *Maybe I'm not so crazy after all.*

Depression sometimes overtook my sanity, so I sought out little spots on campus where no one ventured—under the bushes or trees, or in a private grassy place behind the administration building. I sat on a blanket and waited. Tears often graced my cheeks as I gazed up at the trees and sky in a kind of trance, waiting for the pain to pass. I was accustomed to dealing with it, but now I did so with a belief that God was helping me. I asked God for help while I waited for the pain of overwhelming depression to depart. Usually, the severity would work its way out, but truthfully, I was never pain-free. I recalled my dad's words: "Do what must be done." I focused my attention on remaining grateful for my surroundings, keeping busy with school, and staying distracted to keep the pain at bay. Eventually, these strategies failed me, and I'd find myself practicing the coping mechanism that seemed to help most: hiding out and letting nature heal me. I also had the advantage of some good friends, and a thoughtful boyfriend who liked me. I had more success with my studies than I had in my freshman and sophomore years.

My boyfriend was one year older than I was. He left during my senior year to do six months of officer training in the Marine Corps in Virginia. A new friend, Randy, appeared on the scene. We were truly 'just friends.' Though he was one year younger, he was two years behind me in school. He was not pushy and treated me with respect. He believed he was the honored one if a senior girl gave him attention, so I felt safe and in charge. Randy had no designs on me and was dating other girls, telling me about his experiences and asking for guidance. Though we believed men and women could sustain a friendship, I found myself becoming attracted to Randy.

Pop was a retired Methodist minister who visited our campus cafeteria daily for lunch. Students had the opportunity to visit with him, and because he was so regular, we knew him. One day I cornered him at lunch and told him about my concerns regarding my boyfriend. "He's going to be a Marine Corps officer, and I've been to their parties. The officer social gatherings, and the hierarchy I observe there, remind me of my bossy father. I think my boyfriend is a very fine man, but I'm concerned I can't live his lifestyle. And now I've met someone else I like."

Pop had no hesitation as he spoke to me. His simple answer was, "Search your heart and you will know what to do." No one had ever said anything like that to me, and I felt encouraged. I explained some details, hoping for advice. *Please, tell me what I should do?*

"Search, and God will give you the answer."

I didn't know what to say. I was flabbergasted that someone sincerely believed in me—and in God. *Can I search deep within myself and know what to do? Trust myself? Trust God?* His belief in me and in God was sincere, honest. "Okay, thank you for your help," was all I could muster, but his wisdom took root. I gave myself a measure of credit, my confidence lifted. I searched my heart and mind. I prayed to know what was best for me. A Methodist pastor had ministered to me, but at the time I didn't even realize it!

Since Randy and I were friends, and he had told me his love woes, I shared my relationship concerns about my boyfriend. This was information Randy was happy to hear, and began counseling me not to marry the Marine Corps officer, confirming the idea already formed in my mind.

Meanwhile, the requirement for a fifth year of college to obtain a teaching credential in California became law, and much to my dad's chagrin, I had yet another year of school to obtain it. Still, he was adamant that a woman needed a profession in case she had to support herself or her family. Dad was proud that I graduated, and he honored my need and desire to finish my credential by paying for my first year of graduate school.

One day Randy was searching campus for me. He eventually found me sitting alone in one of my quiet places. I was impressed by his intuition or keen detective work. Always seeking privacy, I sought out new hideaways on campus but secretly began hoping Randy would show up, and he usually did. His gentle encouragement and counsel helped me through bouts of depression. Maybe the appeal was that I didn't have to hide myself and felt a measure of acceptance even when I was overwhelmed and sad. I believed he cared, and I think it made him feel important and needed. He sensed his intuitive gift for counseling.

At that time, I was unaware of Randy's sexual attraction to me. One day, the intercom in my dorm room announced Randy's unexpected arrival. I'd been in deep tears and wanted to be alone. I tried to quell my tears and begged off seeing him, but in his conversation with the desk receptionist, and her ensuing conversation with me, he convinced me to come out of my room. We drove to Cabrillo Lighthouse on Point Loma, only a few miles from campus and for thirty minutes we sat on the bench, silent. Randy's gentle presence comforted me. We didn't hold hands or touch one another, but simply sat in wonder while the fog slowly lifted and burned off. Hundreds of rows of cloud-like ripples formed below the cliff. It looked like a blanket we could walk on. The mid-afternoon sun created alternating patterns of shadows and sparkling rainbows. Then a majestic, soft breeze and warm sun lifted them to the sky and they disappeared. We sat mesmerized by the beauty and power of nature. I felt one with creation, the Creator, God.

Even though Randy and I were still 'just friends,' being together in nature endeared him to me. He was gentle in spirit, patient, and a true friend. He found me in my times of need; I appreciated his concern for me and his tolerance of my ever-flowing tears. The wind spoke to me by gently breathing into the rows of foggy rainbows. It felt like a sign—*I will be alright. The sun is shining, little darlin'.* Rainbows had danced, the fog had risen, the sun had shone and warmed us on our little spot on the cliffs of Point Loma. I confidently hoped for a brighter future.

Randy slowly worked himself into my life. His father had recently died of leukemia, and he was grieving. I related to those feelings. "You are the woman I need," he told me. I was vulnerable—no one had ever needed me before.

Randy's major, behavioral psychology, was coming into its own during the late 1960's and early 70's. Randy was planning to become a psychologist, which of course meant graduate school. *Good! Psychologists make a fair income! He's proficient at it already!* Behavioral psychology intrigued both of us; Randy shared what he'd learned and assured me I wasn't crazy. I did a lot of reading on my own, always exploring and seeking answers.

On a walk at night in May of 1970, about a month after I broke up with my boyfriend, Randy and I witnessed a bold Pacific Bay sunset. The air was balmy and fresh. Later, while sitting in my car, Randy wasted no time in asking me to marry him. Since we had only made out in the backseat of my car a few times, I was a little surprised. He had, however, told me some weeks earlier that I was 'the girl of his dreams.' Just what every fair maiden of twenty years wants to hear and believe.

"Randy, you don't want to marry me," I protested. "You have no idea what a mess I am." Turmoil pulsated through me. I knew that I didn't like the idea of sex very much, but I didn't know why. Part of the feminist revolution of the 1960s was the change in attitudes about having sex before marriage. As the pill became more available, couples found it easier not to wait. Even though there was a 'sexual revolution' going on, I wasn't interested.

My only knowledge about sexual intercourse came from my mother's explanation, which was graphic and somewhat violent, and left me mortified and fearful. But I knew intercourse was a requirement if I wanted a family, and my drive to be in love and have children was stronger than my fear of sex. All of this led me to say with shame, "Randy, I think I have sexual problems." I was confused, but in fairness I wanted to save him from me.

Even though Randy and I had been friends and casually dating for two years, we had not spoken to each other about marriage or sex. I thought he needed to know me better so I tried to explain to him what he might be getting into by choosing me as his lifetime partner. But Randy didn't believe that I had any problems worth worrying about and assumed I was making excuses. He thought he knew me, knew us, and calmly, confidently replied, "We can work through any problems."

"No, you don't understand. You don't know. Listen to me. I'm so mixed up. These problems are too big for us."

"I believe Jesus can help us through anything."

I was stunned. "Wait…you know who Jesus is?"

"Yes. Of course!" He blurted it out as though it was common knowledge. He seemed a bit confused, as if he was thinking, *Doesn't everybody know?* Somehow in our conversations, I hadn't put together that there would be a connection between his dad being a Methodist minister and Randy's knowing about Jesus. "You know who Jesus is?" I repeated, incredulous.

"Yes!"

"Do you really think Jesus can help us through all our problems?"

"Yes, I know he can," he stated.

"Then I'll marry you." I was hopeful there was a way to solve my feelings of inadequacies. In my mind, Randy was the transportation to finding 'the Man.' He was now my stalwart.

Later in our engagement, he said to me, "You need to jump on the train with me if you want to be with me! We are either going together or we're not!"

My spirit sang to me: *My future holds long-sought answers.* So, I leapt on the train with Randy as the engineer. It appeared there was a track to follow, and someone, at long last, to hold onto, albeit by his coattails.

*Lead kindly Light, amid the circling gloom, Lead...me on!*
*The night is dark and I am far from home: Lead...me on!*
*Keep...my feet; I do not ask to see the distant scene;*
*One step for me."*

John B. Dykes

## CHAPTER 5

# Naive—1970

*Treasure the memories of past misfortunes;
they constitute our bank of fortitude.*

ERIC HOFFER

Randy and I waited to tell my parents about our engagement because they made it clear that they thought I'd made a mistake breaking up with my old boyfriend. Mom tried to change my mind about Randy, saying, "You know, your kids could get leukemia because Randy's father died of it! Bad genes. I've got to tell you he reminds me of your dad. He is just like him."

*What? Just because someone's health may not be the strongest, does that mean they don't deserve to be loved?* Mom saw some characteristics in Randy that reminded her of my dad, but I was blind to them. I only had eyes for Randy's good qualities.

Unfortunately, our engagement was fraught with frustrations, anger, and confusion. I'd long been concerned that my issues from childhood would cause unforeseen problems in my future relationships. Randy and I struggled through, little knowing that we were in over our heads.

Our sexual intimacy began with a mixture of fun and fear. In the beginning the sexual foreplay and exploration was great but penetration brought up terrifying feelings for me and I did not know what to do. *This is what I must do if I want to have kids. That is the deal.* When I figured out what foreplay led to, I no longer enjoyed it. Sex became an endurance exercise. I desperately wanted to be 'normal,' and tried to defeat my shortcomings by faking it, but without much success. Shame haunted me, and I was sick to my stomach, always stressed, and my body hurt. I didn't have any idea what was going on with me or how to resolve our problems.

Through counseling, I would later learn why my emotions were intense and unmanageable. The pain I carried was a direct result of having been sexually violated as a child. I knew I was ashamed and that I had sexual problems, even before having intercourse with Randy, but I could not have imagined the depth of forlornness that would invade my emotions and identity when we started having sex regularly. I was lost in shame and anxiety. *What is wrong with me, God? Is there anything that can save me?*

Randy felt rejected by my shame and sexual unease. When I did the dishes, he would hug me or give me a love pat, and instead of feeling close to him, my body stiffened unnaturally. My subsequent avoidance hurt him, and he began to feel shame as well. He told me, "One of my friends told me that you exude sexuality. Even though you are sexy, you aren't really, because you don't like sex."

I defended myself, "I tried to explain this to you the night you asked me to marry you." We didn't know where to turn. *I feel him falling out of love with me, God. I am failing him.* Years later Randy told me, "I married you because we had sexual intercourse before we were married. I felt obligated to marry you after that."

Randy's frustration led him to become critical of me. This led me to accept that I was severely damaged and needed to change. Listen, I said to myself. *Take the criticism as an opportunity to learn to meet Randy's needs. It's constructive criticism. Be brave and face it, then maybe he will love me.* Something about this sounded familiar…

The unrelenting pain made me think of myself as 'a mess.' I did not know what that meant exactly, but it felt like my heart and mind were disconnected. I used all the mind power I could summon to suppress and control any negative emotions. But it was only a matter of time before feelings flooded my being like a river flowing over the bank, and the current swept me off balance and threatened to drown me. What made this particularly terrifying was knowing that this kind of psychological disruption lurked in the shadows and could erupt anywhere, even in public. My disjointedness plagued our relationship.

After I completed my student teaching requirement, Randy and I moved to Berkeley where he completed his BA in psychology. I began a semester-long substitute position in a first-grade class in Oakland. This was a new experience since every child was Black. They did not like having a white teacher and called me 'Honky.' The after-school hours on the campus were unsettling because there was only one other white teacher at the school, and this was 1971–72, during the Black Panther Movement, which began in Oakland. One afternoon I exited the school building and, while walking toward my car, I noticed a group of Black men sitting on the hood. I was afraid to get in, but foolishly braved it, thinking I would look less vulnerable that way. Although I was scared, I didn't want my fear to show. I started the car and waited, thinking, *Are they going to get off?* A few seconds later they walked to the sidewalk, and I drove away like it was no big deal. After that, Randy dropped me off and picked me up. This arrangement allowed me to complete the remainder of the semester. We needed the money, and the pay was good.

We lived four blocks south of the UC Berkeley campus, and we heard gunshots ten times in those five months. In those violent years, Berkeley lived up to its nickname, *Berzerkley*. Randy and I decided to move twenty miles away to Lafayette, where we were allowed to have a three-month-old puppy whose adult weight was only twelve pounds. He gave us some entertainment at night since we didn't have a TV and provided something for us to mutually love. This helped our interactions, but still, our relationship was rocky. We tried, and neither of us gave up on the other. I thought this to be a good overall characteristic of our commitment. We attended church to hear the famous Earl Palmer at the First Presbyterian Church, and I sensed I was on the road to learning who this Jesus was. I was particularly encouraged as Palmer spoke about compassion, social responsibility, and told stories about Jesus.

I managed to function in the world, but I was inexperienced in knowing the secrets of creating good relationships. I had no strategies for dealing with my emotional chaos, which seemed synonymous with pain.

One evening, on my way to a continuing education class, Randy escorted me across a football field that was a shortcut to the classroom. It was twilight and he asked me, "What is the matter with you?" *The matter! Always something wrong with me?* I was probably in one of my withdrawn moments that irked him. It seemed like he never gave me the opportunity to simply be in survival mode. I was exhausted and replied honestly, "I'm in pain!"

"What kind of pain? Where does it hurt?"

"Here!" I put my right hand over my diaphragm and heart. "It never goes away! I cannot help it!" I was angry he had challenged me; I was doing everything I knew, and with great effort, to function within my pain level. And I was busy: teaching, taking classes, as well as being newly engaged to Randy. *I'm doing my best, but it isn't good enough!*

Randy's head cocked sideways, his brow wrinkled, bewildered.

"It feels like someone is twisting a knife in my gut," I said with honesty, though Randy was plainly unable to relate to this description. He tried to talk to me, but I finally burst into tears, escaping to class. I entered late with a red face and puffy eyes.

At that time, I couldn't put my pain into any context that made reasonable sense. Now I was an adult in the real world, not the safe world of college where I could hide out on my blanket watching the ocean. There were no secret getaways, no time or occasion to breathe in the ocean air for two or three hours. I had to take care of the everyday tasks of running a household, teaching, and studying. I was functional at college, but now I was in a demanding relationship where sex was the expectation. With the onslaught of engagement and adulthood, I was over-challenged.

In his effort to cheer me up, Randy told silly jokes and was playful. I didn't know how to respond because in my youth silliness wasn't allowed, but I appreciated Randy's wacky sense of humor, and I began to learn how to laugh. He worked twenty hours a week at the theater box office at UC Berkeley and carried twenty quarter units continuously. By doing this, he graduated earlier and saved money on tuition. On top of that, he was trying to navigate a difficult, immature relationship with a woman who had no Christian upbringing, limited social skills, and was unreliable emotionally. No wonder he was struggling. But we were driven to succeed in our life's goals, and emotions had to be put aside in order to meet the demands.

A few times we were invited to friends' houses for an evening. At the first occasion I didn't say a word all night. When we got home Randy asked me, "Why didn't you talk or say anything?"

"I didn't know what to say."

"Well, try saying something. People want you to talk."

Inwardly I mused, *Why would anyone care what I think? I don't say the right thing anyway.*

On our next visit, I tried to say a few things, but I was always self-conscious and awkward. Driving home, Randy chided me about my comments. "You shared personal information with people. What you told them was too personal." He explained why, and it made sense to me. I had shared too much information and embarrassed him. I believed (and still do) that he was perceptive about people and their responses. His childhood was one of social experience, but mine was one of withdrawal and dysfunction. In my family, our only social contacts were with my aunt, her two adopted children, and my Granny.

Mom wasn't good at social conversations and put up a front; she was uncomfortable with most people outside of our family. I copied her, hiding behind a smile to disguise my embarrassment and insecurities. I, too, was often disingenuous.

Randy usually stayed up late studying, and I went to bed earlier. He noticed that I slept curled in a ball and that my fists were tightly clenched, as if ready to hit someone. He would gently wake me, whispering, "I'm here. Everything is okay. You are safe." He would unclench my hands, straighten my legs, and let me return to sleep as often as needed. This went on for a few weeks, until I no longer slept as if in a battle. "There is nothing wrong with you," he assured me, hugging me gently. "Something must have happened to you to have such habitual tenseness when you sleep." This made me feel less crazy and slightly normal. With his help,

I overcame sleeping in a defensive position, but wondered, *what could have caused this?*

Several months later, noticing my sad demeanor, Randy asked, "Try to remember when this all started. What is one of your earliest memories?"

I prayed *What, God? What now?* God's answers are often deep inside me, but I didn't sense how to start 'unpeeling the onion,' and little did I know that this was just the outer papery skin. I was tired, so I laid down on the bed and took a short power nap. The number seven danced around and around in distinct colors and shapes. When I woke up, I shared this with Randy.

"What happened when you were seven?"

Another blank in my mind. Slowly, a memory glimmered, one that derailed my composure. In a weak and tearful voice, I said, "I was lying on the chartreuse carpet of the recreation room of our house, happily coloring. I said something to my mother, and she responded harshly, making some kind of command, chastising me. I was hurt and angry. I jumped up and ran down the hall screaming, 'No! NO! I hate you. I hate you!'

"She ran after me and caught me in the hallway, grabbing my shoulders and whipping me around. With her hands firmly gripping my little body, she shook me. Her furious, deep brown eyes were about two inches from mine. "Never, ever say no to me!" She snarled. "And you will never say you hate me. Do you understand?" I shrunk under her angry gaze. Her grip on my shoulders frightened me." My knees buckled in limp submission. I was silenced. *Yes, Mom. I understand.*

Randy and I had further conversations about my Mom. My mind jumped back to being in a movie theater watching Disney's *Sleeping Beauty*. "Randy, you remember the Story of *Sleeping Beauty* and the evil witch? Well, when the witch rose up and filled the screen, her red eyes reminded me of my mother. The witch's hands reached out and I felt she was going to grab me. I flew out of my seat, ran up the aisle of the theater and burst through the swinging doors. I was frozen in fear. An usher asked me if I needed help. I was startled to hear a human voice and surprised I was standing in the lobby."

The pairing of the memories of my mother's glare and the witch's scary red eyes brought about a visceral reaction. I knew I was afraid of my mother, but my reaction to the witch in *Sleeping Beauty* revealed its depth.

I never again challenged my mother with a *"No."* I rarely spoke up for myself.

Occasionally I tried, but to no avail. She either could not bring herself to treat me with maternal care or simply didn't know how to. I doubted she could be *for* me. How did it happen that my mother, whom I needed for safety and nurturing, came across as my enemy? I felt agitated and scared, causing me to be on guard. When I was eleven, I sat in the front seat of the car, and Mom reached over and patted my thigh, "I love you," she told me. I tensed up. She was trying, but I had learned not to trust or believe her. Her actions and words meant nothing to me. *I'm not falling for that trick.*

During our engagement we made breakthroughs which further endeared Randy to me. *He will be a great counselor, especially after he has training.* New understanding of how my childhood had affected me didn't lessen my pain. Recently, I learned that whether a person breaks a leg or has emotional pain, the same brain receptors activate. Pain is pain. Brain scans show that the same regions of the brain activate whether the pain is emotional or physical. Broken bones heal and the pain recedes, but traumatic pain lingers.

There were times when I could not cope. On three occasions I walked out the door without a word and tried to disappear. One time I hid under a bush for three hours. I could see Randy searching for me and hear him calling my name, but I stayed hidden, like a terrified child. I wanted to answer him, but for some baffling reason I could not.

I knew Randy was worried about me, so I stopped running away and started hiding under a blanket on the couch. One day I stayed under the blanket for ten hours. Randy tried to engage me in conversation, but after a while he learned that it was best to wait for me to finally throw it off. He could have forced me, but he didn't. When I 'returned,' at that point somehow ready to face reality, I wept a flood of tears. *What is wrong with me? Why do I act this way? Why can't I stop doing what I do not want to do? Why did I forsake our precious time together on Saturday? Who would want to live with someone who behaves like this?* Randy was always gentle with me once the tears flowed. Then, for who knows how long—a few days or a couple of weeks—I became more functional in our relationship, and we were able to share a bit of peace and happiness.

I gradually became more dependent on Randy, causing him to assume the role of caretaker rather than equal partner. The downside was that he began treating me as though I were helpless, which I wasn't. I couldn't understand why he had become so bossy, given that his true nature was kind and gentle.

Years later, Randy admitted, "I purposely criticized you to make you cry. You were easier to be with after a good cry." *Really?* His words pierced my heart. After our quarrels, I began the process of recovering, clinging to a tenuous hold on pride and a sliver of self-confidence. I believed my courage and inner strength would help me face my inadequacies, but my patterns of trying and pleasing only intensified. As our unconscious habits developed, I surrendered power to him, and he eagerly slurped it up.

In retrospect, I realize that my Mom and Dad displayed this pattern, even though I knew Mom detested it. Maybe early on she saw this inter-action developing in my relationship with Randy, and that was the reason she disliked him so intensely. She also disliked him because she found out that we were having sex before marriage. Her disdain toward Randy told me she had no confidence in my judgment.

Randy and I simply didn't have the insight to change our responses to one another. We were co-dependent. He was dependent on me to make him feel like he was the savior counselor and helper; I was dependent on him to reinforce my belief system of trying harder and earning my reward. Our dysfunctions stunted the development of a trusting and caring relationship. Our precious love was in danger of slipping through a sieve. *We are losing each other, and we've only just begun.*

After Randy graduated from UC Berkeley, we moved in with his mom. I was not in favor of this because I'd been offered a fourth-grade teaching position in Northern California. I knew I should take it, but I acquiesced because Randy wanted to be in Southern California with his family. I allowed my needs to take the second stage.

We decided to be celibate at his mom's home until our marriage. We attended church more regularly, and I met a woman, a dear friend of Randy's family, whose name was Evy. Evy and Randy's mother, Vivian, became my Christian mentors. Even though Randy believed in Jesus, he hadn't taught me much about him. I had a new-found faith in Jesus, but I wasn't sure what I was believing in. I reasoned that 'the Man who split time' must have known something more profound than anyone else in history. Why else would the eras have been divided? I was on a search for what Jesus knew. And even though I had some Jesus stories under my belt, the Christian scene still felt foreign. But Randy's family was Christian, and that comforted me. Vivian was in a group led by Sara Robbins, a spiritual leader whose most popular book was *Crushed for Better Wine*, and through Vivian, I was able to meet her. I began to get a sense that my spiritual longings were on a path to fulfillment. Things were slowly coming together in my mind, confirming my belief that something sane and good lived in my heart.

Randy and I were getting along better since we had moved into his mother's house. Kris, Randy's seven-year-old sister, helped fill our days with cheer. Evy popped in to mentor both Kris and me. Evy told me, "We must be very careful to guide Kris in the direction that will help her in life. She is like gold, and we must help mold her carefully." A woman with a purpose. I liked her. I watched her with Kris, and I learned.

Randy was fifteen years older than Kris. We went to the park, played tag and swung on the swings together. She was thin and small-boned, so on our hikes Randy carried his little sister part of the way on his shoulders. "Hey, Gaynelle, look! I'm taller than you!" She giggled. I loved watching him read stories to her as he took on the role of surrogate father.

After our hike, we needed milk; so Kris jumped in the car, and Randy let Kris order the milk at the drive-through dairy store. *He is going to be a great father! And good fathers make good husbands.*

As an adult, Kris shared with me a letter filled with memories of her beloved big brother, Randy:

*My memories are sprinkled with images of you and him. I appreciate the overall memory of how he tried to be steadfast to me. Funny, I recall a time when your arrival caught me by surprise. I was quite young, but I recognized the sound of your little dog running down the hall toward my bedroom. That's what alerted me to the news that you both had arrived. When you were around, the quality of my life improved. Family time was enhanced when you were with us. Those kinds of emotions are hard to put into specific stories, but the awareness that you were there was like looking out the window and discovering unexpected snow, or realizing that Christmas was here, and you didn't even know it! The sound of the pitter-patter on the carpet meant yet another celebration time had arrived. You and Randy made such a difference. Do you remember when my little yellow bird died? Randy put me in the car and took me up to Skyline Drive. We parked. He wanted me to talk about how it made me feel because he thought it was important for me to work through my sadness. He helped me put the bird in a box and bury it in the backyard. Randy always paid attention to my emotions, and I had lots of emotions.*

*Our Dad died on December 4th, so Christmas was a challenging time for our family. But you made it fun. Do you remember the midnight Christmas Eve service? Do you remember the open house afterward? What fun! I would get sent to bed, but even then, I would be listening to the sound of Santa on the roof.*

*Before I started kindergarten, Randy decided I should know the truth. He gathered everyone. He put me on his lap. We were in the kitchen, and he told me the truth about Santa Claus. He wanted me to be prepared. He was assuming the role of his dad, and he did it with such love and good intentions. Do you remember the little angel on top of the tree? He would hoist me up to place it there. Oh, and Christmas morning—it took so long to open the gifts, one person at a time! Randy meticulously opened his gifts to save the paper. And it was not uncommon to see him wearing one of the gift boxes in hopes of earning a smile. He probably felt sorrowful at Christmas, but he tried to lighten our spirits. I remember the beautiful sound of his laugh.*

Planning a wedding usually comes with problems, and ours came from my side of the family. Years before, my mother glared at me and sternly warned me that if I married Randy, I would never see her again. At the time, I didn't know it was a manipulative trick. I shot back an equally piercing look: *I get it, and it won't work.* I thought it was the last time I would see her. I thought this meant she didn't care if she ever saw me again, and if I didn't comply, I wouldn't be part of her life. Nothing new here. I already knew I was a devalued member of our family. Remembering her threat, I went about planning my wedding without her input.

Randy and I weren't married yet, so I figured my Mom's threat was not yet in force. Maybe I had some wiggle room. I was communicating on the phone with my family now and then, hoping for a smidgen of reconciliation, and the possibility that maybe, just maybe, a wedding in the family would be the catalyst. During this time, I went shopping for a wedding dress and picked out a simple, white lace, long-sleeved wedding gown that flowed to the floor. This decision made me feel proud and happy—I'd found the perfect wedding dress. I was excited to share this with my mom, so I called her. "Hi, Mom. Guess what? I bought my wedding dress today! It's a simple white lace dress for getting married in the mountains. I can't wait for you to see it!"

I waited for her response, naively hoping that she'd be glad to know how the wedding plans were coming along. Instead, she yelled at me, "How could you? We were supposed to do that together. You have deprived me of my right to be part of this important occasion. Well then, I am *not* coming to your wedding!" And with that, she slammed down the phone. *Over a wedding dress? You've got to be kidding?* I flopped face down on Kris's bed and bawled. *What did I do that was so wrong? Really, a dress? Can't she love me more than a dress? Will she ever be happy with me, or stop trying to control everything I do?* I saw her withdrawal as yet another manipulative technique, to which I vehemently rebelled. It seemed that the only way to have a relationship with her was to remain as a compliant child, but I was the insolent rebel in the family. My response was to withdraw from the battle and let her have her way. She didn't get a wedding invitation.

No one was surprised when Mom and Dad divorced. I knew my Mom was angry, but I didn't know how my dad was handling things. One day Dad arrived at the front door of Randy's mother's house. What a surprise! Apparently, he wanted to get together with Randy and me for dinner, and because we already had plans with family friends, Randy suggested that we invite my dad to join us.

"Uh, Randy, I don't think that's a good idea."

"Oh, it'll be fine," he declared nonchalantly. He called his friends, who agreed, but I was filled with anxiety. I'd undergone too many argumentative dinner conversations to trust in my father's civil behavior. On one memorable occasion Peggy brought her fiancé home to meet the family. We all had to endure a tumultuous dinner filled with bickering, fighting, and crying. Dad created chaos wherever he went, and we three girls feared his disdain toward whomever we chose to love. I was hesitant about Randy's plan and didn't want the kind of fiasco Peggy had endured.

We were served steak for dinner, one of my dad's favorites. *So far so good.* The couple had recently returned from six months of missionary work in Chile, and we conversed about the local customs and regional food. With no prompting, my father attempted to add to the conversation about cultural differences, "In China, the mothers masturbate their little baby boys to put them to sleep. I always thought this was such a good idea and I've wondered why we don't do it here."

My breathing stopped. Everyone froze in silence. We four looked at each other, at a complete loss of how to respond. Several silent seconds passed that felt like minutes.

My dad had a confused look on his face, *"What's wrong?"* Randy and I were mortified. I was shocked into silence and shame, but somehow, we recovered some conversation and the evening continued.

Despite my dad's inappropriate social behavior, Randy and I tried to maintain a semblance of a relationship with my father and his new fiancé. Surprise: Dad was getting remarried in May. And another surprise: he generously offered to pay for my wedding.

I decided to keep Dad in the loop with wedding details and called regularly to give updates. I ordered a wedding cake from a bakery in Bishop costing $35. When I called him, he blew up.

Yelling at me on the phone, loud enough for those standing in the kitchen to hear through the landline, he said, "You did this without my permission? You didn't even ask me what bakery to use or what flavor cake would be best! Do you think I will pay for anything when you have such little regard for me? I'm not paying for a thing!" I was stupefied. *He's just like Mom! Why am I surprised? I've lived with him for twenty years and should have been wary when he made the offer. I'd let my guard down; I so wanted to believe he cared about me and my happiness.* Randy was furious. He grabbed the phone from my hand and said firmly, "Stop treating Gaynelle this way. I mean it!" After a ten-minute yelling match, Randy put the phone back into my hand and dashed out the door.

"You're marrying a hypnotist who has mesmerized you into wanting to marry him. You're stupid. You should leave him! But you've always been stubborn, you do whatever you want, and you have no regard for my feelings. I'm not coming to your wedding. And I'm not paying for it either!"

A pause, then: "Besides, we'll be on our honeymoon. But even if we were here, I wouldn't come. I don't like this man who controls your mind!"

I screamed something back at him, trying to defend myself. Stabbing pain threw me into an uncontrollable sobbing rage. Years later I would learn that my dad's honeymoon wasn't until August, weeks after our July wedding.

The timing of this argument was four days before my father's wedding, which we'd planned to attend. Randy, hurt and angry, didn't want to go, but I felt obligated and insisted we go anyway. We dressed for the occasion but ended up sitting in the parking lot for an hour and a half, unable to will ourselves into the building to attend the wedding or the reception. It was awkward and I was disappointed, like I'd chickened out. Only eight people in the family were invited, and our empty chairs—Dad reminded me later—made the gathering less festive.

My parents seemed unaware that their degrading words might result in negative consequences for them. Randy, deeply affected by my family's rejection, was hurting and took these attacks personally. Who wouldn't? The crazy interactions with my family weren't good for my reputation with Randy's family, but his dear mother, Vivian, seemed to put up with it. She told us she was praying for us, but this didn't remove my fears. *What does she think about her son's future?* She continued mentoring me in spiritual wisdom and modeled Christian love.

The family and their friends continued to love and accept me, especially Kris, Randy's little sister. *Maybe my sisters will be able to come to our wedding—a small measure of support will be nice.*

I called Peggy, who was a teacher in Chicago where her husband attended medical school. When she said they couldn't make it out because they didn't have the money, I was disappointed, but I understood. Usually, my dad would have paid for such things, but under the circumstances I dare not ask him, and they wouldn't want to take his money anyway.

With Mom, Dad, and my older sister off the guest list, I decided to protect my younger sister, Diane, by not inviting her. She was nineteen, and I figured since Mom wasn't coming to the wedding, it would only cause conflict between the two of them if she was invited. In retrospect, I wish I'd given her the respect of allowing her to make her own decision.

*My dream of this special day is now going to be without my family.* But I was set on marrying Randy. He seemed to love me enough to put up with my tears and dysfunctional family. As much as I desired a relationship with my family, my efforts to reach out to them failed. My overtures were to no avail. When I considered my upcoming wedding, I was acutely aware of the problems that could arise if they attended, so I had no choice but to adjust. I loved the young man I'd fallen in love with at Cal Western. I was grateful that he had tried to protect me from the ridiculous and exasperating covert and overt attacks on my personality. With effort, I kept my pain and disappointment hidden. The safe environment at Randy's house helped lessen my sadness, and I was relieved that I didn't have to deal with my parents since I'd been reminded of how difficult they could be. I knew Randy was a tender man, a good big brother, a loving son, and he was committed to me. I would begin life anew with a Christian family.

I made about sixty simple, hand-written invitations. We made all the preparations and paid for it ourselves. I was proud and pleased; our wedding was going to happen no matter what!

*Let us trust God and our better judgment to set it right hereafter.*
Patrick Henry

*If the LORD delights in a human's way, he makes his steps firm; though he stumbles, he will not fall, for the LORD upholds him with his right hand.* Psalm 37:24

CHAPTER 6

# Blessings at Sky
# Meadow—1972

*Today I will live with hope in my heart.*

CHERYL KARPEN

The memory of my wedding day is precious to me, even though it now seems lost in time and space. Even as the rainbows in the fog at Cal Western had drawn me towards belief in Something beyond me, my wedding day remains a cornerstone in my faith and reminds me to count on God. Evy, along with her husband, Don, were special friends of Randy's family. They owned a cabin on ranch-like property known as Sky Meadow.

They took me under their wings and supported Randy's family, especially after Randy's father died. When asked if we could be married there, they readily agreed. And more good news: Randy's maternal grandfather, Dwight, a retired Methodist minister, said he'd marry us.

Sky Meadow is located on the Eastern slopes of the Sierra Nevada Mountains—the elevation 7,000 feet—3,000 feet above Owens Valley, northwest of Bishop, CA. The view of the valley is spectacular from this meadow, with the White Mountains rising to the east. There were three cabins and a caretaker's cabin on the property.

Randy and I arrived a week before the wedding to prepare a small grass meadow, a quarter mile uphill from the cabins, where we planned to have the ceremony. We stomped down the three-foot-tall dry grass to make a path from the road to the meadow and collected pine cones, lining the path on both sides with them. The summer sun lit up the grass, reflecting a beautiful wavy golden meadow.

With sixty people planning to attend, we rummaged through the cabins and found numerous picnic benches for seating. We placed them carefully, making every effort not to disturb the grass in order to preserve the natural golden beauty of the meadow. Our guests would be looking down on the great Owens Valley. We arranged with the caretakers to have a pump organ from one of the cabins taken to the meadow. A friend of Randy's family who was an organist prepared to play it for us.

Not far from the meadow was a small grove of Ponderosa and Jeffrey pine trees in a large flat area known as 'the campground.' It was a comfortable and protected setting where Randy and I had camped a few times. Our small reception would be held there, and this also provided a place where some of our guests could pitch their tents.

The caretakers were trail-hand cooks for cattle drives in this area. They prepared and served beef stew, salad, and bread for the celebration. We had ordered a two-tiered cake from the bakery in Bishop. A simple dinner for a simple wedding and in our price range.

Our wedding was planned for a Saturday afternoon at 4:00 p.m. Randy's mother and family arrived on Thursday, having driven six hours to get there. Alex, a good friend of Randy's Mom, arrived and was to sing the opening song. Alice, our singing teacher, and friend from college, came to sing the Lord's Prayer. Don planned to tape the wedding with special audio equipment he used for taping bird songs. In May we had rented cabins, located 2000 feet below us, for our guests and Randy's grandparents. Because we rented the cabins in May when it was still cool, we failed to realize the cabins did not provide air conditioning. Unfortunately, the cabins became sweltering saunas in July, and Randy and I felt badly we had failed them in this way.

With all this excitement, my anxiety and fears took over and I was unable to cope. The switch in my brain flipped the day before the wedding, and my emotions swung me out of control. After a week of getting along, Randy and I had a huge argument. "What is wrong with you?" He said hotly. "I hate it when you're like this!"

I shouted at him, "Okay. It's not too late! You don't have to marry me!" I tramped off through the sagebrush in a rage. I wore shorts and my legs got cut with bleeding scratches, but being emotionally charged, I was barely aware of it. If anything, it was a relief.

I returned ten minutes later, crying, blood running down my legs, and we spoke more harsh words. I picked up a rock and hurled it at the windshield of our car trying to shatter it, but it didn't break. Seething with self-hate, I tried a second time with a bigger rock. No luck. *I am such a weakling!*

Randy's family and some guests were now arriving and witnessed my outbursts. I had no idea what they were thinking, nor did I care. But throwing the rock stopped Randy's attack. He reconnected with me in a gentle way that brought me back to him. I calmed down when he held me in his arms and assured me that he wanted to marry me. I again felt loved and believed that in our struggles, we would be okay. I trusted that my real self was who Randy loved. Deep down, I loved her too. I believed Randy would be the balm in my life to heal my cut and scratched-up self. He was the help God was sending me.

And he knew about that mysterious man, Jesus. The wedding was on! The ranch was abuzz with excitement. I concentrated on playing my part by staying present and attending to my responsibilities.

On Saturday morning the vast Owens Valley was on full display with a brilliant blue sky for our rehearsal. Randy's grandfather called us by unusual names, Beatrice, and Leonard, because he said if he used our real names, then he would have married us at the rehearsal. When rehearsal was over, the caretaker pointed at a few white thunderheads coming over the mountain peaks from the west. She pronounced, "Whenever the clouds gather over the mountain like that, it always rains." I did not believe her. *Those few puffy clouds? It's been sunny all week!*

By noon, it was pouring. Though warm, everything was getting a good soak. Our wedding group ate lunch together in one of the cabins. *After all this, we're rained out!* I stood at the open door of the cabin, studying the clouds. Evy walked over to me, and put her arm around my shoulder, hugging me gently, to comfort me. As we stared at the driving rain she mused, "The rain will stop. It will be okay this afternoon. Don't worry. I believe it will be fine!"

I curled my hair and began to get ready for my wedding. Still, there was a steady downpour. Our wedding party took turns getting ready because we had only two bathrooms, one in each of the two cabins we were given to use. The men had one cabin and the women the other. I found Randy during this time and suggested we move the wedding ceremony into the larger cabin. However, Randy's faith was sure, "It doesn't matter if it rains and everyone might get wet, but we are going to get married in the meadow." *Okay then!* My heart smiled. *I so want to get married in our meadow.* Randy's resolve and faith was one of his endearing qualities.

Transporting the cake on the day of the wedding turned out to be a challenge for the friends who volunteered for the job. The uphill grade to the ranch was so steep that the cake slid around in the back of the station wagon. When they got to the top of the hill, they complained bitterly about their task. I muttered an apologetic, *Thank you.* Surely this was all my fault; I felt guilty and inconsiderate. *Why didn't I think of that? I should have had the cake delivered.* I was glad it was delivered intact, and they gave it to the caretakers who were responsible for the dinner.

The wedding party was running a little late, due in part to the rain, but also because our guests, as well as the wedding party, needed to be transported up the hill. It was well past 4:00 when the raindrops became a mere sprinkle. We began the car shuttle up the hill. The rain had quelled the dust till it softened, and the sprinkles came only in little spits and spats. As the bride, I was the last to be driven up the road and I noticed a faint brightening of the sky peeking through the cloud cover. I was in awe of Randy's determination and Evy's belief that the rain would stop. *I am going to live my life with this kind of faith, with earnestness, and the spright-like spunkiness that is the real me.* I felt peaceful and a comforting warmth welled up inside me. *Is this the touch of the Holy Spirit? Is this the peace that passes understanding?! I am safe. Yes, I desire to marry this man.*

*I am fortunate he wants me, considering what I've been through. These people who believe, know something I do not. God is helping me and Randy.*

The mountain meadow sang as the pump organ's music gently floated to the audience and into my heart. Even though we still felt a few raindrops, the sun's rays filtered through the cloud covering and spectacularly lit the sky, highlighting patches of the exquisite Owens Valley below us. Alex began to sing, his deep voice penetrating our little wilderness, "Randy and Gay, this is your day, to stand in sunlight and say…." At that moment, the sun burst through and lit our meadow. As Alex sang the word "sunlight," we and the guests gasped as the sun blazed a spotlight on our meadow. With a smile of acknowledgment, Alex continued singing, *Love is a Many Splendored Thing.*

I felt my future life open before me on our own little hill in the universe. *Something good is happening. The past is behind me, and my future is one full of faith. It is the end of the rain!* I was hopeful and beamed with promise and joy. *God is real, active, and present! This wasn't luck or a coincidence.*

As Randy and I met in front of his grandfather to exchange the traditional Methodist wedding vows, I heard his words, "As the Lord's Prayer is sung, let us listen as Randy and Gay experience the first prayer of their marriage." The pump organ and Alice's voice touched my open heart, and Randy and I stood, holding hands and bowing our heads.

After we were introduced as Randy and Gay Andersen, we kissed, joined hands, and walked back down the center aisle, through the glorious, untouched golden grass. As soon as we reached the end of the aisle, the clouds darted back together, and the brightness subdued. The penetrating rays of sunshine disappeared over Owens Valley, and a gentle breeze refreshed us, subduing the sun's momentary heat. We had perfect weather for the reception and festivities which followed. There was no more rain, yet because of the cloud cover, it was balmy and bug-less!

Vivian, Evy, Don and others who've experienced the power of prayer must have been on their knees. I interpreted the perfection of the day as God saying to me, "It's okay that your family wouldn't come. You're beginning life with Me, and I will take care of you. See what I can do! I will always take care of you." These thoughts gave me comfort, and still do.

God takes pleasure in helping us in our daily and meager lives on this planet. That day was remembered for years among those who attended as a day revered and blessed. All agreed that God intervened for Randy and me. God's Spirit was made known to me in a new and real way. My memory and belief in God's miraculous intervention on this day was my guiding light. *No matter what, we are supposed to be together. We are blessed.*

*His Eye Is on the Sparrow*
*...Jesus is my portion. My constant friend is he:*
*His eye is on the sparrow. And I know he watches me.*
*I sing because I'm happy, I sing because I'm free,*
*His eye is on the sparrow, And I know He watches me.*

Text: Civilla D. Martin Music:
Charles H. Gabriel

*I look to the mountains; does my strength come from mountains? No, my strength comes from God, who made heaven, and earth, and mountain.* Psalm 12:1
*The Message,* by Eugene Peterson

## CHAPTER 7

# Topsy-Turvy—1973

*The truest meaning of success is not to get up
on top, but to get out from under!*

RICHARD GAYLORD BRILEY

Coming back together in intimacy on our wedding night brought back our loving feelings and a sense of normalcy seemed to blossom between us. For our honeymoon we camped across the country, staying with friends and relatives. I had confidence in our ability to provide for ourselves because we were two college graduates, now taking our first trip as a married couple. We were off to experience the world!

One of our visits was to his grandparent's home at a Methodist campground in the Chicago area. It wasn't a campground in the traditional sense, but a group of small white houses with outdoor screened porches. Dwight and Dolly had a 1920's type cabin.

Dwight spoke firmly to Randy about me, "She is a special woman who will need patience and extra care." His voice was resolute but compassionate, and I couldn't help wondering what he meant. I was embarrassed and again thought something must be wrong with me. The conversation was in my presence, so his thoughts were not supposed to be a secret from me.

I asked Dwight, "What is the Holy Spirit? I don't know what that means."

Being a newcomer in the ways and knowledge of God, Christianese lingo still baffled me. He, being a minister, without judgment, explained.

"The Holy Spirit is like the wind or the breath of God." It was early afternoon, and we stood under grand deciduous alders. Dwight looked up, closed his eyes for a few seconds, then lifted his hands upwards as he continued, "The wind blows through the trees, but you can't see the wind. You see the branches of the trees sway, but that is not the wind. You cannot see breath, except on a cold day you may see the steam of breath, but that vision is not breath. You only *feel* the wind embracing your body. You *feel* breath. The Holy Spirit moves like the wind. You feel the Spirit and know it's there, but you'll never see it. Just because you can't see it, does not mean it's not there. The Holy Spirit is like the wind. It is like breathing. It exists. It is God's Spirit. When we take our first breath at birth, the Holy Spirit breathes Life into us. And just in the same way, the Holy Spirit leaves us upon our last breath of life. And the Spirit is good. In God, we move, and live, and have our being. (Acts 17:28) The Holy Spirit breathes in Life. Life we shall be able to see, but never breath."

*My feeling of God's presence is real. What a relief! Like the sun breaking through on our wedding day.* I embraced Dwight's explanation. What I had been sensing and feeling, unseen, were validated. I began to believe in the existence of a Greater Being—that *Something* I always sensed was there. Finally, I could name that unknown presence: The Holy Spirit. *I've felt this all my life! Maybe I'm not so naive after all.* I trusted Dwight Knowlton's wisdom. Smiling to myself, I thought, *One more golden nugget from an experienced, knowledgeable source.*

It was summer but the nights were cold as we drove on I-90 through South Dakota. Late one night we could not find a campground and decided to sleep in the car at a rest area. We wrapped up in sleeping bags, but once we settled in, panic took hold of me. I had never had a panic attack before and didn't know what was happening. "I can't sleep in the car!" I shouted. "I can't."

Randy spoke up, "What? What is the matter? We'll be okay."

"No! You don't understand. I can't do it!" I started kicking the passenger side window. I felt like a caged animal and wanted to run away, but it was dark, pouring rain, and I didn't know where we were. There seemed no hope of escape.

"What happened to you? No one acts like this without a reason. Something had to have happened to make you feel this way. Try to remember, Gay. Why would sleeping in the car be such a big deal?" He wasn't angry with me this time.

It didn't take long for me to regain the memory that prompted my fear. I'd told Randy many times about our family summer camping trips to Oceanside, California. Our small 1950's trailer had no hookups and no electricity; the lamp ran on propane. Campers used community bathrooms common in campgrounds. We parked on Highway 1, and we had only to cross the empty highway to be on the long, sandy beach. Two blocks away was downtown, and three-quarters of a mile north was the Oceanside pier. We camped there for three summers, when I was six, seven, and eight. My sisters, cousins, and I played in the sand and waves, and at night we could hear the calming, pounding surf. Dad came only on weekends to visit, the rest of the week we were with Mom, her sister Georgia and her two kids.

That night in South Dakota, I related to Randy what happened to me when I was six. "Diane and I had always slept in the trailer, sharing a twin bed, with our Mom and Dad, and Peggy slept on a cot inside the enclosed zipped awning. But then things changed, and that's when the nightmare began.

"Dad decided he wanted us out of the trailer, and he announced that Diane and I would sleep in the car when he came on weekends. He put our mattress in the back seat of the Oldsmobile, but the idea of sleeping alone in the car, without adult protection, terrified me. I was determined NOT to do this! When I was forced to get in the car, I couldn't sleep, and soon I began screaming. I screamed so long that Dad came out and spanked me, scolding me to be quiet. But when he left, I started yelling again. I was desperate to get back in the trailer where I felt safe."

As I told this story to Randy, I sobbed uncontrollably. The memory of being spanked because I was afraid and needed my parents wrenched my inside. Randy listened intently, so I felt safe to continue my story: "I wanted my parents to hear me, so I screamed even louder. Dad came out a second time and spanked me again, but I kept it up. He was determined to beat me out of my complaining. I was just as determined that I was NOT sleeping in the car alone and taking care of my sister!

"So my dad used a different tactic. He pointed to a man coming out of the campground bathroom and said, 'Everyone is going to know that you are in the car. If you don't stop screaming, everyone staying here is going to know you're in the car. Now stop it.' I looked out my window and saw a man walking out of the bathroom. That did it. I knew I was vulnerable. I knew that men could overpower me and hurt me. Terrified does not adequately describe the way I felt. I was helpless, and my father's betrayal left me feeling abandoned. My dad knew it was dangerous and he didn't care."

I was dumbfounded, remembering this. "I guess after that, I've always had trouble sleeping in the car. So many beautiful days at the beach were tainted because of this." As I assessed my growing-up years, I understood how my resentments grew, and how I became more scared and insecure. *At six years old, I lost my sense of well-being.*

Here in South Dakota, the memories reactivated. The old panic came up so suddenly that Randy and I were shaken, especially since we'd been tent-camping together for two summers. Awakening that memory gave me a clue as to why I started kicking the window of the car. Understanding the impetus of my overreaction helped me come to my senses and my panic subsided. I laid my head on Randy's lap and sobbed to sleep. As I drifted off in twilight sleepiness, I heard myself moaning, "Mama, please love me. Mama, please come to me."

Still, sometimes we had no alternative but to sleep in the car. I didn't like it, but managed my fear by separating our present situation from my past experiences. I learned that my breakdowns were often breakthroughs. I was strong and courageous in facing my memories, but because of confusing times like this, Randy perceived me as weak. He began treating me like a child, as if he were the all-knowing parent.

During the third week of our honeymoon, we had a fight. The catalyst for the argument is long forgotten, but I recall the outcome clearly. While driving, Randy loudly announced, "Well, we can always get a divorce. That's always an option."

*Whoa! What? We just got married!* Vexation flooded my system, and I threw my purse out the window into the grass along the freeway. My first thought was to get an annulment. *I cannot live with this kind of uncertainty.*

My 'Tame the Beast with Love' mentality won out. Randy's need to be in charge, his need to be all and know all, dove-tailed with my insecurities. Our relationship grew into a codependency; I was dependent on Randy to earn his love and thereby find my value. He was dependent on me to need his advice; to be the know all person, which gave him control of me. He also needed to find his worthiness by being right.

We turned the car around and went back to get my purse.

"Randy, what about our wedding day? Didn't that mean something? What about what Dwight told us? How can we give up now when we've just started? Are you giving up?" No answer.

Neither of us gave up. We made it home to San Diego where we rented a one-bedroom house that had an enclosed patio and a little yard, twelve blocks from Ocean Beach. I loved our first home. It seemed possible that we could begin a life together that would work.

In the autumn of 1972, several California public schools closed due to low enrollment. There were too many baby-boomer teachers and not enough kids to teach. I couldn't get on the substitute lists because full-time teachers who had been let go had priority. This had been our primary source of income and caught us off-guard. Randy took a year off from school to rest, read, and apply to graduate school, where he planned to get a PhD to become a psychologist. This was our plan, but here we were without jobs.

At my insistence, we went to UC San Diego and signed up for odd jobs. We began our own house-cleaning and gardening business, earning minimum wage. We were untrained gardeners and took jobs above our expertise. We bumbled some of our jobs but scraped through working together every day. We enjoyed the sights and activities of San Diego on the weekends.

Randy applied to graduate school, and we discussed our future. Suddenly he quipped, "Psychology doesn't go deep enough. It leaves something short. I'm not going to become a psychologist!"

*What does he mean psychology doesn't go far enough? This is one of the reasons I married him.* I wanted my husband to be a good provider. *Counseling is his calling. Now what?* We were working full time, but the low wages weren't cutting it.

We were flat broke after paying rent and had no money for dinner. One day, while gardening along a busy street in La Jolla, we prayed for money to come to us, foolish as that may sound. I'd learned that if anything was needed, praying was a good place to start. *Trust in a perfect Power, a Power that desires goodness for us.* Walking to the car, I prayed out loud, "Hey God, we need some help down here!" Randy smiled at me.

Plop! A purse landed on the hood of our car. We looked at each other in amazement.

We waited about twenty minutes for someone to claim it, but nothing happened. We found the driver's license and called from a phone booth. We delivered the purse and the woman who answered the door was grateful, "It was on my dashboard and flew out the open window!" She said. Noticing that everything was still in her purse, she gave us twenty dollars. *Hooray! We have enough money for dinner and even more. Who could have thought this up?* How else could I explain this improbability, except that God was taking care of us?

*The LORD will keep you from all harm—he will watch over your life; the LORD will watch over your coming and your going both now and forevermore.* Psalm 121: 7-8

## CHAPTER 8

# Oh, For Goodness Sake

*It is cynicism and fear that freeze life;*
*it is faith that thaws it out, releases it, sets it free.*

HARRY EMERSON FOSDICK

Dredging up memories often caused me headaches or vomiting, especially after a sobbing catharsis. Unbeknownst to me, this was my brain's effort to heal by digging out the roots of my distress. At other times my body could be attacked by uncontrollable shaking, needle-like prickles on my skin, or an uncomfortable fire which felt as though my heart might stop.

Randy and I wanted to dissolve the sexual shame that reared its ugly head after intimacy. "People don't get like this without a reason. There must be a reason" *What happened to me God? Will this ever end?* Peeling my onion brought tears to my eyes every time, and Randy was my only friend in this regard.

In the early 1970s, I was barely able to identify my shame patterns. It would be forty years before brave women came forward to share their stories of how sexual, physical, or mental abuse affected their lives. The gift of time has healed me enough to share what happened to me. I know what happened is not who I am, and I've moved on from feeling guilty or blaming myself for what others did. I learned to practice self-compassion for enduring suffering for a good part of my life. My terrible memories were difficult to recover. They were lost inside my mind and body in an unreachable place. But my pain reminded me that they lived. Though I had purposely pretended certain things had not happened, the denial strategy backfired. I searched to understand the burden of guilt and shame that had been imposed on my sense of self and which became embedded in my core. The symptoms never let up: depression, avoidance, fear, anxiety, and the aching pain throughout my solar plexus.

*What happened to me What caused me to be so ashamed?* But I knew. Of course I did. When I was about three years old, I started obsessively playing with my genitals. I discovered there was something that felt good, and unconsciously, I experimented. I enjoyed doing this in the bathtub, the living room, and wherever it was convenient, and experienced many climaxes. Doing so at bedtime helped me go to sleep. When my mother figured out that masturbating was part of my bedtime routine, she began a vendetta. She smelled my fingers, "You should never touch yourself there," she snarled. Her scowl expressed the gravity of this evil deed. *I'm a terrible girl. Mom says what I do is very bad.* She visited me several times each night, so out of necessity I dropped the bedtime routine. It didn't take long for me to discover that the morning was just as good, but Mom soon caught me and admonished me yet again. I feared her disdain and was ashamed; it permeated my psyche: especially because the harder I tried to be a 'good girl,' the more I wanted to masturbate.

By five years of age, my mother and I were at war. I tried to avoid her, but she was on the lookout. *There's got to be something about this she doesn't want me to know. What can be wrong with this feeling?* My behavior became more obsessive and obvious.

She tried to stop me by enlisting Peggy to tell her when I was 'playing with myself.' I didn't blame my sister for telling my mother. She was my protector against our dad, but she also needed to please our mother. Peggy did not have understood what was going on between me and Mom. My Mom began washing my genitals.

*I am a very bad girl, and my pee-pee makes me a disgusting girl. My mother can touch me, but I am not allowed to.* Even as a small child that didn't make sense.

I absorbed my mother's shame and believed I was a bad person. Fear and shame defined my core sexuality and personality. I unconsciously generalized my mother's shame of me, believing that other people felt like my mother did. *I am a disgusting human being. Everyone can see how sickening I am.* In despair, indeed for survival, I made a child's guess that punishment would relieve the guilt of my evil nature. I began to punish myself by carefully guarding against allowing myself to experience joy in any situation. I had a few friends in first grade, but by third grade I was afraid to interact with kids and became exceedingly shy. I hardly spoke to anyone on the playground. Incorporating my mother's shame of me, I unconsciously shut down good feelings of any kind, sexual or otherwise. By seven, this mental checking of my feeling-barometer was well in place and remained glued to me, especially after my mother chased me down and chastised me in the hallway. This survival strategy started causing me deep mental despair. I was a young sexual being with a normal drive, but the harder I tried to quell my sexual urges, the more insistent they became. I felt worse and worse about myself. Shame permeated my psyche and anxiety plagued me.

To add insult to injury, my mother took me to our doctor for a visit so he could diagnose my confounding problem. He had me undress, and spread my legs for him, while she pointed to the problem area. "What is wrong with her?" I wanted to disappear down a manhole. He touched my genitals gently and looked me over. *Why is this stranger touching me? I must be really bad, because I'm not allowed to.*

The doctor said, "I don't think anything is wrong, Mrs. B." My Mom was frustrated, and after a few months, she repeated the visit. Again, the doctor walked into the room, but he didn't look at me, and he firmly told her," Mrs. B, I am certain that nothing is wrong with your daughter." He was exasperated with my mother and compassionate toward my plight. I was relieved to hear that nothing was wrong with me. These kinds of interactions plagued the relationship between me and my mother. The damage was done though, never to be undone. I never knew if her disgust for me ever left her.

During her adolescence and early adult years, the culture may have reinforced the idea of suppressing masturbation. Many parents used fear tactics, telling their children they would go blind or that their arms would fall off for the evil deed of exploring their sexuality. Thankfully, Mom didn't say that to me, but she invaded my privacy and crossed my boundaries, violating the sense that I owned my own body. This in part, is how I lost a sense of normal boundaries. Her attitude destroyed any possibility of a warm, trusting relationship between us.

These interactions created an icy awareness deep in my soul and sense of sexual identity. It took time to smash it into crushed ice, longer still to melt it away. Maybe later I could begin to forgive. Forgiveness became my life's journey.

*LORD, consider my lament. Hear my cry for help, my king, and my God, for you I pray. In the morning, LORD, you hear my voice in the morning. I lay my requests before you and wait expectantly. Listen to my words.* Psalm 5: 1-3

## CHAPTER 9

# Confirmation

*My life has been very difficult, difficult indeed, but
I am grateful because it developed character in me.*

LORRAINE D, EIGHTY-NINE YEARS OLD

At the time Lorraine told me this, I was nowhere near being grateful for my struggles or my pain. I had read in Romans: "…We glory in our sufferings, because we know that suffering produces perseverance; perseverance, character; and character, hope." (Romans 3-4) I seemed to have developed endurance, and I did defer to hope to keep me going. So maybe, grateful for my suffering? We shall see…

When my dad was ninety-four, we stood on the Oceanside Pier overlooking the incoming surf, reminiscing about our days at the beach. Looking at the bright side, recalling what dad wanted to provide for us, I said, "Remember swimming in the waves? We had those big canvas rafts to ride the waves on… You taught me gin rummy under an umbrella on the beach… I loved taking barefoot walks in the shallows of the surf." Dad nodded, joining in reminiscing about our mutual memories. "And long walks on the pier eating ice cream cones!"

He began to speak of Mom, which was rare, but we had just flipped our minds back to the past when she was alive and present with us. He shook his head back and forth as he did when dismayed or perplexed. "She was always harder on you than the other two girls, and I never knew why." Funny, he'd pipe up with that little bit of information for me, confirming my memories of Mom. He continued, "After her hysterectomy, she was impossible to live with. Back then, they didn't have a clue about hormones, and she was out of whack for a year and a half. Then they finally got it right and she was better."

My mind jumped back in time. I was six and remembered visiting Mom in the hospital. It frightened me to see what she looked like and how she groaned with pain. When she returned home, she was in bed in a dark room. We were not allowed to disturb her; she was unavailable to me or Diane for six months. Peggy, thirteen at the time, fixed dinner, and I helped with the cleanup. My older sister did the laundry and managed homework. She did what she could for Diane and me. I related to her as my Mom.

As Dad spoke, I instantly put my childhood timeline together. I had just turned seven when Mom chased me down the hallway in a fury. *Was it her hormones that had thrown her off balance? Is that why she was so mean that day? Had she ever treated me so forcefully before that day?* I did not know. In terms of sex, it seemed she did.

My dad knew nothing of the chasm between Mom and me. Better to leave some things unknown. After my three-day visit with Dad, as I drove home, I groaned a catharsis of tears. My natural mother-daughter relationship was plundered by a surgery, hormonal imbalance, and my Mom's traumatic childhood. I lamented and longed for the love that my sisters, and other mothers and daughters, had the privilege of knowing.

*Listen…be wise and keep your heart on the right path.* Proverbs 23:19

## CHAPTER 10

# Marital Woes

*Expect the dawn of a new beginning in the dark nights of life.*

LLOYD OGILVIE

As Randy and I uncovered the root causes of my sexual shame, he was released from feeling that he was the cause. After hearing these stories, he intensely disliked my mother. Further discussions allowed for more breakthrough moments that helped me find a measure of purpose in healing my pain. I began to understand much of the impetus behind my unconscious responses. I thought Randy understood me better, and that this would help heal our relationship.

What was supposed to bring understanding and compassion toward me, became his excuse for arguments. Randy found it convenient to flagrantly blame me for any problems, real or perceived, using the excuse that I was 'damaged.' If I tried to defend myself, it created the chaos Randy seemed to thrive on. One blowout happened on our way to work because, naturally, there was something wrong with me. Random criticism kept me anxious, a good strategy to help him stay in power and keep me off balance.

This particular day, we stopped at the beach to fight it out, but I ran off into the crashing winter waves to douse my anger. His hateful criticism incited my uncontrollable rage, making me look crazy and unreliable.

Years before, as a teenager, when Dad yelled at me, I kicked the sliding glass door but never broke it. In another argument, when Randy screamed at me, I reacted as I did when I was a teenager—by kicking the glass door. This time it shattered.

My extreme reactions seemed to stop Randy's personal attacks on me for a short time, but his condescending verbal admonishments were increasing. I noticed a pattern: my outburst allowed calm and normality for a week or two. *Is this the only way I can stop Randy's attacks on me?*

One night, he pointed to our twelve-pound dog, "You're like this dog I have to take care of," he said, sneering at me. I knew this was a farce and tried to ignore his frequent demeaning comments. He threatened divorce, knowing how much it hurt me. I felt worn down; I lacked the confidence to leave or to meet his requirements to be a valued wife.

It was as if Randy found a treasure in a pretty bottle on the beach, something inside with the possibility of easing his grief. When he took the bottle home, he thought he could drink sips that would soothe his troubled soul. He hoped my love, with my heart entrusted to his hands, would heal him. But we both had real issues, and when he shook the bottle (me) up, what poured out was the residue from my childhood. As much as I wanted to help Randy and be the balm he needed, I needed to be valued. As much as I wanted his love to heal me, neither of us could become that for each other.

Once Randy decided he didn't want to become a psychologist, the next option for him was seminary. He applied for a Rockefeller Fellowship and was awarded a one-year grant at Colgate Rochester Crozer Divinity School in Rochester, New York.

*Well, this will be an interesting enterprise! Getting paid to go to graduate school! Sounds good to me. I'm always up for an adventure.* I surmised that seminary had something to do with God and church work, but had no clue what that entailed. I was relieved that we weren't going to be gardeners or housekeepers.

The estrangement from my family continued. I loved them, but was wary of their criticism or anger. I feared a confrontation would flip me back to the past. My sense of *self* was fragile and my emotions unsteady. For now, I was thankful my family was leaving me alone, though I missed my sisters. Later I would learn that they missed me, too. I continued hoping for change. My hope was to believe God is for me and to trust God with my future.

*God will never, never, never let us down. If we have faith and put our trust in Him, He will always look after us.*

Mother Teresa

CHAPTER 11

# Meeting the Christian Community—1973

*Justice is an instrument of Love, Power is an instrument of Justice, And Law is an instrument of Justice and Power.*

DR. KENNETH L. SMITH, 1973

The theological seminary was located on Goodman Avenue at the top of a hill overlooking Rochester. We were given a one-bedroom apartment for married students on campus. This was my first Christian community, with people who called themselves 'believers' or 'Christians.' I felt accepted and valued as a member of this unique group of graduate students. They openly shared their beliefs, experiences, and faith in Jesus. Throughout the year, I learned the meaning, purpose, and power of Christian community. I had found a family at last—the Family of God.

I got a part-time job at the University in Rochester, and Randy began classes and worked part time at the seminary. As his wife, I was allowed to audit classes, which I enjoyed because there was no pressure or requirement to write papers and take tests. My favorite class was a study of the life and ministry of Dr. Martin Luther King, Jr. The professor, Dr. Kenneth L. Smith, was one of MLK's professors and had worked with him during his ministry. Dr. Smith was on fire with personal, theological, and ethical insights about King's life, and I learned biblical principles through the lens of the Civil Rights Movement. This class provided my first breakthrough into the complexities of comprehending Jesus as the catalyst for liberty, justice, and equality.

Throughout the '60s, I'd been keenly aware of the Civil Rights Movement. I listened to King's speeches, and in high school read his book of sermons and speeches, *Strength to Love*. A Baptist minister, Dr. King spoke and wrote eloquently about God's love, and I agreed with the principles and was encouraged.

At the time, I didn't know King's focus was based on the biblical precepts of Jesus' teachings and life. My sophomore year in college, in April of 1968, King was assassinated. The events of the Civil Rights Movement and its purpose burned in my mind. The three assassinations of major leaders in the 1960s concerned me for the mental health of our nation.

Now it was 1973, and Dr. Smith's poignant teachings about Jesus' life and ministry became pivotal as I progressed in my biblical understanding. I experienced the power of intellectual thought with the serious study of the ministry and the teachings of Jesus. This was my first introduction to the four gospels, the parables, the community life Jesus experienced, and his resurrection from death. We delved into the narratives of the nature of healing miracles. Martin Luther King reflected on the Israelites' enslavement in Egypt, comparing it to the enslaved Black people in America. King compared the political movements in Israel during Jesus' day to our modern times of political unrest concerning Civil Rights. The powers that were in Israel didn't want to hear Jesus; the powers in this country did not want to hear Dr. Martin Luther King, Jr.. Both had a commitment to truth, that caused disagreements which led others to murder them.

Dr. Smith presented a segment in the class called "*A Summary of the Intellectual Sources of the Thought of Martin Luther King, Jr.*" We discussed MLK's legacy at length, focusing on the non-violent strategies he developed, along with those of Gandhi and Jesus. Dr. Smith focused on civil disobedience and why a responsible society must work toward 'Justice for all.'

The implicit work of the church is "to draw people away from false assumptions, and to find creative solutions where the church fosters freedom and justice, and to keep the two from destroying each other." Dr. Smith addressed King's theological assumptions as a model for change. He said, "In King's thinking, the Church does not have a mission—it *is* mission. The church does not have a ministry—it *is* ministry." The function of the church is clear, but the nature of the church involves people, and so the nature of the church varies from community to community.

We listened to recordings of Dr. King's speeches. One speech, from his book *Strength to Love*, really affected me: "We are greatly mistaken to think that Christianity protects us from the pain and agony of mortal existence. Christianity has always insisted that the cross we bear precedes the crown we wear. To be a Christian, one must take up his cross, with all its difficulties and agonizing and tragedy-packed content, and carry it until that very cross leaves its marks upon us and redeems us to that more excellent way, which comes only through suffering."[5]

MLK understood the effects of oppression upon the human soul and mind, and I admired his intellectual emphasis. I could relate to the suffering and helplessness the Black people endured. Dr. King asked the Black community to have compassion on their oppressors by following the teachings of Jesus. In response to oppression and hate, he led a movement of nonviolence because Jesus said, "… I tell you, love your enemies and pray for those who persecute you." (Matthew 5:44) This inspired and reassured me: *"The wrong shall fail, the right prevail, with peace on earth good will to men."* [6]

*I'm on an empowering path. If justice, peace, and non-violence is the church's aspiration and purpose, if this is what Randy and I will be working toward in his career, then I am all-in.*

The biblical world with Jesus' teachings and the modern world we live in, are interdependent and intertwined. People came to Jesus with human needs. They were sick, debilitated, poor, afraid, and anxious about social problems. People begged for help. And Jesus welcomed them. Both ancient and modern people are drawn together by a variety of human experiences. The Bible taught principals that I could relate to. The disciples who were close to Jesus modeled for us, even in modern times, how to live—in peace, love, and with sacrifice. Our abundant lives do not make us different from those who came before us, those who suffered. We may have more, but we are the same sick, debilitated, poor, and anxious people. *Jesus welcomed them; he welcomes us; he welcomes me.* This new way of thinking provided a way for me to face the challenges in finding a healthy path for my life.

MLK taught about the importance of responding to oppression with prayer and non-violent resistance, which is what Jesus did. Jesus met/ meets the needs of people who seek him. "Jesus Christ is the same yesterday, today, and forever." (Hebrews 13:8) God's love is constant and sure and stretches over the eras. God's way, revealed to us in Jesus, carries us through the generations. God is always acting on behalf of the oppressed.[7]

Randy's grandmother, Dolly, died on her and Dwight's sixtieth wedding anniversary. It was my twenty-fifth birthday. I thought this significant; she lived her life knowing Jesus and serving others in the church, and I welcomed the opportunity to follow in her footsteps with my marriage to a pastor. *It is my turn to carry on. My deep longing has been to serve, and I am happy my life has meaning.*

Soon afterwards, lying in bed one Saturday morning, in that waking twilight sleep, I heard an audible whisper, *"Follow me. Follow me."* I felt breath on my neck and was startled. Raising up on one elbow, I was surprised that Randy wasn't by my side. "Randy? Did you just say something to me?"

"No. I'm getting ready to take a shower," he yelled to me from the bathroom.

I rested my head on the pillow. *Am I dreaming?* I rested, but again, in my ear were the audible whispering words, *"Follow Me. Follow Me."* Something indescribable entered from the top of my head, tingling and working through my veins, down my body, into my toes. I felt as if I had been washed through. Peace touched the core of my soul. I relaxed fully and sank into the mattress. The vision of a protective umbrella covered me, us, our future, and my parents and sisters. *All is well.* The feeling enveloped me in peace and harmony I had never known and lasted throughout the day. Jesus spoke to me, reached out to me, and was leading me into a relationship with him. The words 'peace that passes understanding' had new meaning for me.

I began having conversations with Jesus, and my relationship with 'the Lord' began in earnest. However, the idea of God as a Father grated on me because my concept of a father was authoritarian and fraught with pain. Years later, I told a Methodist minister how I felt about my distrust of God, also known as *Father* God. He explained, "This is how I see it. The Trinity is a threesome: God, Jesus, and the Holy Spirit. The Trinity is the Ever Three and the Ever One. Think of it as holding a triangle. If you hold one side of the triangle, you hold the entire triangle in your hand. Such is the Trinity. Then think of yourself safe inside the Triangle." *In other words, as I cling to Jesus, when I pray to him, I also hold on to God and the Holy Spirit. Praying to Jesus is not exclusionary.*

"Think of it this way," he continued, "The Trinity represents one Person who has different roles, like a person who is a child, then a parent, and then a grandparent. One person, many functions. Jesus promised that the Father would send the gift of the Holy Spirit in his name. The Spirit works in us to teach us and help us to understand Jesus and to become like Jesus, the Christ. The Spirit is known as the Comforter or Advocate. But Jesus alone promises the gift of peace. Jesus' sacrificial action shows us the depth of God's passion to assure us of God's secure love for his people forever.

"God is the Heavenly Parent, protecting and guiding all his children, which of course includes adults. We identify God as Father because Jesus called out to his Abba, Hebrew for 'Father,' when he was dying on the Cross. But we must always remember… we are made in God's image, male and female alike… and thus, God's character is both father and mother."

*A-ha! A mini sermon from my pastor friend. Thanks again, God. This Trinity idea has been a mystery to me. How do you know just what I'm needing? This makes sense to me.*

*Take delight in the Lord and he will give you the desires of your heart.*
Psalm 37:4

# CHAPTER 12

# What Now?

*Delay is preferable to error.*

THOMAS JEFFERSON

At Christmas Randy wanted to return to California for the four-week break between semesters. This didn't make sense to me; we needed my job, and June was not far off. Our friends encouraged us to stay. Most of them were staying and had invited us to share Christmas gatherings with them. I was against taking a winter road trip across the country. As had become customary with Randy, my opinion didn't count for much, and his need to make the decisions steam rolled over me and our life together. I allowed this by not taking equal ownership for our plans. Packed and ready to leave, our friends gathered round our car, a 1970 Volvo my dad gave me as a graduation present, imploring us to stay at least one more day, warning "You shouldn't travel! Wait out the storm." Randy refused. They joined hands and prayed for us to be protected and have a safe trip.

I pleaded with Randy, "It's too risky. God is trying to lead us. I don't think we're supposed to go." Randy's determination to leave and go back to California won out.

Snowflakes appeared on our windshield as we drove down the long driveway away from the seminary at 9:00 p.m., our little dog in the back seat. Randy planned to drive through the night.

When I awoke in the early morning, Randy accused me: "Why can't you stay awake with me when I need you?" *He knows by now that I don't—can't—pull an all-nighter.* I endured his yelling with patience and acquiescence. We were in Ohio, on an unplowed, snow-covered four-lane freeway. It had snowed all night, and we were traveling at 35-miles-per hour in heavy traffic. I felt helpless, frightened for our lives, and my only solace was praying that God would help us. *Please help Randy drive, God, and keep everyone safe on the road. Protect us, please.*

I offered him some respite, "Let's stop and take a break. Let me drive, I've had sleep." He wouldn't budge. We continued moving at this snail's pace. Snow was predicted for the next 1,000 miles. *How long will it take us to get to California at this rate?* I drifted off late in the morning, awakening with a start. "Wake up, wake up!" Groggy, my sleepy eyes widened as I saw an orange sedan spinning out of control in front of us. Randy swerved sideways and slid on the ice. We fish-tailed into the orange sedan. The impact swung our car broadside across the left lane and halfway into the freeway's right lane. In slow motion, we slid to a stop, while vehicles around us collided like bumper cars, the ice canceling any friction that would have stopped them. There we sat, broadside across nearly two lanes of the freeway. Oncoming traffic and a semi-truck were headed directly for us.

*Oh God, save us now!* I silently prayed. *We will never survive a direct hit!* The truck couldn't slow down but moved onto the shoulder and plowed through the snowbank. The driver missed the front of our car by a centimeter. I know, because as it barreled by, I saw the bottom of the truck's trailer scrape the paint off the hood of our car. Bam! We were hit by another car! We careened across the ice, an impact that damaged the engine so that our car was dead on the highway. What seemed like hours had happened in mere seconds. All traffic stopped. I believed that the prayers of our friends at seminary, much like the prayers of friends on our wedding day, were answered.

When the police arrived, everyone, including Randy, got a ticket for unsafe driving in these severe weather conditions. The road was cleared, but how that happened is a blur. Our car was towed to an auto shop, and a highway patrolman took us to a motel and arranged a room for us. *We are alive! No injuries, God! A miracle—again! Oh, thank you, dear God!*

Though shaken, I was awed and happy that we'd survived uninjured. We didn't have enough money for the motel, but the manager put us up out of compassion for our misfortune, and even brought us beef stew for dinner. Our predicament wasn't caused by misfortune; it was flagrant irresponsibility. What foolishness to drive all night during a heavy snowstorm in December!

This was a glimpse into the truth of my life, living with a man who made poor decisions and rarely took me seriously.

"Let's get the car fixed, stay with your uncle in Cincinnati for Christmas, and return to school." My suggestion fell on deaf ears.

Randy called his Mom. She wanted us home for Christmas and offered to pay for our flight. I counted our blessings. "See, things are working out for us, Randy."

Though I interpreted this event as being 'saved' and proof of God's protection, Randy nearly had a nervous breakdown. When the policeman admonished him, Randy couldn't bear it. Staring him in the face was evidence of his imperfection, and to him, our blessings were incidental. I reminded him, "We received the most wonderful gift from heaven—life! Honey, we're alive!"

"You are such a Pollyanna!" He snorted, not wanting to hear about being saved or gratitude.

We caught a flight to California late in the afternoon the next day, leaving the car at the shop. After Christmas at his mother's, we flew back to Rochester for the second semester. We were penniless, without a car, and in debt.

During the next few months, we struggled to get food on the table. I had to give up my job because I was gone in December and early January. My position was filled by someone else. We arrived back at seminary with no transportation to get anywhere. Randy's part-time work at the seminary barely met our needs. The grocery store was a long block away from the seminary, in addition to a quarter-mile walk down the driveway of the school. We walked up and down the icy hills in our California tennis shoes. It was extremely difficult to get anywhere. I slipped and sprawled across the icy sidewalk, and the groceries scattered everywhere. I worked to suppress my anger. I blamed Randy for putting us in this predicament and the loss of my car. But anger was pointless, so I tried to focus on the positives of graduate education and remain grateful that our lives were saved.

Randy and I were thinner and hungrier than usual, but we were managing. One evening we found ourselves out of food with not a thing to cook—not even flour and sugar for cookies or brownies. A bare pantry and a bare refrigerator. Randy didn't get paid until the next afternoon. It was a beautiful April evening, and instead of complaining we took our dog outside for a walk between the apartment buildings. Looking at the twilight sky, I conversed with God: *Well, Jesus, this is okay. We can easily go without food for twenty-four hours. People all over the world do it, so we will make it. It's just for a day.*

"Hey, Randy and Gay," a young man's voice beckoned. He and his wife lived directly above us. "Have you guys had dinner yet? We've got extra—it's a Chinese dish we made with pineapple. Come join us!"

The next morning, friends saw us walking, and said they'd fixed too many potatoes, "We'll cook up some more eggs. Let's have breakfast together." I will always remember how delicious that breakfast tasted. The significance of the Christian community became real to me. God provides for people through one another. A simple concept, but new to me.

Lunchtime. Another couple invited us for sandwiches. Unbelievable! *How can God continually provide for us like this?* Our 'save' on the freeway and these provisions increased my faith in God miraculously intervening in our lives. *When we goof up or make bad decisions, I can count on God*

When I think back, I wonder if our poverty was obvious to everyone, or if Randy had told people we were out of food. He said he hadn't, which only made sense, because Randy's pride would never have allowed him to share what looked like failure. Our failures were God's opportunity to show us his love.

Randy bought me my first Bible for Christmas. I wrote my name in it followed by 'child of God.' When the spring semester started, I took a class for credit. I needed four more units at graduate level to complete my California Teaching Credential. I embarked on reading passages in the Old Testament, and studied diligently. The stories were new to me, and I was excited to learn more. I currently had an A from tests and papers, until the last requirement came up, which was an oral exam with the professor.

I was anxious. I'd had no experience in verbalizing any knowledge I'd gained, especially from the Bible. For the oral exam, three students met with the professor to respond to his questions. When I tried to answer, words fumbled on my tongue and my voice cracked. I avoided answering further questions and failed. I was embarrassed.

I complained, "Randy, the expectation to answer so quickly is unfair."

"I don't think so," he said. "Ministers are expected to be able to speak and have informative conversations with others. It's part of the job."

Randy passed the exam with flying colors. He convinced my professor to give me a one-on-one chance to answer questions. My verbalizing was skimpy, but I passed the class with a C, meaning I still failed the oral exam requirement. Nevertheless, I loved learning about the Prophetic Tradition of the Old Testament and was eager to learn more.

In pursuing a career in church work, Randy had an advantage, and he knew it. His father was a Methodist minister and the youth pastor of the churches he led. His mother's father, Dwight, the one who'd married us, was a minister, and his father before him. Randy felt a responsibility to follow in the footsteps of this rich family heritage. He had unconsciously learned from his father the skills needed to be a good pastor. Maybe it was his background that led Randy to feel that psychology didn't go deep enough. However, Randy had told me numerous times at seminary, "I'm never going to be a minister like my dad." This was a lifelong promise Randy made to himself. *Hmm... what does that mean for you, Randy, and us?*

The conflict of being in seminary yet wanting to keep his promise to himself was eating him alive. He was anxious and angry; he carried an uncontrollable fear that he might be a minister like his father, and this conflict led him to a barrage of panic attacks. "It's that car accident," he guessed. He didn't know the real impetus of his panic attacks, and this anxiety caused significant struggles for us. I tried to help him as he had helped me.

*Marriage is about sticking together, right?* We made it through the school year, but Randy hardened his resolve to never become a minister. He concluded that he would never continue seminary. We needed our car, which was still in Cincinnati. Friends drove us to Randy's uncle, and we retrieved our car and drove home to California. We barely had enough money for the trip, and I was disheartened with uncertainty.

*What will be next for us?* Seminary taught me the basics of the Christian faith that had eluded me for so long. I trusted that Randy and I were supposed to be together and that our time in seminary was part of a greater plan. I had an opportunity to live out my newfound life in Jesus and follow his teachings.

*Surely goodness and mercy shall follow me all the days of my life and I shall live in the house of God forever.* Psalm 23:6

CHAPTER 13

# Mental Paralysis

*If you must walk on coals, let the energy carry you.*

DR. KENNETH L. SMITH

Emotional pain is like a fire burning in the veins. Studies show that physical pain and emotional pain activate the same nerve endings in the brain. My emotional turmoil caused me physical aching and knife-jabbing pains. When I accidentally hurt myself, something as small as an abrasion or cut finger, the physical pain triggered my brain's nerves and caused my emotional pain to intensify. I usually cried, making me look like a cry-baby over a scrape or a toe caught in the door. I thought I was abnormal and was embarrassed. Other times though, when I was emotionally disturbed, I clawed my arms or pulled out my hair. This physical pain helped quell my severe emotional pain.

The two kinds of pain are intertwined; one affects the other. Imposed physical pain can alter the sensory nerves with a stimulus that eases emotional distress. "Pain (physical) may actually be functional in many ways," explains Brock Bastian, a psychologist at the University of Queensland in Australia. "…leaders in the field describe an intense overlap between emotional and physical pain." In his study, he asked participants to focus on an episode in their past that made them feel guilty, while submerging one hand in a bucket of freezing or a bucket of tepid water. Those with their hands in icy water kept it there longer and felt less guilt over time. Bastian's conclusion was that guilt motivated them to prolong their exposure to physical pain as a prescription for psychological pain."[8]

*Ah, so I'm not crazy! I'm like all other humans who have emotional or physical wounds.*

❧

Upon our return to California, Don and Evy invited us to be caretakers for a month at Sky Meadow Ranch where we got married. The regular caretakers were going on a cattle drive and they needed someone to stay in their cabin to watch over the property. We would get a stipend that would support us for a couple months. I saw it as a retreat to beauty and peace and hoped for respite after a difficult year. It seemed perfect for us, and we gladly accepted.

Randy had no idea what path to follow now that he'd dropped out of a possible career in church ministry. The isolation of the ranch sent Randy into a disgruntled, anxious state. In a panic, he begged our doctor friend to prescribe low doses of Valium twice a day. He was also drinking a six-pack of beer every night, which we didn't have the money for. Mixing the two drugs together can lead to addiction.

Nearly two years had passed since our spectacular wedding day. One cloudy day Randy and I walked up to the wedding meadow. When we got there, Randy prayed for the sun to light up our meadow, but not a ray of sunshine broke forth. "Why doesn't God bring out the sun for us again?"

"God already sent us the sun when it meant the most to us. It was in God's timing, not ours. We didn't even ask for it. I didn't know a person could ask for the rain to stop, or for the sun to shine." I remembered the certainty that Evy expressed to me the day of the wedding, when Randy's Mom, Vivian, and Evy prayed for the rain to stop.

While I admired the beautiful view, Randy waited and prayed. I suspected his upset had to do with our car accident six months prior. While I had compassion for the anger and fear he struggled with, I could not tolerate the drinking. Randy and I wanted a family, and I had a firm boundary that I was not going to live with, or expose my children to, a problem alcoholic. My dad was a functional alcoholic, and I wanted no part of that lifestyle.

The blame game was convenient for Randy. He was skilled at criticizing others, and I was an easy target. Whenever anything went wrong it was always my fault. We did not talk about his deep fears or emotions. We didn't know how to share or compassionately communicate, so we bumbled and fumbled without intelligent direction. Randy was consumed by the life decisions looming ahead for our lives and it seemed he had come undone with worry. We returned to San Diego and rented an affordable one-bedroom apartment next to the freeway. I was pregnant, having conceived under the trees one afternoon at Sky Meadow. We hoped that the joy of a child would bring us closer. We had two months' rent and had applied for an assortment of jobs, but we could not get things to work out. I did not want to eke out a living. *Should two college graduates settle for low-paying wages? Maybe — but I could no longer be a gardener.*

Continual failures were exasperating, and Randy drank more, up to three six-packs of beer a night. Added to that, again, we were broke… "I will not stay married to an alcoholic," I said firmly. "We have a baby to care for, and we are two college graduates who believe God can help us. We must do better than this!" At my insistence and threats to leave him, Rand did stop drinking. *He does love me and wants to stay married. He wants our child.* I grabbed at anything to stay encouraged.

In the end, our three-month stay in San Diego was a bust. We went back to Fullerton where Randy got a job in landscape maintenance. The job was forty-five minutes drive from where we lived and barely supported us. We rented a small apartment in Anaheim and attended church with his family, but we had to borrow money from his mother to make ends meet. In May, our first son, Abram, was born. Randy treasured everything about him. He held him, rocked him, played, and talked to him. In the following months, with each passing day, I watched Randy heal and come back to a recognizable, normal person.

Randy's grandfather, Dwight, arrived for a visit shortly after Abram was born, to see his family and his new great-grandson. One night Randy's family came to our apartment to baptize Abram and me. Reverend Dwight poured water in a bowl and prayed over it in the name of the Father, Son, and the Holy Spirit. *Ah, the Trinity.* He held two red roses in his hand which he dipped in the holy water. He sprinkled Abram with the water from one rose, and me with the other. Then he handed me the roses. We were baptized!

We were dedicating our lives to be followers of Jesus. Another little miracle etched itself upon my heart: *Who would ever guess I would be baptized with my son?* This experience had a powerful, peaceful effect on all of us.

Shortly after Abram's birth, Randy was fired from his job. We had no savings or income. We were aware that our neighbors were also barely managing; they ate expired food they found in the dumpsters behind grocery stores. I was shocked and beside myself when they brought us outdated items like bologna, hot dogs, yogurt, and other perishable foods. *Here we are, God. We are eating outdated food from concerned neighbors we hardly know!* I don't recall if I ever thanked them. Though grateful for this provision, I was more disconcerted about our circumstances. We couldn't pay our rent, and the sheriff came to our door to inform us we were evicted.

It bothered me that we reneged on the rent we owed. This was a valid opportunity to practice self-reproach. As a child, I learned to amplify my failures and berate myself before my dad had the chance to do so. If I verbalized my mistakes, dad would agree, but the good thing was, he didn't raise his voice at me. I decided to share with Evy my concerns about failing to pay our rent.

She confidently told me, "God does not condemn you, dear." She got her Bible and read John 7:53-8:11 to me:

> *Then they all went home, but Jesus went to the Mount of Olives.*
> *At dawn he appeared again in the temple courts, where all the*
> *people gathered around him, and he sat down to teach them.*
> *The teachers of the law and the Pharisees brought in a woman*
> *caught in adultery. They made her stand before the group and said*
> *to Jesus, "Teacher, this woman was caught in the act of adultery.*
> *In the Law Moses commanded us to stone such women. Now what*
> *do you say?" They were using this question as a trap, in order to*
> *have a basis for accusing him.*

*But Jesus bent down and started to write on the ground with his finger. When they kept on questioning him, he straightened up and said to them, "Let any one of you who is without sin be the first to throw a stone at her."*
*Again he stooped down and wrote on the ground. At this, those who heard began to go away one at a time, the older ones first, until only Jesus was left, with the woman still standing there.*
*Jesus straightened up and asked her, "Woman, where are they? Has no one condemned you?"*
*"No one, sir," she said.*
*"Then neither do I condemn you," Jesus declared.*
*"Go now and leave your life of sin."*

Evy explained, "This is the power of Jesus' life. You see, Jesus does not condemn you."

The idea of God's love and forgiveness lessened my guilt. *Am I forgiven? I am not condemned but forgiven?* "Try to love yourself as God loves you!" Evy told me.

*Hmm…* I practiced this simple experiment and found that my faith and peace of mind increased.

The joy in having a precious new baby didn't lift me, and this unnerved me. *What is wrong with my brain?* My joy turned to fright as the familiar 'avoid feeling good at all costs' syndrome unconsciously kicked in. Though it's entirely normal for a new mother to feel tentative and unsure, my deep-seated responses and fear thwarted my positive feelings. The lack of pleasure and fulfillment when I nursed Abram frightened me. The delight of motherhood seemed out of reach for me. I hoped with all my heart that my baby wouldn't pick up on my discomfort.

I searched for answers in books and learned what my baby needed; make eye contact, hold him tightly, make sure he feels secure, talk to him often, look and coo at him when he is nursing, I trusted that if he didn't sense my unrest, he would be okay, but my insides were still troubled. *Why am I scared when I hold my baby?* It didn't make sense. I knew that I ought to feel gratified. A couple times I ran down the street trying to run away from myself, but returned immediately. I loved Abram. *What is wrong with me?* Sad and scared that I was missing out on real life. I never wanted anyone to hurt like I did.

After much prayer and discussion of my fears with Randy, I overcame the fear of enjoying my dear son and felt the stirrings of freedom to be a nurturing mother. I had a lot to unravel. It seemed that when I felt happy, I believed I would die. As much as I knew that was crazy thinking, I unconsciously acted as if my survival depended on rejecting the warmth and natural motherly feelings I had toward my baby. It was as if that very survival depended on staying out-of-touch with my emotions. I slowly became aware of the thought patterns of guilt and self-rejection as I unwrapped more packages of chaos. When self-degrading thoughts jumped into my head faster than I could slap them away, I waited a few minutes and did all I could to force them from my mind. This short time of guilt about my happiness in having a baby was yet another opportunity to forgive myself and let my awareness further allow warmth and joy in my heart. *May my fear drop to the ground. Help me, oh Lord, to feel the joy of my baby and motherhood.*

Abram's first three months of life were a reflective time for me. I read *Be Here Now* by Ram Dass. Since our engagement, Randy and I had lived in Berkeley, jump-started my teaching career, got married in the mountains, taken seminary classes in Rochester, New York, stayed a month at Sky Meadow, and I gave birth to Abram and was baptized with him. *I think we're making progress, Lord.*

I hadn't read the Gospels yet, and as a new disciple, I decided this was required reading. I looked forward to the stories about Jesus, learning from his wisdom and parables. But I wasn't prepared to meet the man of sorrows: the heinous acts of humankind and the pain Jesus endured. My heart ached, and I cried for his pain and mine when I read about his death.

Out of financial desperation, we moved back to Randy's mother's house. Randy did odd jobs for food money. One night I overheard Vivian visiting with her dad on the phone as she explained our situation. As she walked down the hallway to our room, I heard her announce to the family, "My dad is coming back for a few more days!"

Dwight understood the gravity of our situation. Shortly after he arrived, he went to visit his colleague, the President of Claremont Theological Seminary in Upland, California. When he returned, he announced, "Randy, you've been given a grant from the school for three years! The president recommended a matching bank loan of $3000." I was awed. *This is fantastic news! And the seminary is only thirty miles from Randy's Mom's house.* Randy protested, "I'm not sure I believe in Jesus and his life!" *What? News to me!* But Randy's grandfather would have none of my husband's excuses. He and Dolly made it through WWII and the Depression, and even when life held challenges, they knew action had to be taken.

Dwight spoke without pretense, "Preach it 'til you believe it!" I can still hear his voice: "It is an honor to serve God, and he will bless you." I remembered that Dolly served in the church as a pastor's wife, and I looked forward to doing the same. I felt my life would have a purpose if I were to follow in her footsteps. *God honored and blessed them, and God will do the same for us.*

*God has intervened in our personal affairs. We needed direction and suddenly we we're off to graduate school at Claremont Seminary.* We rented a two-bedroom apartment off campus so we could keep our little dog. The loan was in our bank account two weeks before school started, and we had enough money to enable me to stay home as a full-time Mom. I felt exceedingly blessed that I didn't have to work and enjoyed Abram with my whole being. I loved my walks with him, feeding and caring for him, and being home, even if we had less money. I didn't mind having 'Frankenstein' furniture (nothing matched). We didn't have a couch for a year, just pillows on the floor, and we used an old bed from Vivian's garage.

Randy made a desk out of orange crates and plywood, and we bought a simple breakfast table from a thrift store. Kris's old crib and highchair served well for Abram.

We were in a new season, and I felt thankful for all that had been provided. It seemed like after the last year of difficulties and failures; Randy had no choice but to accept something he could do well. He broke his self-promise never to become a minister and decided he was 'called' (by his grandfather?); the need to support his family and provide fresh food and housing motivated him.

Meanwhile, I absorbed the Gospel stories and my understanding and faith deepened. I took into my being not only what he taught and modeled, but what he endured. He walked his talk. I was drawn to and spellbound by so many thoughts. I was in awe of Jesus' confidence, his stand for justice, his compassion for the marginalized, and especially his brilliance. I couldn't get enough. I read the Psalms and other literature. Whenever Abram was asleep, I rocked him in my arms and read. I prayed faithfully and believed. *With Jesus' help, all will be well.*

*When you pass through the waters, I will be with you; and through the rivers, they shall not overwhelm you; and when you walk through the fire, you shall not be burned, and the flame shall not consume you. For I am the LORD your God, the Holy One of Israel, your Savior…. you are precious in my eyes, and honored, and I love you…* Isaiah 43:2-4

## CHAPTER 14

# A New Beginning
# 1975-1979

*Faith is the first factor in a life devoted to service.*
*Without faith, nothing is possible.*

MARY MCLEOD BETHUNE

After Randy completed his second year in seminary, he received a part-time internship as associate pastor at a Methodist Church in Whittier. Meanwhile he continued his graduate studies and commuted to Claremont. The position included a comfortable, furnished, three-bedroom, two-bath parsonage with a backyard for one-year-old Abram to play in. This was the kind of setting I grew up in, and these new surroundings comforted me. I maintained our home, determined to remain a stay-at-home-mom. My vision was to be the mother I wished I'd had. I gained self-confidence by nurturing, attending to, and respecting my child. My insides began to thaw; I trusted that my happy feelings would not cause me, or my family, harm.

Again, the church community took an interest in us and helped us along our journey toward ministry. The Methodist women planned a baby shower for me, and we received twenty-one homemade baby blankets, clothes for Abram, and a new sewing machine. *So, this is how God takes care of people! God sends his people to help one another. I'm part of this new family!* Their generosity reminded me of our seminary communities at Rochester and Claremont. I was relieved and happy. The congregation gave us money at Christmas which paid for clothes for Randy and me, and Christmas presents for Abram. *Blessings upon blessings. Thank you, Jesus.* But trouble was lurking around the corner.

While walking Abram in his stroller, I noticed a black car parked across the street. No one was sitting in it, but I got a creepy feeling that made me rush back home.

Something seemed amiss. The car was there every morning for several days for two or three hours. I had an unsettling niggle that someone was watching me. I stopped taking Abram to the park each day, and Randy took me to the store because I feared walking alone. But this scenario continued for three more weeks. *Well, it's got to be someone visiting a relative and I just haven't seen the person arrive or leave.* I resumed my walks but always with a wary eye on the car. My mind flashed back to the memory of being twelve years old when an old lady in a black car followed me home from the bus stop. She called out to me to get in the car, saying "I will take you home." I was terrified that there was someone in the backseat who would jump out and snatch me. I ran away from her, up a different street than my own, walking into a neighbor's backyard as though I lived there. This routine played out for three more days, but I didn't feel secure enough to share my fears with anyone. Stories I'd heard from teachers about kids being kidnapped rattled me. I noticed that the woman did not follow anyone else who was on the bus, only me.

As I pushed Abram in his stroller to the mall a block from our house, that same foreboding feeling haunted me. I remained suspicious, but the long walk across the parking lot seemed safe enough. On this beautiful January day, I decided to stroll along the sunny mall's open corridor. I cheerfully sang songs to Abram, when a wary feeling came over me. *I feel like I'm being followed.* My heart jumped into my throat and adrenaline pumped through my body as I scanned my surroundings. *Nothing. Where is he hiding?* I hurried inside JC Penney, seeking the safety of other people. I stayed there while Abram was distracted playing with toys. *There it is again. I am being followed! How did he get in here?* I had kept my eye on the door, but no one had come in. Now I was really frightened, and even though I waited a while longer, the feeling would not leave me. I couldn't see anyone or anything out of the ordinary. Finally, I dashed for home, nervously checking behind me as I ran through the parking lot. Abram smiled, enjoying the good ride! The entire experience left me feeling anxious, and that strange but familiar terror gripped me.

The car was across the street for weeks, then it disappeared. Though it was a strange pattern, I began to feel calm as I practiced letting go of what I thought must be old fears playing videos in my mind.

Two weeks later, in the late afternoon, Randy and I took Abram for a walk to the mall, and who should we 'happen' to run into as we crossed the lengthy parking lot? What a shock to see my mother and her new husband—well not so new, but new to me—hurrying toward us. I'd carefully hidden myself from her; it had been six years since we had last seen one another. Stunned and ambushed, I was unable to speak. Randy stepped up and started the conversation. When he agreed to go out to dinner with them, I could only gape at him with incredulity. I sat unwillingly in the restaurant, but did not engage in conversation. I'd been trapped and I counted the minutes for it to be over. *How did she find me?* I thought it funny that Abram, eighteen months old, threw peas at my mother. She was upset that I didn't stop him. I knew it was childish, but it pleased me because he was doing what I wished I could. *She is offended. Good!*

As soon as we got home, Randy demanded, "What happened to you? I've lost you. You're not the same! You didn't say a word at dinner." Seeing my mother triggered my anxiety and sent me directly into shut-down mode. I felt violated and struggled to regain my equilibrium. Shame dogged my heels as I berated myself for not having control over my reactions. Then I felt guilty because of that shame. A roller-coaster of emotions enveloped me. The enjoyment I had learned to embrace in my role as a new mother and wife, escaped like steam from a boiling pot. I hoped Abram would not sense my hopelessness and fear. To get through this period of disconnection with myself and Randy, I needed antidepressants. This helped me to begin the daily journey toward recovery, though it would be four months before my brain switched back to a sense of feeling normal.

Randy's internship was over in August. He was relieved, and as we drove back to Claremont, he said, "I'm so glad this job is over. I feel like a used paper cup." *What does that mean for our future?*

We'd left our pretty little parsonage and moved into married-student housing at the seminary in Claremont. Because of campus regulations we had to give away the sweet dog we'd had for seven years. We made a few friends, and a special perk was that the California Botanical Gardens was fifty yards from our door. This delightful garden provided the beauty we needed for respite and became our go-to spot. This was Randy's fourth and final year of seminary to earn his Doctor of Ministry degree.

I was still recovering from the shock of having my mother back in my life. She came to our apartment a few times to visit, at least calling first to ask us when a good time would be to visit. I felt oppressed and caged. I could not say *no*. Randy seemed okay with her visits, and he led the conversations. I thanked God he could socialize with my mother because I didn't have it in me. Every time I saw my mother, my unhealthy past with her was triggered. My mind threw me back in time, and I was thrust into shut down mode. I didn't seem to have control over this, and after each visit it took several days to get my equilibrium back. I took care of the things that needed to be done, but I struggled to be present and lost my spontaneity. At least it didn't take me four months to recover!

On my Mom's third visit to our apartment, she came with her husband. I mustered enough courage to ask her, "How did you find me?"

She hesitated, looking uncomfortable before admitting, "I hired a private detective." My foreboding and fearful feelings were confirmed; like a hunted deer I'd been stalked. I didn't talk for the rest of the visit, for fear I'd start screaming at her. I wanted to describe to her the terror at being surveilled by her detective, but I could hear her condescending voice minimize my reaction, saying in a patronizing voice, "What are you so upset about? It was just a private detective. He didn't hurt you. And anyway, I wanted to see you."

Over the next year my mother visited because she wanted to see Abram. My interaction with her were uncomfortable, and I needed three to four days to recover after each visit. Randy was exasperated with this situation. With his workload, school, and a thesis due, he needed me. But after her visits I wasn't available. I needed to tell my mother not to come over, but I did not have the emotional strength to tell her the truth.

Finally, I called her and blamed Randy for the decision to end her visits. Although we asked her not to visit, there was no hiding from her now, no freedom. She could always find me even if I wanted to conceal my whereabouts. The knowledge that she could reappear made me feel less confident on many fronts. I felt like an animal with one paw clamped in a trap. Irrational fears haunted me: *is my mother back in control of my life? Why can't I go back to the freedom I felt last year? Why isn't my faith in Christ overriding my fears? My faith hasn't disappeared, but what has happened to me?* I was out of sync.

Randy graduated from Seminary in 1978 and was accepted and ordained in the United Methodist Conference. He was appointed an associate minister in a large church in southern California. We were provided with a furnished three-bedroom parsonage.

We'd been married for six years, and this was our ninth move.

Abram was now three. With a professional job in place, Randy wanted to have a second child, but I wasn't confident about it. I remembered the confluence of joy and fear, the conflict of being afraid to feel happy when Abram was first born. A fear in me rose up when I first nursed him and coursed through my soul warning me that if I allowed myself to enjoy warm feelings, something terrible would happen. I had identified my irrational fear and I resolved it enough to entertain the idea of having a second child. Randy and I made love a few times without protection, and I was pregnant within the first two months.

That autumn, there was a knock on the door. The UPS man handed me a package from my mother; I knew it was a birthday present. I refused to sign for it and sent it back. *You can't just buy your way into my life*, I thought self-righteously. In retrospect, I don't think she was really trying to buy me. At that time, I didn't understand why I couldn't trust her enough to accept her overtures. They may have been the only ways she knew how to reach out to me. *I am sorry, Mom.*

I sent her a hand-written letter that Randy penned, trying to explain why I needed to limit our relationship, but she never responded. I wrote a second letter asking if we could get counseling together, thinking this could open a door for us. This time she wrote me back and said she was not interested in doing counseling with me.

Randy and I had only a little money, and his school loans and our doctor bills took all our extra income. At that time insurance did not cover pregnancies. We couldn't afford orange juice. Being pregnant increased my anxiety. I monitored my fears daily to keep from shutting down, but this required a lot of thought and emotional energy. Despite my best efforts, things were not working between Randy and me.

One night Randy fell asleep on the couch for two hours, and Abram played on the kitchen floor while I washed dishes. I was six months pregnant, and my back ached, but I was happy when the task was finished. When Randy woke up, he stumbled into the kitchen, and with little effort found something to criticize, "Why did you do the dishes now?"

*What kind of question is that? Why can't you be grateful that I did them and you didn't have to!* But these were only my thoughts; I dared not vocalize them. I'd been accustomed all my life to enduring unjust criticism. If such a scenario happened like that today, I would confidently walk out of the room, "Feel free to do the dishes in your timing from now on."

We fought continually; I was emotionally beat-up. One day I threw my wedding ring in the grass. Our innocent little boy was witness to his parents' constant anger and unhappiness. This caused him distress and insecurity, manifesting in an inability to fall asleep at night, a pattern that would last throughout his childhood. Soon he developed an anxiety about being away from home, as though he felt responsibility for the well-being of his family. Abram came to believe that if he was home, he might be able to prevent a catastrophe.

A calm healthy marital relationship seemed unattainable. My pain deepened as I fought for dignity, for the freedom to experience the me I knew was there. Randy was tired, unsatisfied in his new job, and exasperated with our relationship.

*Where is the Randy I thought I knew, a young man who'd once been so kind, thoughtful and generous to me and is now so angry? He excludes me from any show of warmth or compassion.* Romantic feelings for my husband fell away day by day.

*I'm getting ready to give birth, and this is my mate. How will this affect Abram?* I felt so sad for our little boy. Abram's anxiety was growing, even though I was always there for him. I made every effort to reassure Abram that he was loved and important, playing with him for hours and always held him close.

When I was seven months pregnant, my nerves frayed and frazzled. Randy had become my adversary, offered me no kindness or support, and criticized me at every turn. I was stressed; I felt I wasn't 'good enough,' or 'I couldn't do *it* right.' Nothing I said or did made any difference to him. One warm afternoon in February, we drove out to Irvine Regional Park, a six-minute drive from our house. It seemed like the perfect getaway for the three of us, a time to relax in a beautiful country setting with grass and tall trees. But as soon as we set up our blanket, Randy announced, "Gaynelle, we are going to stay here until you tell me what is going on. What's wrong? Ever since you got pregnant you haven't been yourself. Something is driving you crazy and I can't stand it anymore!"

I had tried so hard to make things work for our family and his comments deflated my worn-out emotions. Looking at Abram, our wonderful little boy, I plopped down in the grass and started to cry. Abram had looked forward to going to the park with his Mom and Dad and now he was entirely ignored. A short distance away, in the tall grass, Abram entertained himself on the logs and made up his own games, as he often did while we were 'working on problems.' I felt sad because my Abram needed attention and deserved safe, fun-loving interactions with us. *Will this ever change? Are we trapped forever? Where is God and why can't God help us?*

I continued to plead with God: *What is it I need to know? Have mercy on me, Lord.*

*Don't you see how hard I'm trying?* After a few minutes and without any thought, I proclaimed, "Randy, I'm not allowed to have a baby. It's not allowed!" I flung my arms into the air, fell back into the grass, and as I laid back, I gazed at the bright sky and tree limbs waving in the breeze.

"What do you mean, *you're not allowed to have a baby?* Of course you are."

"You don't understand. The baby belongs to my mother. It's not mine. I'm simply not allowed to have another child. Abram made me so happy but something terrible will happen if I have another baby."

Randy was stupefied. I couldn't believe my words either. They floated in the air, and I heard them again for the strange, alien words they were. *What? My baby isn't for me? It doesn't belong to me? Why does it belong to my mother? What is going on? I am obviously going to have a baby. Why do I feel that I am not allowed to have my baby?* These thoughts brought to my consciousness the irrational and deep fear I had of my mother. I thought the baby belonged to my mother, because claiming anything as mine felt dangerous — as if my very survival was at risk. To need, to want, or to have something of my own meant I could be annihilated.

My words sounded over-the-top crazy. *This is not how a normal person thinks and feels.* I was thrilled to be pregnant again and loved feeling life growing inside me. But apparently, I lived with an unconscious conflict between wanting my baby and being afraid to enjoy that bond with my child. *Randy is right, something is wrong with me. How could it be that the baby, my baby, growing inside my body, doesn't belong to me?*

Haunted and oppressed, it slowly dawned on me that my mother had made me feel as if my body were dirty and that I was, too. She alone could wash my genitals, and then she took me to a doctor who was allowed to touch me. She disregarded his words that I was a normal child. *What a tangled, nauseating mess.* The message was that I was not allowed to feel, to touch, or to have a say about my own body. A child cannot create a sense of self-worth, and I was not allowed to feel happy. I didn't believe that my body belonged to me. That's why I felt like even my baby didn't belong to me. *Is it any wonder I have difficulties seeing my mother?*

I paid close attention to my feelings, practicing mindfulness before it earned that name. When my anxiety flared up, I created a new self-talk system along with prayer to encourage myself to get to the other side of it. I prepared myself for joy, the same joy I experienced when Abram was born. It is my baby, and I love this child. I will be happy when our baby is born. I kept up this self-talk during the rest of my pregnancy. God gets the credit for the insight, and I give myself credit for determining to overcome absurd thought patterns.

My skills from mothering Abram kicked in when Noel was born. I was more relaxed and confident. We named him after Randy's grandfather, Dwight Knowlton. Experience, the great teacher, gave me assurance that I was a good mother. I calmed down, noticing that joyful, relaxed feelings attended me.

After Noel's birth, things were calm between Randy and me. For five months we got along, focusing on our boys. But then, with no warning or mishap, Randy created drama and chaos. During a terrible fight, as I held five-month-old Noel in my arms, Randy totally lost control and began a rant that lasted for hours. "You're a terrible mother!" He yelled, making sure Abram overheard. "You're worse than your own mother. I can't believe how inept you are!" *Is he intentionally undermining my feelings of self-worth and Abram's confidence in me?* After four hours of his venting, I broke down in sobs, my infant son still in my arms. I recognized the dysfunctional pattern that emerged: my distress seemed to satisfy his broken ego, and he stopped his attack. But not before reminding Abram, "See how mixed-up your mother is?"

*Is he jealous that I've become happier? Am I his scapegoat because of his own problems that he doesn't seem able to face?* Happiness or contentment continually eluded me. I chased something I knew to be close by, even possible, but every time I saw that beautiful butterfly it fluttered away as though it had never existed. Joy and happiness occasionally crept into my spirit, but I didn't count on it to be a daily part of my life. Just when I thought peace was in reach, when I decided to risk trusting that joy was possible, someone who should have been close to me and safe, wanted to destroy it. To survive, I continually acquiesced. *Is there anything I can do?* If there was, I didn't know what it might be... *Do good people actually exist?* Then I remembered my Granny, and the people who'd helped us in our times of need.

I was financially dependent because I wanted to be home with my kids. I consoled myself as best I could with thoughts like, *Randy's a good father. He'll find a way to love me so that I feel safe again.* I concentrated on Randy's relationship with our sons, but I noticed he continually negated my family contributions. *His disparagement of me might have lasting effects on my relationship with my kids. Will they grow up to see me as pathetic and helpless, and not a mother to be respected or regarded with dignity. Is that intentional on Randy's part or is it his own insecurities and frustrations in life?* I will never know for sure.

Abram told me when he was an adult that he waited for his dad to come home and he would 'tell on me' so he could get me in trouble with Randy. "We ganged up on you, Mom. Dad said I didn't have to do what you told me. I know it must have been hard for you to have a son who didn't respect you. I'm so sorry about this, Mom." This understanding and compassion came from my son thirty years later.

I'm not sure I made the best decision staying in the marriage. My kids loved their daddy. I had learned to endure criticism at an early age, and I was good at it. I wanted a good father-son relationship for them. If we separated and I went to work, I would need to put them in childcare. It was my responsibility to raise and teach my children the values I wanted them to have, not someone else's. In order to stay home and keep the family together, I became creative at saving money instead. I sewed up the holes in our underwear and socks, made all the meals, and stayed true to my vision of having the needed time to be the mom I wanted my sons to have.

*What good is it for someone to gain the whole world, and yet lose or forfeit their very self.* Luke 9:25

CHAPTER 15

# Tinder and Flint—1980

*It is worse than folly...not to recognize the*
*truth, for in it lies the tinder for tomorrow.*
PEARL S. BUCK

Randy's uncle, Dwight's son, was the District Superintendent in the Wisconsin United Methodist Conference. Randy grew up in Illinois and Indiana, so it was no surprise when he told me, "The churches in the Midwest are different from those in California. I need to find a church that better fits my style of ministry." Like Brer Rabbit, Randy believed *there must be a better rabbit hole.*

After not quite two years as an associate minister, and after numerous prodding phone calls from his uncle, Randy accepted membership into another conference. We were to serve two small rural Methodist Churches, five miles apart, in Southern Wisconsin.

During this time, I pleaded with my husband. "Go visit your uncle and find out more about this. Get a feeling for the churches you'll be serving. You're good at discernment, so find out if this is something you really want to do." However, he was certain that the culprits for his unhappiness were the churches in Southern California, so he ignored my suggestions and forged ahead with his plan.

The parsonage in California was furnished, so we had very few belongings to pack up. As the moving van drove away, I had a terrible foreboding feeling and was certain we'd made a big mistake. Too late! His replacement was on his way and he would minister to the people that I had deemed family. We sold our car, and flew to Madison, Wisconsin.

*Oh God, nothing can be done to change this. We are really going to need your help!* Off on another adventure? I mustered up hope and courage and tried my best to portray an upbeat attitude for the sake of the boys. Once we got there, the reality of our situation set in. We had no support except for his aunt and uncle, people I didn't know, who lived ninety miles away. Randy had rarely spoken to them over the years. *Now what? There is nothing else to do but tough it out. Randy had burned our bridges.* We needed to find a way to adjust to our circumstance and work toward a more cohesive family. At least we were in this 'together.' I was dependent on God. I prayed: *Help us to learn to love and appreciate each other, Lord. Here we are, just the four of us. We need each other and we need to bond as a family.*

Randy's uncle loaned us a car that we could keep until we were able to buy one. Then we drove to what was to be our home, ninety miles southwest of Madison. To my dismay, our new home was located on a busy two-lane highway. In addition, the small, white 1930s house was in the corner lot of the church cemetery. Our parsonage had three tiny bedrooms, one of which was Randy's office, and one bathroom. We walked into an unfurnished house. There were no carpets. The linoleum in the kitchen was sorely outdated, stained and impossible to clean. The oak floors, once a luxury, lacked varnish and were severely scratched. In the kids' bedroom was a single pane window ten feet from standing gravestones. The moving van delivered our dishes, clothes, bedding, and sleeping bags. The people from the two churches Randy was now pastoring started furnishing our place with the stuff they no longer wanted. Lucky us—we were back to Frankenstein furniture. Thanks to unwanted guests that came with a donated couch, we had to flea-bomb the house twice. The Salvation Army picked it up where we'd left it on the curb.

Quickly we learned that many things were different in Wisconsin. We had sold our car before leaving California, but when we got to the Toyota dealership in Madison, the gigantic car lot was empty. The salesman said, "You have to order a car, and it'll take two months for it to be delivered." Looking for any car on the lot, I knew he wasn't kidding.

Believing that God keeps his promises to care for us, I prayed: *Please send us a car.* We filled out paperwork to order a car.

Three weeks later, the salesperson called. "The person who ordered a Corolla station wagon didn't want it, and you're next on this list. Do you want it?" *Hallelujah! This is exactly what we need; yes, we want it.* We drove to Madison to pick up a yellow station wagon. Not my favorite color, but, hey, it was an answer to my prayer. I grew quite fond of that little yellow wagon.

I wanted a carpet for the kids' room, so I bought small rectangular samples from a carpet store for $1 each. I hand-sewed them together with carpet needle and thread. I bought more squares for our living room and bedroom. Our Frankenstein carpet now matched our furniture.

Now that we had our own car, we drove the two hours to Madison, the only place to get a Wisconsin driver's license. While Randy filled out forms, I cared for the kids in the car. He returned and told me the fee was $16. Then I went to get my license, and when I returned I said, "Hey Randy, my fee was $9." He looked perplexed and wanted to get his $7 back. The four of us returned to the window, and Randy said to the clerk, "You charged me $16 and my wife $9. There must have been a mistake. I would like $7 back please."

"No mistake," the clerk replied.

"So why is there a difference in the fees?" I asked.

"You were born in an even year, and he was born in an odd year." Baffled, we laughed.

On Labor Day the temperature dropped. The beautiful colors of autumn were a trade-off for living in a cold climate, but the next day a tornado wind brought huge black clouds, and I watched as the leaves blew off the trees. They blew so hard and fast they smacked onto our large living room window where they stayed glued for several days. The next day school began for Abram. He was in kindergarten, and as we walked to the school two blocks away, we noticed the trees were bare.

We were bundled up in our warmest jackets, gloves, and hats. To people in Wisconsin, this was autumn, but to me, September was winter. The playground equipment was from the 1950's and one freezing day Abram slipped off the icy ladder of the slide and broke his wrist.

Our new town had only eight hundred people and they all knew one another. We were outsiders, and no one trusted Californians. Even the kindergartners discriminated against Abram, who was friendless in school. The people in our church and community seemed suspicious of anyone who would move from California to Wisconsin. None of the women befriended me. *Was this the friendly Midwest Randy envisioned?* The only person I forged a friendship with was an eighty-three-year-old woman who lived down the street who didn't happen to attend our church. Noel and I visited her frequently and we both enjoyed our visits and looked forward to each new one. She enjoyed making cookies for Noel and watching him play. I couldn't figure out why I had no other friends, so I concentrated on my children. I jumped into the church community as I'd learned to do but received no friendly support or recognition.

One Sunday at church, a couple celebrated their 50th wedding anniversary. I congratulated the woman and she commented, "I've been married to Walter for fifty years, and I've lived here all these years with him, but I still don't have a friend. I have never been accepted in this town since the day I came!" Interesting information. *I wonder in all these years if she had tried to prove herself worthy, show them that she is "good enough" and now has given up. Well, I'm not going to live here for fifty years! I guess I'll never have a friend here either.*

"As winter arrives, old people die," I was told by several people in our church. "In November and December, old people just can't seem to face another winter, so they give up and go on." Randy was responsible for ministering to the church families and he performed eight funerals in eight weeks, each for very elderly folks. The funerals were scheduled on his only day off, and the burials took place in our backyard. Randy walked fifty yards back home for dinner. For nine grueling weeks he had no break or even one day off.

As an adult, Abram commented about our time there, "Not many people can say they learned to ride a bike and hit a baseball in a cemetery, Mom. It makes for a good story now, but it wasn't so great then." *No kidding!*

Ten weeks after we moved in, there was a knock at the door, and there stood my Mom and her husband, Jack. I was speechless. A large suitcase sat on the doorstep. "I came to stay with you for a week!" My Mom announced. Jack hurried inside with her suitcase in hand and dropped it in the living room. My mother followed him. She said a quick goodbye to Jack, who, without a word, practically jogged back to their car. He was gone before I knew what had happened. I looked at my mother, flabbergasted. Uninvited, she bombed back into my life in, of all places, a tiny town in Wisconsin.

Noel was in the living room with me, and I introduced her to her grandson. "I brought this for you." She handed me a black and white portrait of me taken when I was three. Noel was now two, and I noticed that he and I looked alike as children. The photo was a treasure to me and broke the ice a bit. My mother wanted to be with her grandkids, and by golly, she would not be denied.

I kept my same routines, but we were awkward. I didn't know what to say to her, much less how to converse. I struggled to ask her questions about her life; I simply didn't know how to get through to her or provide opportunities for her to get to know me or my kids.

When I look back at this time, I can't remember her helping me with food preparations or washing dishes. She ate meals with us at the table, but there was no other interaction with her. Silently, I did my duties and relied on Randy to provide some kind of meaningful conversation. We did not have extra beds, so she must have slept on the couch. I was not even mad. I was just voiceless. She read the newspaper and didn't converse, just as when I was a teenager. I'd been working on a patchwork quilt for our bed before she arrived, and it was good to have a project to do while she was there.

She didn't ask me anything about my life or why I'd been away from the family for so long. She didn't ask me about my kids, or our church. Maybe she was as clueless as I was. Her lonely time in the house reflected our life-long relationship. After four nights, she accepted there would be no resolve or conversation, so she called Jack. "You might as well come pick me up," she said with resignation. There was a quick exit, no hugs or words of goodbye, and that was that. We gave up on each other.

The experience with my Mom, my aching loneliness, and the suspicion that I was rejected by church members, was upsetting and depressing, but my hurt remained internal and unexpressed. It was at this time that I decided to give counseling a try. Fortunately for us, the Methodist, Lutheran, and Presbyterian Churches had joined together to provide a counselor for ministers and their families, though we had to drive to Madison, ninety miles north.

The counselor got straight to the point. "Can you give me a picture of how you see your mother?"

I thought for a moment, "It's like I'm learning to play the piano. I'm just a little girl. She is a black vulture sitting on the top of the piano, and every time I make a mistake, she pecks at me!"

The counselor probed further, "What bothers you most about her?"

I told him two more things: "She is ashamed of me, and I can't say *no* to her. You don't say *no* to my mother." I was in tears.

He simply answered, "I can say no to your mother."

I looked at him in disbelief and thought, *What? You can say no to my mother? No, you can't.* A few moments of silence passed. *I'll bet he can...but I can't. Or can I?* Something about this conversation stuck with me, giving me helpful insight.

*Do not conform any longer to the pattern of this world but be transformed by the renewing of your mind...* Romans 12:2

## CHAPTER 16

# Two Churches, Yoked Together

*Hi God, I am just a mess.*
*It is all hopeless. What else is new?*
*I would be sick of me if I were You,*
*But miraculously, You are not.*
*I know I have no control over other people's lives,*
*And I hate this.*
*Yet I believe that if I accept this and surrender,*
*You will meet me wherever I am.*

ANN LAMOTT

R andy preached twice every week now that he was responsible for two churches. I listened, absorbing knowledge about the Man. One day after church Randy barked at me, "Why is it that you are the only one in church with a grimace on your face? No one else frowns at me, and I'm so tired of looking across the congregation and seeing you scowl. Why are you like this?" *Why, indeed?*

*Here we go again. Something is wrong with me.* My stomach knotted and my throat tightened as though a ball of wax was caught there, and for a few minutes, I could not speak or swallow. *I'm scowling? I didn't know that.* I checked in with myself over the next few weeks in church. I became aware of a sickening feeling deep inside me. *Something dark is going on inside me. Are my deep feelings what shows up on my face?* I pleaded with God: *tell me what it is about church that makes me feel so hurt and angry?*

After thinking and praying about it for a few weeks, the answer came to me. *It is my mother's father, my grandfather.* Within seconds my mind had my answer—something terrible released from the vault of my memories. Until this moment I'd blocked out of my mind my grandfather's abuse. *Dare I relate another abuse story to Randy?*

Unlocking the door to this trauma provoked my awareness. The memory rushed through my being. When I was six, I was molested by my grandfather on Saturday nights when Diane and I were left in my mother's parents' care. The next day they took us to church. I was afraid and confused when they dropped me off at Sunday school with strangers. Seeping back into my memory were the details. I remembered how the night before church my grandfather's hands were all over my body. I couldn't get away from him because he pinned me down, and how I screamed for help but my grandmother, being deaf, never arrived. Even when she wore hearing aids, it didn't make much difference.

The memory of being powerless infuriated me. I had carried the abuse deep inside me for years. I had chastised myself because I wasn't strong enough to get away from him. I'd learned to 'check out' as he was touching me so I wouldn't have to feel anything. I remember looking down on my body, knowing it was happening, but not feeling it. It didn't occur to me to tell my grandmother or mother. I didn't realize how wrong and hurtful this was. My grandfather didn't rape me, but he touched me in all the inappropriate places. Part of me knew something was wrong, even though I didn't tell my Mom. When he finished with me, he tried to molest my three-year-old sister, who was sleeping next to me. I jumped out of bed without a thought. I kicked him in the shins and pummeled him with a windmill of my skinny arms and little fists to distract him and protect her. I'm lucky he wasn't violent, because he could have easily knocked me to the floor.

Though I was to pay the price of his increased sexual abuse, I was determined I wouldn't let him hurt my sister. One Sunday morning after an ugly night at my grandparents' house, a woman at the church who was a stranger to me, leaned down with her face near mine and said, "Oh your grandfather is such a wonderful Christian man. He gave the coat off his back to a man who needed it!"

I'd overheard this story circulate around the family. *He's a Christian man? Then I never want to be a Christian, whatever that is!* When I was twelve and my breasts started to develop, my grandfather was still molesting me. Up until then I wasn't positive that what he was doing was wrong, but when he fondled my breasts, I got it. *This is bad. No more! I need to get away.* When I finally told my mother about what grandpa did to me, she commented nonchalantly, "Oh, he's just loving you. That's just what old men do."

"Mom, I will never go to their house again," I said, and this time she listened. I never had to go through that again.

This memory was bouncing around in my mind. My child's mind had made an association that abuse and church were connected. I'd already known that I distrusted the men in church. I saw them as shams, men pretending to be godly but who abused little girls. As my memories awakened, I realized that I needed to separate the disturbing images of my grandfather from being in church and from the men in church. I told myself, *they are not related. The two have no relationship in real life. These men sitting here in church are probably not abusing children. It's not fair to them to think this.* Finally I was able to keep the frown off my face while listening to Randy's sermons. I tried to be friendly, and instead of disliking church, I started learning more about Jesus from my husband, something he'd promised me years ago.

A couple months later I found the courage to explain this to Randy, and his reaction was quick and judgmental. "You and your stupid family," he ranted. "I got cheated when I married you!" I knew *we* were cheated but it wasn't my fault. He didn't give me a hug or a shred of compassion. *What about how I feel? You aren't the only one who was robbed!*

Thirty-three years later, after my mother died, I found out from my cousin, Judy, that she had the same awful experiences with our grandfather. And Judy's mother, Mom's sister Georgia, had told her the same thing I'd heard: "He's just loving you. That's just what old men do." *My poor mother and aunt.*

"That's just what they believed then," Judy commented, shaking her head. It was one more puzzle piece falling in place in the overall picture of our family's dysfunction.

When I happened to come across a photo of my Mom when she was twelve, I saw a familiar expression on her face. *I recognize how she's feeling! I see her shame. She was molested by her father.* This explains why she justified her father's behavior when she said, "Oh, he's just loving you." Her denial of my abuse belied the abuse she experienced as a child. She couldn't face the awful truth and perhaps blocked out her painful memories just as I had done. She created a belief system that told her that her father's abuse was love. She had created an 'excellent' excuse against the ravages of being sexually violated as a child.

The two country churches Randy served shared the expenses of a pastor. I met a woman named June who attended the sister church five miles away. She often stopped by our house in the mornings when Randy was working. We both had young kids, and she seemed to want to spend time with me, so a simple friendship began. At the time I didn't notice that the person who she really liked was Randy. He had suspicions about June and told me he didn't like her coming over, even when he wasn't around.

During the winter months I began writing a cookbook, *Unhooking with Sugarless Cooking*. I kept my kids off white granulated sugar and used apple juice concentrate, raisins, and dates to make desserts like cookies, pies, and brownies. I seemed to have a knack for this and invented all kinds of recipes. I developed a relationship with a woman from the church who offered to type it up for me, in the days of typewriters. The whole thing turned out to be a two-year project and it kept me occupied during the dreary winter days while also providing needed goodies for my family. Soon we were able to self-publish the book.

The churches Randy served were near the Iowa border and Dubuque. We laughed at the old, ornate overarching sign inviting people into the city: 'Dubuque, a town to live in.' Isn't every town a town to live in? We gathered up the boys once a week, and while Randy made hospital rounds, I played games with them in our cold car. Our big treat was to go out to dinner, usually for pizza.

The population of the town we lived in was eight hundred. The sister church was in a town twice as big, all of 1,500. Both churches were in Wisconsin's dairyland. It was strange to me that the two churches, only five miles apart, would not relate with each other in any way other than to share the expenses of the Methodist pastor. One town was Welsh, the other was Celtic. The Celts made remarks about the Welsh being un-friendly, and the Welsh had a negative take on the Celts as being uppity. Each group justified their position. *Isn't this a brand of ethnic prejudice? Tribalism.* No wonder I had no invitations for friendship; I simply didn't belong.

In less than two years, Randy wanted to move again—none of us liked living in a church graveyard. Due to Randy's leadership, the larger church had grown in numbers and Randy could see that they would be able to afford their own minister without the support of the smaller church.

Randy was brilliant at orchestrating the separation of the sister churches for our benefit. The lure was plain to see. The other parsonage was a modern new house with a dishwasher! No gravestones in the yard! And a larger and more modern school for Abram. Our son had struggled to flourish in the two years of unacceptance in our tiny town. Randy convinced the larger church to separate from the more dependent one, where we presently lived. In my heart I felt that separating the sister churches was unfair, but I also knew that I had no influence once Randy was determined to do something, and yes, the changes would be good for our family.

The final separation left the little church hurt and angry at us, who they'd dubbed 'the Californians.' Now they were dependent on a student pastor instead of an ordained minister. But the people of the larger church had long wanted to be unlinked from the smaller and were ecstatic.

On a Sunday afternoon, almost the entire church showed up at our house to move us. There were so many people and trucks that they emptied everything in our house in just over an hour.

They drove five miles and moved everything back into the new parsonage. They took care of every detail: beds were made, kitchen set up, and cupboards were full. The bath towels were stacked in the bathroom cabinets, furniture was in place, and all our clothing was hung in the closets. And this only took three hours! *Wow! This is the way to move!* I was thrilled. I thanked them all, grateful I didn't have to spend another three months setting up our house. To top it off, some of the women took time to befriend me. I felt supported and no longer lonely. We started a prayer group in our home, and I was grateful that I was experiencing the power and love of Christian community once again.

Noel was three, and though there were times when Randy ragged on me, I had grown to feel more confident as a mother and wife. I prayed: *Should we have another baby, Jesus?* Randy and I decided to try. We had only been together three times in our married life without protection, and we'd had two babies. It only took another two times of unprotected sex, and I was pregnant. I prayed faithfully that all would go well, happy and content to be pregnant again. *I'm not feeling any guilt, and I know the baby belongs to me.*

On a summer day, we took the kids to a nearby park, but I soon began to feel some cramping. I rested the remainder of the day, but as the cramps continued, I knew that I would miscarry. It was early in the pregnancy, and we hadn't informed anyone yet, but I was distraught. Randy seemed relieved. I miscarried early that evening and lay in bed alone. He didn't offer a kind word or support me to help mend my broken heart. I was disappointed to learn that he didn't really want another baby, but we went on with life as though nothing had happened. I couldn't shake my sadness or disregard Randy's apathy. *How can Randy be glad that we're not having another child?* I continued to rely on God in prayer and felt it would be wise for me not to get pregnant again.

Depression dogged my heels as we continued to misunderstand one another and argued continually. I was barely functioning; I had too many things to cope with all at one time: the miscarriage, Randy's apathy, and the need to remain pleasant with my children when I was running on empty. I was moved to numbness. I felt alone because I was alone. Even though we were in a much better setting for our family, the health of our marriage was in peril. I prayed, *Jesus, if you are real, show me how to find happiness. Please save our marriage. Help me out of this abyss.*

My counselor in Madison referred me to a psychiatrist because he felt I needed a doctor who could prescribe medication. On the first visit, the doctor inquired, "Tell me about a time you were happy. What has brought about your happy times and feelings of joy?"

"I don't have any," I replied bleakly. I couldn't remember if I'd ever been truly happy.

"Not one?" He asked, puzzled.

"Nope. None." *That's how depressed I am.*

He was a good listener as I shared about my mother, father, and grandfather. Then I described my failing marriage and my angry husband. The doctor wrote out a prescription and added some encouragement: "I want you to take this for a while. When you start to feel better—and you *will*—I want you to really pay attention. Notice those moments when you feel a little lighter, a little more yourself. Try to hold on to them. Try to recreate them. See, no one can feel happiness or a sense of well-being if they've never *felt* it before. The brain can't invent what it doesn't know. We have to show it the way. Turn it on. Flip the switch, so to speak.

The medication will help you with that. Learn, and after some time has gone by, we can reevaluate." *Switch my brain. That sounds reasonable.*

The medication helped immeasurably and immediately. Since I couldn't be pregnant while on medication, I realized I wasn't supposed to have a third child. *This is God's intervention.* I noticed the change in my feelings immediately and Randy noticed it, too. *Is this how other people feel?* I relinquished my emotional defenses. I felt like a whole person, not jumbled up. Everything was better: sex, eating, church, simply being. I felt freer. I had more joy with my boys. *So, this is what Randy has been missing in me all these years? What a loss for us all. I've missed out on being me.*

Even though our lives resumed with more calm, Randy wasn't happy about my renewed spirit. "If you have to be on medication to function normally, then you're more of a mess than I thought," he said in front of our children. This aspect of my recovery backfired.

"Damned if you do, damned if you don't," my father would say. As much as I dislike this kind of negative thinking there was no doubt about where I stood with Randy. He had an uncanny timing, as did my mother and father, to spew out repugnance and disgust. They purposely stomped on my little butterflies of happiness. I was in a no-win situation.

I suspected that Randy had given up on us, something that began long before this time. Now there was no mistaking it. His heart and mind seemed to be far away, and his body language confirmed that our marriage was over. We were still in bed, but not together, not in love.

*God, what's happening here?* I kept pleading for an answer. For weeks I asked God for insight to know what to do. But then a strange answer seemed to come from Heaven. In my mind I heard, "You and Randy won't be together in eight years." *What? God, is that you? Is Randy going to die of leukemia?* I felt certain that God was communicating with me because that thought was far removed from what I could have imagined. *Eight years? Why eight years?*

*Well, things can change, right?* I encouraged myself with the stories in the Bible where God answered prayers. At night, when we prayed with the boys, I added to the prayer, "And God, please help the love in our family to grow." I believe God directs and helps us even when we make bad decisions. *Maybe God will guide us and help us to love and respect each other again. But…why did God specify eight years?*

Our move to the sister church was the church June attended. Her children were the same age as ours and she made a point to visit us more often. I was happy to see Noel, who was not in preschool, play with friends. I myself was in need of friendship, but my need made me blind to the fact that she was scheming to catch Randy's eye. I noticed he enjoyed her attention.

One day he announced, "I need to tell you that I love June, and we are having a sexual relationship." I didn't know how to process this betrayal, but my body did. I vomited. My husband was sneaking off at night after the boys were asleep. Even worse, he reported to me daily about their relationship, as if I was his best friend! Bad enough that he was having an affair and was disloyal to me; but he was a minister, and she was his parishioner.

I was done. I couldn't stand lying in bed next to Randy and hearing him call out June's name in his sleep. One night, after everyone was asleep, I packed the car, planning to wake Abram and Noel and take them with me back to California. I sat in the parked car, Visa card and checkbook in hand. It was November, with the possibility of snow, and I wondered if I could make the drive to California safely with two small children. *Is this too risky? Would Randy cancel the credit card and leave me stranded?* My mind raced. *What would I tell the kids?* Abram had started doing well in school and was enjoying his first friends. He went bike riding in the woods and built forts, doing what boys his age are supposed to do. *God had blessed us. Why does Randy have to spoil everything?*

I rationalized. *We have a comfortable home to live in. Already we'd moved Abram all over the country, ten times since he was born. He was in his second school in second grade. Move him again?* I heard my mother's words, "All men cheat on their wives and as long as your husband comes home to you, don't worry or think about it." *What if I can't find a job? If I start teaching, Noel will have to be in preschool all day.*

*Where will I go? Home… to my mother? Did I marry a man like my Dad? Am I a victim of the generations or what I hear Christian folk say, caught in generational bondage?*

It was clear that leaving would be too hard on my little ones. Driving alone with the boys would be dangerous. Flying home with no plan was not smart. My children were secure and attached to their father. *I can't do this to them. Their world will be turned upside down. Better for my world to be unstable than theirs.* In this swirling emotional storm, I feared that no matter which path I chose, it couldn't work out. Alone in the dark garage, the best I could do was to take the path of least resistance. Silently, I took everything out of the car. No one woke to witness what I'd almost done, and I never said a word about my plan to anyone, but the option to flee with my children stayed firm in the back of my mind.

While Randy and June continued with their relationship, I took care of the kids, studied my Bible, and prayed. When I came across verses about forgiveness it occurred to me that forgiveness was my challenge. I was still seeing my counselor and he warned me that once a man starts looking for another woman, the marriage is usually over and can't be saved.

June, who was adept at finding time to spend with Randy, wasn't wise about keeping knowledge of their affair from her husband. Or was that her intent? Her husband readily found Randy's love notes in June's Bible, hidden in the back of their closet, and he went crazy. He drove circles on our front lawn in the middle of the night, revving his truck and destroying the grass. He also made incessant threatening phone calls.

All hell broke loose in the church. Randy and June denied the affair, and June found a way to destroy Randy's notes. The scuttlebutt was all over town and reached the highest ranking members in the Methodist Conference. Within days, Randy's boss, also his uncle, called him. I learned from a parishioner that June had a reputation for seducing previous pastors in the church. Randy had been duped. Maybe June intentionally wanted to cause trouble, or was she a broken and unhappy woman who had a need to exercise power over men? I was grateful that the community protected my sons from the gossip because neither of them found out until they were adults.

At the time the news of the affair was making its way around town, Randy's Mom and stepdad came for a visit. Vivian wanted to see not only us but other relatives in Wisconsin, which included her brother, Randy's uncle, who was the District Superintendent in the Methodist Conference. I didn't think I should reveal anything about the mayhem in our lives. Randy kept his door shut and barely acknowledged his Mom as he moaned in despair. He was nauseous and unable to cope. He sounded sick so everyone believed that he was. He didn't eat. Hosting his family became my responsibility. His Mom and step Dad slept in our bed, Randy was on a single bed in an extra room, and I slept in the kids' room. I never imagined I would be living in this kind of nightmare.

Nightmares have the potential to get worse, especially if we aren't healthy ourselves. In all my criticism of Randy's behavior, I want to be honest about my own. People are often selfish, and my psychiatrist was no exception. He knew of my distress and sensed my bitter disappointment about Randy's affair. He was fully aware of my inability to say *no*. At the end of a session, as I walked out the door, he put his arm around my waist and pulled me toward him and kissed me goodbye. Confused, hurt, and too stunned to know how to respond, I accepted his behavior. I wish I had found another psychiatrist. I returned the next week, slightly fearful. We didn't have a counseling session, we had sex. He had the upper hand and knew how to manipulate my unhealthy acquiesce. There was a part of me that wanted to know why Randy did what he did. My mind swirled with Randy's blatant misbelief that an open marriage—sex with others outside of the marriage bed—was fine. In fact, he believed it to be a good thing. This added to the weird sexual messages I'd already received throughout my life. "You're missing out on a lot of fun," he told me. I make no excuses for myself, but these things contributed to me succumbing to sex outside of my marriage. In the end, this experience wasn't fun or pleasurable, but the surprise was that it didn't cause me distress. I was already used to my body being used. Randy didn't love me, but he used my body, and I dutifully acquiesced in hopes of winning his love and affection. My mind flipped back to the helpless little girl who had to endure her grandfather's ugly smile and strong, groping hands. This sex didn't seem much different. *Is that what a woman is supposed to endure? Is that her purpose in life?*

In forgiving myself, I felt obligated not to condemn Randy for his sexual misdeeds. I let him off the hook and worked to more fully comprehend what forgiveness meant. Sizzle. Sizzle. This was hellfire and it was costly: grief, loss, and betrayal seared our souls and slashed any relationship I falsely believed we might be able to salvage from these ruins. Our sins would have been unredeemable if not for God's mercy.

I stood by Randy, hoping I could be of support and comfort, and that my love, like Belle's in *Beauty and the Beast*, could restore some measure of trust and appreciation. I vacillated between hope and despair. Maybe we never had a love or marriage worth keeping. Maybe the day I threw my purse out the window was the day I should have left. Yet my mind always returned to the memory of the sun breaking through the clouds, shining on us as we took our marital vows. *What marriage doesn't have its woes and betrayals?*

An inquisition of sorts was held in our home to investigate Randy's affair, where Randy's uncle and several Conference leaders led the inquiry. Lying, more my idea than his, was the name of the game. I had no thoughts of integrity—I didn't even know what that meant. Keeping our provision, our livelihood, was all that mattered to me. Randy had already lied about his affair, but in his heart, he wanted to admit that he did, in truth, have sex with a parishioner. Sixteen years later, he made the same decision. This time he was kicked out of the Methodist Conference.

A history of lying had woven itself throughout my family for generations. My father lied when it was in his best interest, which made me think it worked. Of course, in the greater reality, it doesn't. Randy and I denied his affair to the panel of church investigators and no action was taken because there was no proof. Everyone knew the truth except Randy's mother, our family in California, and, thankfully, our children.

The church community was not fooled, and Randy suffered through two months of judgment and shame before he chose to retire from church work and leave the ministry. It was an admission of guilt. We had made a place for ourselves in the world, in the Midwest no less, where Randy so desperately wanted to live. But Randy tossed our lifestyle in the trash like used paper cups. Our kids suffered from the effects of our dysfunction and began to display rebellious behavior, something we had not witnessed before.

Too bad for Randy that he was a first-rate preacher and leader in the church. The congregations grew under his leadership. But he had a love/hate relationship with the church. He didn't feel pride or honor in serving. Though he was intuitive, effective, and socially brilliant, he was overwhelmed and burdened by his role as pastor. "Preach it until you believe it," his grandfather counseled, but to no avail. Randy was a fourth-generation Methodist preacher, he felt pressure from everyone in the family, all of whom placed him on a pedestal. He tried to meet their expectations. In truth, he stayed in church work only because to him there were no other options. Who he really was, what he really believed or how he wanted to behave sexually directly opposed the standards of the Christian church's theological dogmas. It was like living a double life: the appearance of a self-righteous pastor who knew deep inside he wasn't. The conflict caused anger and his family suffered.

So in my Pollyanna thinking, I kept hoping for resolution. I'd always believed that people were capable of changing their perspectives. Though I considered divorcing Randy, I did my best to honor my wedding vows and reflected on the metaphor of the sun bursting through the clouds after the rain.

This challenge fell squarely into my need to prove myself good enough and earn my reward. But it also emboldened Randy to exercise power over me by never allowing me to be 'good enough.' In reality, Randy had left our marriage mentally, emotionally, and physically. I found myself in the loneliest of places, married legally, but not in any other way. I wonder if my counselor was right? *When a man seeks another woman, the marriage is over.*

*Well, it's for better or for worse. I guess I got the worse part.* Randy was in his own private hell, feeling trapped in a bad marriage and in a job he hated. *My Mom stuck it out. I will stick it out, too, for the sake of my sons. Hopefully they will not know about their parent's loneliness and disconnectedness.* Though Randy and I were distant from one another, we continued doing things together as a family, spending quality time with the boys. Thank goodness we knew the importance of assuring them that they were loved and valued. Years later Abram related to me, "I told Noel not to worry about your quarrels and that we would be okay."

Two days after Noel's fourth birthday, we headed back to California. We had no vision for our future. Randy didn't have a job, we didn't have a home, and we had no foreseeable income. Traveling back to California, I wondered: *How will we get through this? Will we be able to feed our children? Will we be eating expired food from trash cans?*

I thought about Jesus's life and what he said. His life teachings, promises, and his love was my rock of hope! I prayed for the Savior to save us, reminding myself that he suffered, and his life was not easy.

I believed God knew what I was going through and would support me, lift me up. And feed my family. I focused on God's love and lived in faith that Jesus would show us what's next. *This is my trust walk.* I figured God was watching how I would deal with this.

*Look at the birds of the air, they do not sow or reap or store away in barns, yet your heavenly Father feeds them. Are you not more valuable than they?* (Matthew 6:26)

*I am convinced that neither death nor life, neither angels nor demons, neither the present nor the future, nor any powers, neither height nor depth, nor anything else in all creation, will be able to separate us from the love of God who is in Christ Jesus our Lord.* Romans 8:38

## CHAPTER 17

# Plumes of Smoke—1983

*It is absolutely crucial...to keep in constant touch with what is going on in one's own life story and to pay close attention to what is going on in the stories of others' lives. If God is present anywhere, it is in those stories that God is present.*

FREDERICK BUECHNER

Our route back to California depended on where we could find friends or relatives to visit and stay with. We met Randy's distant cousins in Chicago, and Iowa. They welcomed us with a meal and a place to sleep. They packed lunches for us before we went on our way.

This was a time when reservations were not required so it was easy to camp. We visited Yellowstone National Park and many other beautiful state parks. We pretended to be on vacation and not two homeless vagabonds with children in tow. We made it fun for the kids, hiking and swimming, cooking on a camp stove and eating outdoors, and sleeping in our tent. (When my boys became men, they pieced together their childhood story and realized that, at that time, we were jobless and homeless.) After a month of 'camping' and 'vacationing,' we were broke.

Randy called his mother, and she again graciously accepted our family into her home. What a relief when we reached California, home at last. I called my mother to let her know we were back. I reached out in hopes of establishing a more trusting relationship, however part of my motive came from fear. I might need her as a backup in the future if Randy and I broke up, and I hoped she would be there for me. A month later I got a letter in the mail from her and a check for *$6000. What a Godsend!* When I called to thank her, she invited me to go out to lunch.

When we met, I noticed she had changed. She wasn't uptight, and our conversation was pleasant, warmer, and more genuine than I'd ever remembered. The tension between us gradually melted away. *Her husband, Jack, is a good man, and I think his love and appreciation of her has helped her heal. She had to heal from Dad just like me.* I wondered what it would be like for me if I was married to someone who was caring and supportive.

I was in for some surprises in our new relationship we were forging. She said softly, "I was wrong to let my father abuse you when you stayed at his house. Gay, I'm so sorry." She gave me a sincere apology, but I was disarmed and still so damaged I could barely respond. I'm sure she wanted to hear words of forgiveness. *Say something.* But I still had no voice when it came to my mother and could not offer any words of consolation or forgiveness.

After living for two months with Randy's Mom, we used part of the gift money from my mother to move into a two-bedroom apartment in Poway, fifteen miles east of San Diego. Again, we had no furniture so we made the best of it, sleeping with our camping pads and sleeping bags. We didn't even have Frankenstein furniture, not yet. We ate our meals on a picnic blanket in the empty living room, and with Pollyanna thinking, we pretended it was an adventure, though it was not easy.

Randy, always looking for a different career, a way to avoid his internal conflict, used a good portion of the money from my Mom to enroll in a private graduate school in San Diego to earn a master's in psychology. *Maybe this will be the answer.* The money my mother gave us was almost gone so I applied for a teaching job in the area.

Just as we were settling in, and before I could gain an interview, Randy received a phone call offering him a part-time associate minister position in Modesto, California 400 miles north of Poway. He would also pastor for a country church 30 miles away. Although he didn't want to be in the ministry, we were out of money, so he accepted the offer. We had only been in Poway for two months and Abram, who had adjusted to another new school, was yanked out of his third-grade class. This move pushed my son over the edge. He had moved ten times with us now, not including in and out of his grandparents homes. He began acting out with rage at school, and I was unsure how to help him.

Randy returned to the ministry to support the family. The two churches were supposed to provide a full time income and we were disheartened and deflated to learn that once again, Randy's pay was inadequate for a family of four. I signed up to substitute teach three days a week while Noel was in preschool, but we still struggled to make ends meet. For the fall semester, Randy commuted 400 miles to graduate school in San Diego for two days twice a month. We'd already paid for it, so he felt obligated to follow through. The money we needed went to that school instead of our pockets. After that semester, he quit, our money had been squandered. *I follow this man into one quagmire after another; bad decisions are his specialty.*

Twice we traveled to Southern California to see my mother and her husband, Jack. It was an expensive trip for our family. Being with her brought up feelings from my past. She had years of healing, and I welcomed her lighter spirit and happier countenance. Jack loved her. She no longer had to endure criticism and rejection from my Dad. Her familiar movements and voice comforted me. I was glad to meet my real Mom, the one other people seemed to know and like. I always suspected there was a lovely person who was hidden from me.

One night while lying in bed at her house, she sat on my bed and talked with me, asking me questions. I was overjoyed that she was interested in me. This was what I'd hungered for my whole life, and I hoped it was the breakthrough we needed. This rare interaction gave me a feeling for what could have been. I treasured this precious time and kept the memory alive.

My Mom read stories to my children as they sat on her lap and got to know her, building on the positive visit we previously had with her and Jack. Deep down, though, I was sad that I had no memories of sitting on her lap. My self-defeating thoughts raced: *my kids are good enough for her, but I never have been.* But I was learning that she had healed and grown over the years, as I had. When I was a youngster, she didn't have the experience or wherewithal to give me time or seek a relationship with me. I believe she had wanted a loving relationship for us as much as I did, but neither of us had acquired the knowledge to overcome our dysfunctions.

I learned to give myself compassion, and in turn developed compassion for her. This eventually led me to forgiveness, but even though this was over thirty years ago, I still had this unproductive thought: *If only I'd known then what I know now.*

The following spring Randy was offered a position at a small church no one wanted to serve in the Northern California coastal mountains. He surrendered to being stuck in ministry in order to support our family. This was the dues he had to pay to move upward within the hierarchical system of our third Methodist Conference. So off we went. *I wonder what Randy will do this time? God, keep him from making a mess of this!*

In May, Abram turned nine and Noel five. As soon as school was out, we packed up. My stomach ached as we drove away from the home where we had lived for only eight months. Move number eleven for Abram and move number 18 for Randy and me. Looking back, it's pretty obvious I was following a man who wanted to run away even more than I did.

Abram felt like he'd been kidnapped. He hadn't had many opportunities to make friends, and now the ones he had made in third grade were left behind. His distress caused him to sob a catharsis of tears on our four hour trip to a new town, new school, and new church. I could find no words to comfort or calm him. Finally, after a heart-wrenching drive, we arrived in Tiny Town, my name for the village where our new church and parsonage was. It was late afternoon when I saw the little hovel of a house, built in the 1940s. It was next door to the church, and while it didn't have a fenced-in yard, at least we weren't living in a cemetery. I walked through the front door and winced at the odor coming from the old carpet. The living room was dark, so I flipped on the overhead light switch. Zap! It sparked. *Oh God, we've moved into a fire trap. Please don't let us burn up in this house!* Warning bells went off as I took stock of old broken electric heaters recessed in the walls. As if on cue, Abram stumbled into the house and threw up, hot with fever. Soon Noel had the flu, and the next day Randy succumbed. I hoped I was strong enough to fight it off, but two days later I was down. I wasn't sick, I was sickened. *Please, not a repeat, Lord! I was hoping for a reset. We desperately need a reset.*

I faithfully sought sanity and peace of mind from the Man who'd whispered in my ears, *Follow Me.* "Come to me, all you who are weary and burdened, and I will give you rest. Take my yoke upon you and learn from me, for I am gentle and humble in heart, and you will find rest for your souls. For my yoke is easy and my burden light." (Matthew 11:28-30)

I turned to Jesus and prayed for my family. I was concerned for my children who were not experiencing the peaceful and secure home I had hoped to provide them. In this regard Randy and I were dismal failures. I tried my best to believe something better was around the corner. My hopes for stability lived silently in my heart, but often my dreams evaporated like morning mist rising off a clear blue lake. The accumulation of so many bad decisions afflicted any sense of harmony I tried to create. We shouldn't have left Randy's first appointment in Southern California; it was a good position and a prestigious one. Each decision to move since then had led to another debacle. It was as though we were being sabotaged at each turn, except the saboteur was my husband.

In a marriage, when one partner travels the path of wrongdoing and missteps, both partners face the consequences. By staying with Randy, was I complicit? *Will God save me? Can God save us?* Hope in God was my only handhold. *God, must I suffer the consequences of Randy's bad choices?* I guess so.

Part of Randy's salary package was that the church provided for a parsonage and paid the electric and water bills, along with the upkeep of the house. It was the responsibility of the church to provide wood for our heat. The primary heat for the house came from an old-fashioned wood-burning stove, and one of the parishioners made firewood available to us. We drove to his farm where he showed us a pile of huge, unsplit rounds of tree trunks. Next to the unruly pile was a log splitter. This of course meant heaving the large rounds and placing them correctly in the splitter.

The fellow who provided the wood was in his seventies, so naturally, he expected Randy to heave the logs into the splitter and learn how to use it. Randy complied. It was dangerous, and I was anxious that Noel and Abram were close by. Even though I was uncomfortable with this arrangement, I became the buffer between the log splitter and my boys. We dutifully carried the smaller pieces and threw them in the man's pick-up truck. He drove to our house, dumped the wood in our drive-way, and drove off. There lay a huge pile of split wood small enough to carry in the house and fit in the wood stove. The next few days I moved and stacked all the wood outside the back door. *Is this the expectation of the pastor and his wife when living in the country?* I tried to be grateful for what we had been given, but I was hurting. I was disgusted and Randy was furious; but whenever Randy needed or wanted something he always managed to work it out. He resolved to meet with the parsonage committee and advocate for someone else to split the wood and deliver it. We, more accurately, I, still had to stack it, but we had a source of heat, and I was relieved that the harder, more dangerous work was out of our purview.

Every day I dusted the ashes off the mantel, dining room table, and furniture. I vacuumed every day, sickened to think of the ashes we were breathing. I brought in firewood, cleaned out the fireplace twice a week, and kept the fire going during the winter nights. Country living wasn't easy or dreamy. Thankfully, this was a California winter, warm by Wisconsin standards.

An eighty-five-year-old woman whom I'd befriended in church shared with me some of her childhood experiences in the early 1900s. She said, "Monday was laundry day and every week my sisters and I took the laundry to a large black kettle next to the stream. We filled it with water from the stream, lit a fire, and boiled the water. Then we dropped the clothes into the water and boiled them clean. We pulled out the clothes and hung them to dry. During the summer months we played in the stream, and we found other games in the winter. The next day we ironed our clothes." *I'm so glad I have a washing machine and permanent press clothes. And I'm upset about the chores of stacking wood and cleaning the fireplace?*

The light switches continued to spark. I asked the parsonage committee to fix them and though they said they would, they never did. The good news was the fire department was only fifty feet away. The unwelcome news was whenever there was a fire in the community, the alarm blasted across the town to alert the volunteer firefighters. The sound bolted me out of my skin.

One of my brightest memories was being near a wide, gentle flowing stream that was just two blocks from our house. The water flowed from a mountain spring and was clean and sparkly. It was shallow enough that the kids could lay on their tummies and cool off and practice some swimming safely. I had no fear of them being swept away or drowning. We enjoyed daily refreshment there.

My older sister, Peggy, lived forty-five minutes from our house. She had two girls who were close in age to Abram and Noel, so they finally got to meet their cousins on my side of the family. Peggy and I started rebuilding our relationship.

Randy brought home a stray three-month-old, Heinz-57 variety pitbull that happened to jump into his car. It adopted us as soon as it walked into the house. Abram announced, "This is my dog. Corky is his name!" Secretly, I wanted to get rid of it. I put it out in our unfenced backyard, hoping it would wander away.

Ten days later, while I was substituting, the principal walked into class. "There's a dog wandering around the schoolyard," he said. "The kids tell me it's your dog. I'll stay with your class while you take it home." I looked outside, and sure enough it was Corky. So I reluctantly took him home. Randy built a ramshackle barrier to contain the dog. He made it out of freestanding objects and attached them to the nearby trees. He used trash cans and old curtain rods that he nailed vertically into boards so that he could string wire between them and the trees. It was a fence we could afford. I laughed as I watched his ingenuity as he invented something to keep 'our' dog from wandering. *Ha!* If we'd had cell phones back then I'd have a great picture of Randy's creative, penny-pinching project.

The church hated the look of that makeshift fence. They built a six-foot fence to enclose our backyard and make it safe for our dog and children. Corky became a playful, gladsome member of our family, especially for Abram and Noel, and that silly dog brightened our spirits. Living in ranch country afforded the children new experiences. A church member invited Abram to a party at his ranch to brand the cattle. When Abram returned several hours later, he told us he had eaten rocky mountain oysters off the grill. Randy and I hadn't a clue what that was. We later learned that they were the testicles of cattle that had been castrated that day. *Oh yes, country living!*

I steadfastly reminded Randy of my love. "I love you," I said regularly, encouraging him with hugs and embraces, though nothing came my way in return. I could not remember the last time he had said that he loved me and deep in my gut I knew he no longer did. *At least he's not lying.* Even though he wanted to have sex every night, I knew it didn't qualify as lovemaking. By the time we arrived in Tiny Town we had been married twelve years, and I had learned to enjoy sex, but it was too late. I lost hope for us but decided to stay for the sake of my precious sons. I prayed to God for rescue and relied on my faith that something bigger than me was at work. *Can God change people? Is there hope for us?*

Noel was in first grade and Abram in fifth, when a fourth-grade teaching position became available. After I applied and got the job, the District Superintendent requested that we have a chat. *Gosh, I haven't even started teaching. Could I have done something wrong already?*

After the regular chit-chat, the superintendent told me he'd seen pastor's wives take teaching positions in the past. His voice was calm, and he seemed kind and sincere. "For some reason it just never works out," he said. "It's not a promising idea in a community this small to be teaching children where your husband is leading, serving, and ministering to their families. I would encourage you to decline this position and wait for a better opportunity." I listened, but this made no sense to me. *Why would there be a conflict of interest just because we were two professionals working in the same town?* I was so taken aback by his comment that I forgot to ask him to elaborate.

I was bored in Tiny Town, but most importantly, I wanted to start my teaching career. Randy and I talked it over for about three minutes, and we immediately agreed that I should take the job.

*Why didn't I listen to an experienced superintendent or ask questions as to his reasoning?* I wanted to do it and was unwilling to consider the ramifications of taking the job. This was an opportunity too good to pass up and I needed something meaningful to do.

The school was larger than I realized, serving a fifteen-mile radius of country folks. We had a good relationship with the people at church, and did well with my teacher colleagues, but the schoolyard was an entirely different story. It was common for kids to scuffle aggressively with each other on the playground. One day on my way to the office, I heard commotion in the boys' bathroom. I called, "Teacher coming in!" As I opened the door, I heard, "Get 'em Abram! Yeah! Get 'em." There was my son pummeling another boy, slugging him repeatedly.

I stopped the fight, mortified. Now I saw what my kids and I were up against. Might was the norm. Abram was usually the strongest among his peers and these boys, who grew up with a fighting mentality, used him by encouraging him to fight their fights. Suddenly, he was now a hero—*Strike one!*

Not long after that, from across the street I heard a bunch of boys yelling and screaming. I flew out the front door into the vacant lot next to our house to discover Abram on top of a boy in a scuffle. I scolded, "Stop it! No! Get up!" Separating them, I said, "We must work this out.

This must stop!" I marched them down a short block, pushed open a squeaky, unpainted gate and approached a shanty house. The boy's Mom threw open the screen door and took her stance on the porch with a shotgun pointed directly at me.

"Get off my property, you bitch of a teacher. And don't you ever come back."

Instinctively, I put my hands up and stepped in front of my son. I can't remember if I said anything, but we backed off until we were out the gate, at which point she angled the gun toward the ground. *Whew! The Hatfields and McCoys—Strike two!*

Randy called the police, and they visited the woman's house. I think the experience may have had an impression on Abram because I did not hear anything about fighting and didn't have to pull him off anyone after that.

Susie was in my class and came to school with bruises, sometimes on her cheeks and arms, and once with a black eye. I tried to befriend her and gained her confidence. She shared tales of her home life with me and though she never indicated her dad in any incidents, I sensed something. I reported my suspicions to the principal (teachers are required by law to report abuse.) A few days later the principal nonchalantly strolled into my classroom and said he would take my class while I attended to something in the office. I had no idea what to expect and when I got there, I was greeted by the Child Protective Service representatives who had come to ask questions about Susie. When I returned to my class, it was obvious that the kids knew my conversation in the office was about Susie, and her flashing eyes let me know she felt betrayed.

That night I received a threatening call from Susie's father, "I better not see you in a dark alley! You better watch your back." I feared for our lives for several nights. *What might he do?* This was our second encounter with the police in my first three months of teaching.

I had lost Susie's confidence, and the abuse didn't stop. She protected her abuser, no doubt out of necessity. *Strike three! Am I out?* It sure felt like it, but I had a teaching contract to fulfill. I needed to go to work and keep trying to get base hits or maybe a double or triple.

I did have some home runs. The children in my class showed improvement and tested at a solid fourth grade level in reading and math at the end of the year. That was my focus, and I had succeeded. My class also came in second in the school science fair, and the bonus was that I developed friendly relationships with some of the other teachers.

I got up at 5:00 every morning to correct papers, make lunches for the kids, fix breakfast, then off we went! Every afternoon Abram and Noel watched TV in my classroom until 4:30 while I prepared lessons for the next day. This was wearisome as they wanted to be home. They also missed having quality time with me. We hired someone to do the weekly cleaning, but Randy didn't like having another woman in the house when he was working in his office. Considering his past behavior, I decided to do the cleaning myself. My energy steadily drained as the year progressed.

Because Randy and I were busy, there wasn't much time or opportunity for Randy to fight with me, but his uncontrollable rage needed an outlet, and his target became our ten-year-old son. After preaching one Sunday, he began a two-hour tirade, wildly berating Abram for all manner of imagined faults. When Abram yelled back at his father and I attempted to defend my son, the argument spun out of control. I felt disheartened. We have dragged Abram, my sweet Abram, into our horrible fighting cage. Abram and I never knew what prompted Randy's outbursts, which made the situation even more difficult.

One memorable afternoon, in distress after one of Randy's long rants, Abram smashed his fist through a window. Luckily, there was only a small cut on his finger. When Randy saw Abram bleeding, he stopped his rampage. *Is this what it takes to stop him? Does it take trauma and chaos to calm this man?*

Abram was beginning his march toward becoming a young man. Sensing the subtle changes in Abram caused Randy to assert his authority over him. He intended to make sure that Abram would never challenge him in any way, now or in the future. I became an enraged mother bear. Now it wasn't just me I was defending; I was defending Abram from these unwarranted attacks.

Despite these bouts with his father, Abram deemed his dad to be his best friend. Through it all, Randy continued to undermine my relationship with Abram, doing all he could to make me out as the problem. *How convenient.* This gave Abram unwarranted power over me, a power he shouldn't have had. He became firmly steeped in the belief that I was not worthy of his respect, and this damaged our fragile parent-child relationship. When I asked the boys to help me with the dishes, Randy quipped, "I don't want them helping you because you will ruin them!" *What an excuse for me to do all the work, and for them to believe I was not a fit mother.* Witnessing Randy's disrespect, Abram saw no need to respect me either. I understood my predicament clearly. Randy's twisted undermining of me caused both Abram and me the sorrow of an unhealthy relationship. That Randy intentionally robbed us in this way caused a deep sadness that would burn through my heart and soul for years.

Amid this dysfunction, I somehow maintained my sanity in my daily life and was proud of my teaching ability. A strange feeling of peace during this tumultuous time had come over me. I could feel the power of the Holy Spirit blowing through me, like the wind. This must have been what helped keep me, and our family together.

I was never quite sure how all this was affecting Noel. He was a quiet and giving soul, who declared at six years of age: "I don't want to be like you guys. I'm not going to fight with you!" Noel was the peacemaker of the family. As an adult, he told me, "I never believed all that stuff Dad said about you, Mom."

Tiny Town was only eleven short blocks long and three wide, with one grocery store, one pizza shack, and no stop lights. A two-lane highway ran through the middle of town. Noel made a friend from school who lived a few blocks from our house. Kevin was a pleasant boy who played nicely with Noel. His eyelid was curled with extra skin that slipped over his right eye, and though it didn't block his vision, his eye was noticeably different. I called it droopy eye, medically known as dermatochalasis or ptosis.

There weren't many desirable playmates for our kids in this small community, and Kevin and Noel were good friends. After a few months, Noel's opposite eye, the mirror of Kevin's, became noticeably droopier. After a few more months, Noel's eye looked like Kevin's. Research shows that this sometimes occurs when people have a strong emotional connection; it is an unconscious response and can become a syndrome, sympathetic dystrophy, mirroring symptoms of another person.

*Hmmm…Should I restrict their playing together? That's not right or fair. Noel never mentions it; he doesn't even notice. I never said a word to anyone.*

A woman from our church attempted suicide by running her car engine while the garage door was closed. Someone found her before she died, and she was saved. Her nine-year-old son was in my class and Randy counseled and prayed with the woman several times the following week. She needed mental health professional support until she was stable. She attended church the next Sunday and I was able to speak with her kindly and compassionately. I understood the sorrow of sinking into despair and knew about the desire to end pain. In her distress, she tried again the second week, and succeeded. Her son found her that morning, adding to the tragedy. Three days later this devastated child rejoined our class, numb, and disconnected. Tragedy permeated the atmosphere, and I was helpless.

Grieving children were expected to keep on keeping on—and their teacher, too. Randy performed both the memorial and funeral services.

Unknown to most people in our church community, our family was concurrently grieving because of our own family's loss. Randy's four-year-old nephew had died two months earlier from a rare genetic immunity disease. Randy was heartbroken, but he was in the familial leadership role and was expected to officiate at the memorial service. We mistakenly allowed our boys to view their cousin's small body, which made the stark reality of death all too real for them. During bedtime prayers, Abram added this plea, "And God, please let my Mom and Dad grow old, old, old." Randy's nephew's death also increased our worry of losing our children in some unforeseen circumstances.

A family who had moved from the Bay Area joined our church. They had a seventeen-year-old boy. After church, the children usually played in the our fenced yard, and I noticed that the new teenager joined in the games with the younger boys. I dutifully kept watch over the kids. Two of the boys, whom we shall call Tom and John, were in my fourth grade class. One day after teaching a lesson, Tom approached me after school to inform me that John had been molested upstairs in the church attic by the new seventeen-year-old boy. My stomach flipped and a current of panic parched my mouth as I asked again for clarification of what had happened.

Randy and I spent a lot of time discussing the situation. The next day, I informed John's parents. I had trouble finding words and felt as though I didn't communicate well with John's parents even though Randy coached me about what to say. That this happened in the church building and with two families in our church left Randy dealing with the ramifications. These kinds of situations were his specialty and he dealt with it well, making sure no one in the church became aware of what had happened. He met with each family individually and then had a meeting with both families. He led them to get legal advice and counselors who could help them work through these tragic circumstances.

The advice from the superintendent came back to me: a pastor and a teacher serving in a small town is not wise.

I thought back on the advice Randy's uncle had given him when we arrived in Wisconsin: "It's simple. The job is to baptize 'em, marry 'em, and bury 'em. That's how folks' bond to you. Teach and preach the Gospel. Do that and the congregations will follow you." It made me wonder: *Could Randy ever believe what he was teaching and preaching? He must know that he doesn't 'walk his talk' with me. Maybe moving from town to town and conference to conference prevents any kind of bonding with people in the church. He doesn't want to be too close with anyone. No taking chances on being known! Too much vulnerability. Did Randy sabotage his career in fear that people might recognize he was faking it? Getting out of Dodge before they find out?*

I wanted to enjoy people and develop friendships. I longed for a normal marriage relationship with my husband. I did not know the particulars of what normal might look and feel like, but I knew we were not experiencing it. Randy was not interested in developing a relationship with me, or with the people in our churches.

I finished my first year of teaching disheartened and defeated. *If this is what I must go through to teach, I quit.* I was depleted and it showed. The following year I stayed home.

My idea that *I don't matter in our family* shattered when I saw the difference I made to my sons by staying home with them. *I have been absent for nine months, instead of keeping things stable for my children. I am more important to our family than I knew.* In that deeper knowing place within myself, I knew that my leadership was essential to their well-being. With this information confirmed, I turned my thoughts toward healing. Contentment seemed within our reach and a measure of peace grew among us because I stabilized our home life. This was a first-hand revelation as I began to consider myself a loving, contributing human being with influence. *I can let my little light shine, shine, shine.*

My teaching salary hadn't provided much additional income for us. We went out to eat pizza twice a week. We paid someone to stack wood and do other chores I usually did. We purchased a second car and took on the expenses that came with it. We were disheartened when we discovered that our combined income put us in a higher tax bracket, leaving no savings in the bank. Altogether, there was nothing that could compensate for the lost time with my children. I never wanted to play ball in the teaching arena again.

That following summer my dad re-entered my life with a single phone call. "Gay, this is your father calling. We are in the area and are coming for a visit, and we plan to stay a couple of days. We will sleep in our motor home." *Ok, I suppose I can manage this.*

A day later, my dad and his wife arrived. As they walked in, I received a call from a church parishioner who said the water heater in the church was broken. My dad overheard the conversation, "Well let's go take a look at it." I had watched him fix things all my life and I trusted him in this regard. Sure enough, he fixed it in two hours. *Yay! One problem solved! Who would have guessed my dad would be a Godsend and save us time and energy?* I was hopeful that this would be a good visit for all.

Randy showed up and found us in the church kitchen. Dad had just finished the job. Randy could not control himself and yelled, "You come to my house and take over! You had no business fixing this!" *Really Randy? No hello? Not one word of greeting?* Dad was confused. He shook his head in dismay as I tried to calm everyone down. There I was, in the middle of a heated argument, defending my dad, of all people! Randy backed off and we tried to go on with the visit.

Dad and his wife decided to stay despite the conflict. Soon they left in their motor home and a half hour later reappeared with pizza, which they set on the dining room table.

"Pineapple and ham!" They said with big smiles. They had gone to the only place in town to get prepared food; I imagined they saw the pizza as a peace offering. Unfortunately, no one in our family cared for pineapple and ham. *Oh well, we can go with the flow.* But Abram took one look at it and disappeared into his bedroom.

Randy could not pass up this opportunity to create more chaos. "I can't believe you planned dinner without asking us and didn't even check to see what kind of pizza we like!" I was flabbergasted and so were they. *All this hullabaloo over pizza? Randy reminds me more of my dad than my dad does! Guess my Mom was right when she told me, nineteen years ago, that Randy reminded her of my dad.*

We sat down to eat, but my dad, already offended, was soon on the attack.

"Where is Abram? Why isn't he here with us?" Dad took it upon himself to go get him. Abram, who'd only known his grandfather for eight hours of his life, felt no compunction to comply when my dad ordered him to the table. Agitated and true to form, my dad began to berate my character, "What kind of mother are you, anyway? You should make him sit with us. You're teaching him to be rude!"

"It's okay, Dad. Maybe he's not hungry," I offered meekly.

"You don't know how to parent and teach your kids manners."

"He is free to make his own choices, Dad. If Abram skips dinner and is hungry tonight, then that experience will show him that there are consequences to his choices." *Next time he'll think twice before hightailing it to his room at dinner time.*

I felt courageous about my response, but Randy felt the need to use his sharp verbal skills to lay an opponent low. Randy was the instigator instead of my dad, and I was put in the position of trying to stop their ridiculous squabble. But when either of them was provoked, it was like entering a dog fight! I was sure to get bitten. Later that night, Randy and Abram commiserated. Neither my Dad or Randy ever recovered from this conflict, each one blaming the other. My Dad carried his anger and hurt with him for the rest of his life.

The saddest part was that my dad and his wife had tried to visit me and their grandchildren. They showed up unannounced without regard for the needs and plans of our family. Their visit fit in with their travel plans, much as when they didn't show up at our wedding because they had other plans.

*I am so torn up and frazzled, Lord. I can't stand their behavior. Why do I still want to love them?*

They stayed two nights and three days and then were ready to leave. I followed them across the front yard to say goodbye, and as they climbed into their little motor home, I said, "Well Dad, it was an interesting visit." I couldn't muster a kind goodbye by saying I was glad they had come. When they arrived, I was hoping for some semblance of reconciliation. Alas, it could not be. Bravely, I added, "I guess you came because you love me!"

"What do you mean by that? Of course I love you. Why do you think I worked so long and hard all those years?" His eyebrows raised in confusion as he turned and sank into the driver's seat. With a slight wave, they drove off. My father, who had worked to provide and support us, was impoverished in terms of what we needed emotionally, or how his actions and words hurt me, my sisters, and my Mom. It required significant mental effort to be grateful for what he was able to give me and to believe that he meant well. Granny once told me, "Saying a person 'means well' is not a compliment."

I would not see him again for several more years.

Before Dad's visit, I was able to maintain normalcy and a sense of healthy identity. Over his three-day stay, I used my strong willpower to be kind to everyone and to provide for their needs. But as their motor home disappeared around the corner, I walked back into the house and plopped into a chair. At my first deep breath, my unpredictable switch flipped me into 'off.' I recognized the change. *This is exactly what happened to me ten years ago after being with my Mom when she met me unexpectedly in the parking lot after hiring that private detective.* I felt forlorn and out of touch with myself and my family. My sense of well-being darted out the window like a frightened bird. *Oh, God, not again!* I wondered what this visit would have been like if it just could have been friendly instead of hostile. *We are not a normal family.*

Two and a half days was supposed to be a small dose of Dad, but the fighting between my father and Randy overwhelmed me. I felt under attack. I no longer felt safe at home or even at church. I continued to perform my motherly and wifely tasks, moving about with the same patterns and language, but deep inside I was disconnected from being able to love and or receive love. Shut-down mode was in full force. My recent discovery of knowing I was a valuable member of my family sloshed into a mud hole. I was depleted and unable to function normally. Having gone through this weird phenomenon before, I hoped this mode would be temporary.

In early autumn, four months later, my internal switch flipped back to normal. *There it is! I'm back!* I took a long, cleansing breath. *I feel like me again!* Though I was relieved and grateful, this on/off switch that lived somewhere deep inside me left me feeling deeply insecure. I knew I had no control over it and that it could rule my being. I was on edge and less confident. *Where did it come from, Lord, and will I ever be free of it? What happens in my psyche to cause this?*

I'd made it through another strange episode of, well, I did not know what. Randy didn't respond to the newfound me. His response was no response, like the walking dead. He couldn't muster any happiness for me, or for us. He was detached and despondent, much as after his affair in Wisconsin. He was finished dealing with my 'absences', incapable of hugs or any manner of affection. He didn't care about me in any way.

I imagined how my children viewed me now that Randy was treating me like I was invisible. I worried they would grow up and treat their wives as Randy treated me. I was concerned they would feel they had a right to power over women. To be valued and respected by my children, I was intentional in my relationship with them. I took them to the nearby stream to play, planned bike rides and walks, and ended our days with an engaging book. I gave them lots of touch by massaging their hands, feet, and lots of back rubs. I helped them with their homework and tried to meet their needs. But Randy's apathy undermined my confidence. He consciously, or unconsciously, attacked my positive efforts to pull our family back together.

In October, Randy asked for a transfer to another church. Once again, the process of changing churches began. Desperate, I prayed about everything. I firmly held on to Jesus as my best friend who would protect and value me. I prayed for Randy's new appointment to be in a church in a town that had values that matched ours. We needed a normal school setting and a place where guns and fists were not the accepted way to solve problems. I hoped for a house with forced heating and air conditioning, a safe home with a carpet that didn't smell bad. We needed to get out of Tiny Town. Noel's left eye had become droopier, so much so that his eyelid nearly covered his eye to the same extent that Kevin's did. I did not know how to deal with that problem. I prayed for a new car because our little yellow wagon needed repairs. I shot high, and audaciously prayed: *God how about a Toyota van for our family?* I knew that the needs and desires of my heart were already known by the Creator.

And even though I believed God had answers to our problems, I had learned that they rarely came in the tidy packages of my imagination. Circumstances arise that we have little control over, and answers to prayer appear in strange ways and with mixed consequences. There may be unexpected difficulties, and sometimes, in the process, unforeseen blessings sprout from these difficulties. It becomes obvious that through prayer come answers. Usually the answers arrive differently than we might have expected. Yet they become our blessings. We give thanks. Because I was bonded to Randy in the sharing of our lives and of our sons' lives, and because every week I learned more about Jesus, I still believed Randy was a blessing to me. It was impossible to let go. With blinders firmly attached, I clung to hope, because I believed that the words of Romans 5:5 were true: "...hope does not disappoint us."

*May the God of hope fill you with all joy and peace as you trust in him, so that you may overflow with hope by the power of the Holy Spirit.* Romans 15:13

*I believe our emotions—all of them—belong in our prayers... Our prayers represent not just what we say, but who we are, with all our complex longings and feelings.*

Thomas Jones

## CHAPTER 18

# On the Lighter Side

*Far away, there in the sunshine, are my highest aspirations. I may not reach them, but I can look up and see their beauty, believe in them and try to follow where they lead.*

LOUISA MAY ALCOTT

When we were on vacation and away from his church duties I could believe that Randy liked me and enjoyed my company. I still loved and cared for him and encouraged myself with positive thinking. *There are good times that keep me with Randy. I love our trips together. I love and need my family.*

I experienced a good measure of peace during our camping trips in nature. We saw the geysers at Yellowstone National Park, walked on the shoreline of Lake Yellowstone, and threw rocks in the water. The boys particularly liked watching the bison and elk. Sequoia National Park was the closest national park to us in California and became our favorite go-to camping place. Because Randy was a preacher, he led an ecumenical outdoor church service on Sunday in the amphitheater. In exchange, we had a free campsite for a week. Randy carried our young son, Noel, on his back as we hiked Crescent Meadows, enjoying the flowers, and swimming in the small lakes in the park.

Randy's free spirit was released in our travels. He joked and made-up stories that kept us laughing. We made up songs and sang them while cooking dinner on our camp stove. We didn't fight, not at all, so I relaxed and could feel my damaged self start to heal. This always encouraged me. *We do actually get along. What happens in the real life demands of working?*

We took three, 4,000-mile round trips between California and Wisconsin with Randy driving until midnight while the boys slept in the back seat. We stayed in campgrounds because we couldn't afford motels. Randy and I could set up the tent and spread out the sleeping bags in twenty minutes. Randy gently carried Abram and Noel from their cramped sleeping arrangements in the back seat and tucked them into their comfortable bags.

In the mornings, Randy slept in while I played with the boys. I entertained them with frisbee and wiffle ball and we kicked small soccer balls and played football. I chased them, and when I caught them, they giggled as I tickled them. Sometimes we woke up to discover a children's play area with ladders and swings, something that helped them burn off energy before resuming the trip. These were precious times when I had lots of fun. Love welled up in my heart for our little family.

I read John Muir's writings, Henry David Thoreau's *Walden Pond*, Washington Irving's *Tour on the Prairie*, and other nature-oriented works which kept me in touch with the wonder of God's creation. I read lots of stories to the boys, and we laughed at the antics of Garfield the cat and Odie the dog.

Because Randy and I fell in love and got engaged in wondrous San Diego, it became another favorite place to take the kids. The San Diego zoos were fabulous adventures for our young boys. We frolicked in the ocean, dove under the waves and boogie boarded in the warm summer water. Again, no arguments and peace in our family.

My time with Abram and Noel kept me as sane and happy as any mother might be in my circumstances. When the boys were older, we played soccer on the front lawn, basketball in the backyard, and walked our dogs in the parks in the evenings. Romping and wrestling on the living room floor brought us close, and I laughed as they tried to pin me down. Our physical play was healing for me.

I stayed engaged with life's many blessings and watched the developmental milestones as my boys grew.

It's well-documented that a person's ability to respond to others with compassion and acceptance directly correlates to how their needs were met as a child. Throughout a child's development, expressing one's needs and having support is essential for a child's sense of his social standing and sense of belonging. I learned this in psychology classes, but my greatest teachers in this regard were my childhood longings, my unmet needs. I was committed to doing my best for Abram and Noel, guiding their growth and development so they could be happy in their relationships and become well adjusted, contributing adults to society.

Bonding with a person's caretaker is essential to leading a balanced life, mentally, emotionally, and physically. A baby cries. The baby communicates. My boys and I bonded, and I gained confidence in myself. I recognized a gift that God had placed in me: I was gifted in teaching young children. It came naturally to me to guide my sons, and as I noticed positive results of their growth, my self-esteem and sense of well-being were enhanced. I was needed and loved; I was 'Mom.'

As a child, I knew in my mind what I needed. My parents didn't know how to care for or even listen to me; they weren't able to meet any needs other than provision. But God has given each of us a deep knowing of self so that when given leeway, a person can develop and express his/her thoughts. Since I didn't have these opportunities, I resolved to provide this kind of environment for my children. I am grateful that God answered my prayers to be the kind of mother who was able to guide my children by recognizing their successes, strengths, and abilities. I deliberately encouraged a sense of confidence to help them learn and trust their instincts. And I made sure to give them many opportunities to make decisions about their lives, even at a young age. Though Randy may have been controlling, I was not. Today my adult sons make decisions easily, without self-doubt. With self-confidence, they know what is needed, and can articulate and act upon those things in an acceptable manner. This gives me satisfaction and parental pride and joy.

I also had the opportunity to shine in the role of a pastor's wife. Some spouses resent the expectations in their role as a pastor's wife, but I thrived. Dolly, Randy's grandmother, and Vivian, were my role models. I understood the social structure of the church, and it pleased me to be a trusted member.

My spirits were lifted as I enjoyed getting to know people in the church. This enhanced my self-confidence and improved my social graces. After ten years serving together, Randy commented, "You have become my biggest asset in the church." *Wow! That's a rare compliment. I've made the grade!* His compliments contributed to my joyful continuation in doing ordinary, helpful activities like making meals for potlucks and taking meals to those who were sick. I prepared for community events such as health clinics or election voting booths. I taught Sunday school. I was gratified with positive feedback from the parishioners which made me feel like I was where I needed to be.

Behind the scenes participation in the church worked for me because I avoided long-winded interactions that overwhelmed me. In this way I didn't have to compromise the defenses lodged deep in my brain. My giving came naturally. I took heart in believing I was "serving the Lord." I was supporting my husband's work as a good wife 'should.' I thought by making life easier for Randy, surely he would acknowledge my contribution and love me for it. Serving can be doing the right thing with an ulterior motive. It seemed like a win-win situation and built my self-esteem. I cared for my children in ways that exceeded the standard of my parents. All these experiences gratified me and brightened my life.

My identity became following the teachings of Jesus. Though I loved doing and serving, I loved God more. *See what great love the Father has lavished on us, that we should be called the children of God!* (1 John: 3-1) And that is what we are!

*The LORD your God is with you, he is mighty to save. He will take great delight in you, he will quiet you with his love, he will rejoice over you with singing.* Zephaniah 3:17

CHAPTER 19

# Unbelievable—1987

*There are not too many miracles. If there were, we might become*
*careless and lazy. If there were not any, we might be destroyed.*

J. RUFUS MOSELEY

In January 1987 Randy received a call from the Methodist Conference with an appointment offering him a church position as pastor of a struggling church in Chico, California. We knew the layout of the town because that is where Randy's mother lived. We had a positive feel for the community from our many visits to see Vivian. A huge draw for us was family support, along with Randy's sister, Kris, and her new baby. This was what I imagined when praying about Randy's new assignment. A normal town with regular schools. A place where people reject the Hatfield and McCoy mentality. *This looks like a good place to raise children.* I hoped I was right. Out of over seven hundred churches in the Conference, God chose Chico!

Randy met with the pastor-parish committee for an interview, and I was graciously invited to be part of the process and meet the people who would approve his appointment. I felt visible. The church had suffered a recent loss of their beloved pastor and attendance had significantly declined. The Conference was aware of Randy's record for growing a church congregation and had chosen him for that reason.

The interview was fantastic. The people on the pastor-parish committee were warm and welcoming. *Friendly and thoughtful people, a small but functional church building, and an active township. Thank you, God.* The committee accepted Randy as their new pastor that night.

As we wrapped up the interview, a man on the committee was called away for an important telephone call. A few minutes later he returned, "Randy, I have bad news. That call was to let you know that your house in Tiny Town caught on fire. Part of the house burned, but most of it was saved."

We stood there in shock, my heart dropped into my stomach. I assumed that it was caused by faulty electrical wiring. *Oh God! You protected us when the house we lived in was a fire trap. You saved us!* The flames came while we were safe in Chico. I wanted to fall on my knees to give thanks for blessings that can't be measured. *This could have happened while we were sleeping.* I was awed, speechless with gratitude that God had heard my prayer on that first day I entered the old parsonage. We stayed that night in Chico and returned to our partially burned home the next day. A church leader walked with us into the smoky mess, and I stood in the boys' bedroom where the fire started. My legs shook and I was weak-kneed when I saw the beds, burned from the bottom up. I feared I would drop to the floor and cry. Thank goodness the fire department was next door. They had seen the flames bursting from the windows and rushed right over. But Abram's Millennium Falcon model spacecraft that he'd received for Christmas melted, along with all the boys' toys. No other rooms in the house were burned, but everything was smoke-damaged. I walked out feeling bitter-sweet, unsettled, and angry that the parsonage committee had not done its job to keep us safe. God had kept us safe. I was in awe and my trust in God increased. *My life, and my family have been touched by God. Jesus DID answer my prayers. I am humbled.*

Randy had to deal with fallout from disgruntled church members. He hated the idea that some parishioners blamed him for having burned their parsonage even though they failed to perform essential maintenance. I couldn't comfort him with my thoughts of looking for the positive and being thankful we were alive. He swatted me away and turned his back saying, "You are such a Pollyanna." His reaction reminded me of his difficulty in being grateful after our near catastrophic car accident on the interstate in the Ohio snow. *I happen to like looking for the silver lining.*

The church rented a small, furnished A-frame home with two bedrooms upstairs and a small room for an office downstairs. It was clean, had newer carpeting and linoleum and, best of all, was five miles north of town in a gated community where some of our church friends lived.

Our little church made ends meet by running a thrift store, which Randy started. The women in the church got things from the thrift store, and before we moved in, they had made our beds, organized the kitchen, and had towels and bathroom necessities in place. Within three days, the church people had provided for us and helped us set up the house.

I felt safer in our new gated location. *Oh, if we could have lived here all along instead of in Tiny Town.* This was my second experience of church people showing up and working miracles. To me, this generosity was the witness of the Christian community sparked 2000 years ago by Jesus' teachings and ministry.

Our beige dog, Corky, came with us, but we had no fenced yard and he had to be chained to a stake. After he broke the chain and chased a skunk, I gave him a tomato juice bath. What a kick! "We have a pink dog!" Abram laughed.

Because Abram was scrapping with the boys at school without consequences, and Noel's eyelid became droopier, I decided to homeschool them for the final four months of our time serving the Tiny Town church. I taught them three or four hours a day. Noel's eyelid began to lift; Abram did a lot of reading, and he wasn't fighting at school. We had a decent home and traveled to town only on Sundays.

Even though we had a safe place to live, when we drove to and from Tiny Town, I had imaginations of my dad hiding behind a tree and jumping out with a gun ready to kill me. An irrational fear to be sure, but my mind couldn't shake the image. I had similar kinds of dreams at night, and the distressing illusion did not leave me until we moved to Chico.

The fire department reported that the fire was caused by a faulty rheostat in the obsolete electric heater in the boys' room. Because none of the heaters worked, I assumed they were not getting any electricity. I checked daily to make sure the heaters didn't flip on, but I didn't know about rheostats or that if one is faulty, it might turn on and off incorrectly. The heat dried out a nearby wooden bookshelf and it caught fire. The fire seemed random. Or was it?

Thanks be to God that this fire started when we were in Chico and not when we were at home. I think this is why people say, 'God is in control.'

All was well, except for the soot in the parsonage. The smoke from the fire left soot on everything that didn't burn; pots and pans, vases, meaningful do-dads, lamps and chairs. It invaded every tiny crevice of the silverware and the covers of every book. The dishwasher didn't cut through the greasy soot on the kitchen ware. I spent the next four months moving our belongings and scrubbing everything we decided to keep. I did all this work because Randy continued his sixty-hour-week ministerial work. Peggy, my sister, came up to help me, a blessing that reassured me of her love. *Her company is the best.* Mom generously sent $500 to help us. I was in such a weird place mentally, I'm not sure I ever said thank you to her, so *Thanks Mom.* Fortunately, Randy had invested in renter's insurance and our claim was covered in full. This gave us some extra cash, and four months later we moved to Chico in our paid-for new Toyota van! No more Frankenstein furnishings either. *Maybe we've arrived! Does that happen?*

*"For I know the plans that I have for you"* declares the LORD, *"plans to prosper you and not harm you, plans to give you hope and a future."* Jeremiah 29:11

## CHAPTER 20

# Walking On Coals
# —1988-1990

*It is worse than folly... Not to recognize the truth,*
*For herein lies the tinder for tomorrow.*

PEARL S. BUCK

Since I married Randy, I've survived a car accident in Ohio, lived penniless after Abram was born, ate outdated food from trash cans, lived amongst tombstones in the Midwest, endured my husband's marital affair and been saved from disaster in a house fire. *What is next?*

We moved into a lovely middle-class three-bedroom parsonage with new wool carpeting and fresh paint. There was a small space for a home office for Randy and a one car garage. *Looks like the parsonage committee does their job! No more fires to build or ashes to clean out of a wood stove.* We ordered new furniture and new beds, a first for us. Our family was welcomed by the parishioners, and we settled into our new home. Chico's summer heat reminded me of living in Riverside, California, where I grew up. A friend in the church told us, "There are only two things I don't like about Chico, July and August."

It was Abram's thirteenth move, but hey, who's counting? Noel was in third grade, and Abram was in seventh, one of the most difficult grades for kids and teachers alike. Two days after school started, we received a call from the principal's office. My stomach rolled over. Randy and I met the vice principal who oversaw discipline. Abram was waiting for us in his office, his right elbow resting unnaturally on the arm of the chair with his fingers pointing upward.

The vice principal explained, "I believe Abram has broken his index finger. He hit another boy on the jaw." *Here we go again.*

I explained about our experiences in Tiny Town. He listened with interest and related his experiences when he was a vice principal at a junior high located seventeen miles north of Tiny Town.

"I was the vice principal at the middle school. I oversaw discipline, as I do here. I began my usual program of teaching the children right from wrong, and I had to expel children for aggressive behaviors. Some parents were angry, and I received threats at school and at home. One warned, 'You'd better be careful walking down a dark alley, because I will be there,' and another told me, 'I want my son to be able to fight and defend himself.' And another parent threatened my life. I noticed I was anxious and fearful, and I worried I might become unable to keep doing my job in the manner I thought best. Last year, after five years there, I came to Chico. I am very familiar with what you and your family were dealing with in these small mountain towns." I took a deep breath of relief, appreciating that someone understood our situation.

The vice principal looked directly at Abram, "You know, son, fighting is not how we do things here. I understand that fighting is what you learned to do, but you must unlearn it, because it will not serve you well in life. We solve problems in other ways. No more fighting, do you understand?" Abram nodded his head in agreement.

Looking at Randy and me, he continued, "His broken finger is a sufficient consequence for Abram. I am not going to suspend him, and I expect he will learn from the pain in his finger to avoid fighting when problems arise." *Ah, a thought of kindness and forgiveness and letting consequences be part of the learning process. We will be safer in Chico.* We thanked him and left with Abram, who stayed home for the rest of the day. Abram had to wait three days for the swelling to go down before the doctor could put a splint on his finger. I felt as though God knew our problems and sent a person with authority to guide and direct Abram's choices in his life.

At school, Abram became friends with a boy his age, Jay. I mention this only because this was the first time Abram had the opportunity to experience a lasting friendship. They played basketball in the backyard and spent time together at school. In most ways they were very good for each other, but as they became older, they encouraged one another with crazy ideas, like sneaking out of windows in the middle of the night, or after they learned to drive, finding college keg parties.

I suppose that's only common for teenage boys, but their effort to exert their newly found power does pose challenges for parents. In Randy's effort to control Abram, twice he pinned him against the wall and one time he put his hand around his neck and throat, frightening me out of my wits. We were supposed to be instructing our children not to fight! Consequently, Randy and I began our usual sparring, but it was difficult to defend myself or my kids against Randy's wit and strength. And still, I kept making excuses and pretending that our marriage was okay, that deep down we really did love each other, and that God would help us overcome our dysfunctions.

We  made some visits to see my Mom and Jack. I usually was depressed after seeing her, which provoked Randy's irritation and resentment toward my mother. I became the target for his frustrations. He decided we should limit our interactions, but I needed more opportunities to heal my mother/daughter relationship. Mom lived 500 miles away and traveling that far was time consuming and expensive, something we couldn't afford to do often. My mother's visits to us were few due to Randy's disrespectful and controlling attitude.

On one of our visits to Mom's, she gave me her favorite watch. I was pleased and began wearing it day and night. Three weeks later, I had a dream:

I walked into a room where my Mom sat in a chair wearing the red robe she wore when I was a child. I said something to her, I have no idea what, and she stood up and blasted me with anger, disdain, and disappointment. Furious, I ran down the hallway and jumped out the open window. Luckily for me, there was a green canvas canopy right below the window. It sliced open when I hit it, and I conveniently landed in a huge pile of peas. Uninjured and fuming, I abruptly jaunted up a beautiful, wide, red-carpeted staircase as my left hand pulled me up the mahogany railing. I was determined to confront my mother and stand up for myself. When I looked up the staircase, she was walking toward me. Her face matched her robe. When we met on the stairway, she grabbed hold of my right wrist. *She had me! I couldn't get away.* I looked up into her witchy-red eyes that burned through me. My knees buckled and my body gave way as I crumpled onto the staircase. "I'm sorry, Mom," I said meekly.

I awoke, startled, disturbed to realize that I was still afraid of my mother, so much so that even in my dreams I had relinquished the ability to stand up for myself. I glanced at my Mom's watch to check on the time. It had stopped. We took it in to get it fixed and were told it was unfixable. I was disappointed, sad. *Her watch represented our relationship. Broken.*

In *Scientific American Mind*, Deirdre Barrett explains the power of the dream, "When you fall asleep, you enter an alternative state of consciousness, a time when true inspiration can strike.

"Dreams are simply thoughts in a different biochemical state. We continue focusing on all the same issues that concern us while we are awake." Rapid Eye Movement, REM, sleep inhibits our cognitive, logical brain areas making them much less active. When the sleeping brain takes over, problem-solving dreams can emerge that explain our deep feelings of fear or anxiety, happiness and joy.[9]

News came in October of 1988 that my mother had melanoma cancer. The doctors would not meet with her until January, so there was no prognosis. We made three weekend trips to visit her and Jack, and each time we saw her she was weaker. In December she was in a wheelchair and in pain, and by January she was in bed on codeine. That was the last time I saw her. I wanted to stay and care for her, but Jack emphatically sent me away. The hospice nurse who witnessed our conversation compassionately told me, "You will be alright. It is time to go. You must be strong, dear." I walked out the door feeling unwanted and unwelcome. I had no way to retrieve my claim on healing time with my mother. My opportunity to care for her needs and let her know I appreciated her and loved her was denied. I felt as if a raptor had snatched away a little love bird that lived in my heart. When news came three weeks later that she'd died, we attended her memorial service, which I found very meaningful. A few days later Jack, who was the executor of her finances, informed my sisters and me that we would each be receiving a fair sum of money. Looking directly at me, in profound seriousness he said, "This money belongs to you. Keep it in a safe place and separate. No one else gets to use it but you. It does not belong to your husband; it belongs to you. Remember that!"

I failed to follow his advice. The right action would have been to honor my Mom's wishes, and keep the money separate in case I needed it for some unforeseen reason. I had hobbled myself throughout the years by complying with Randy's wishes, and I let this opportunity to exercise personal power pass me by. To make Randy happy, I put the money in our joint account. I thought maybe I could buy his love.

I read Elizabeth Kubler-Ross's book, *Death and Dying*, and was committed to giving myself time to grieve and heal after my mother's death. She suggested setting time aside to grieve. After the kids went to school, I stayed attentive to my need to let my bitter tears soothe my broken heart. I allowed myself to feel, to experience my pain and sadness, while the kids were in school. I pulled myself together in the afternoon and evening for the sake of my family. I set time aside for grieving in the morning, and then later carried on with normal life with my family.

I often sat in the backyard on the porch steps, teary-eyed. Randy walked through the back door holding a puppy. "The puppy jumped in my car! I thought she might cheer you up!" *Hmm…just like Corky jumped into your car?* It was a two-month-old Newfoundland-Labrador puppy, and as soon as she put her little head on my lap to comfort me, she became my dog and Corky's girlfriend! I named her Samantha.

One morning in May, I awoke with a happy smile. It had been three months since my Mom died. In Ross' book, she wrote that if one permits oneself to grieve, then at some point the sadness will mostly be over. A person can continue without the devastating feelings of great loss and accept one's new reality. *Thank you, God. I am healing.*

One day Randy observed, "You seem relieved about your mother's death." I had thought this, even while grieving, but I didn't want anybody else to know. I'd indeed grieved over the loss of an opportunity to recover a mother/daughter relationship, but I was also relieved, simply because I no longer feared her disappointment, judgments, or rejections. I could finally stop worrying about never being good enough for her to treasure her second daughter.

God gives us the gift of one another to love and enjoy. Our human weaknesses can result in self-inflicted tragedies; we miss out on the joy and comfort that was supposed to be the adhesive that makes our lives meaningful. With God's help, I found healing and forgiveness, and the embers of rejection cooled.

I began substituting again in late May, and when the inheritance money arrived, I deposited it in our joint bank account. I was trusting my husband as I thought 'good wives' were supposed to do. Within a few weeks of seeing money in the bank, Randy decided to quit his job and soon we were living solely on my inheritance.

A parsonage is a home owned by the church and used by the pastor and family. It is factored in as part of the pastor's income. Because Randy quit his great church job, we no longer had a house to live in. Out of necessity, we decided to invest in a home of our own and made a down payment on a house in Chico with my mother's inheritance.

Then, much to my dismay, Randy decided we should drive back to Chicago to see his uncle. I argued with him, but to no avail. So off we went. Randy made the decisions, even though it was my cash in the bank. *Money, my money, squandered.* Thriftiness had never been part of his resume. We had no income that summer. In the fall, he got a part-time job teaching two introductory psychology classes at Butte Community

College. The next semester he became one of the career counselors for twenty hours a week.

I substituted regularly in Special Education classes. Teachers encouraged me, "You are so good at this, and the kids always like you to be my sub. The children need someone like you. Why don't you go back to school and get a Special Ed credential? Think about it."

I didn't think long about teaching in Special Education because I knew I was gifted working with children. Since there were only two openings in our area for regular teachers, and there was a definite shortage of Special Ed teachers, I decided to return to college to get the credential. Three weeks into the semester I attended an introductory class without having enrolled.

I advocated for myself to join the class, and the professor accepted me. I assured her I would catch up. The requirement to earn the additional Special Education teaching credential was thirty-seven units. Randy and I would have two full-time incomes in a year or two. It seemed like a worthwhile investment.

That fall I interviewed for a Special Education position at an elementary school. I was reluctant to take it because it was sixty miles away, but the interview committee pleaded with me to take it, reassuring me there was a carpool I'd be able to join. I was an intern, and I didn't get paid much, but it was a new beginning.

In November, my younger sister, Diane, called and invited us to join them for Thanksgiving. I was glad to be invited but it was another 500-mile drive to southern California. My dad and his wife were going to be there, and this would be my first time seeing them since the pizza fiasco in Tiny Town. I figured that between Diane's family and mine, I would be supported when I saw Dad again. I was determined to reestablish adult relationships with my family. We decided to make the trip, and I brought pumpkin pie. When Diane opened the door, delight flowed through my heart. My younger sister, with her shiny, beautiful blue eyes, gave us a warm welcome. *Oh, she's happy to see us!* We hadn't talked much, so we had to begin anew after all, we hadn't truly known one another for twenty years.

"I've been praying for you to come back to the family," Diane said. "I told God, I just want to see my sister again!" I was relieved that she was happy to see us, and I was touched by her vision and faith. Yet I thought: *how is it that I am offered relationships with my sisters now that Mom is gone?* I had never been included or invited to any holiday before she died.

I followed Diane into the living room and there was Dad, ready to say hello. When I saw him, I tried not to let my body stiffen with anxiety but what happened next caught me totally off guard. My body flashed with the fire of sexual feelings toward my father. The only memory of any- thing remotely like this was when I was sixteen and a young man gave me the finger as he passed by. But here I was, at forty years of age, feeling sickened, embarrassed, and terrified by my response to my father. *Does it show to everyone else?* I tried waiting for the feeling to go away, but it would not leave. *This is not normal; this isn't the way I'm supposed to feel. This is wrong. Why is this happening to me?* I didn't know what to do except leave the room, and thankfully, when I did everything inside me calmed down. This sexual feeling was new to me. I did not have strong sexual feelings toward Randy that were like what my body was feeling. *Is this the way I'm supposed to feel when being sexually intimate with my husband? Is this the feeling of being 'turned on?' Are these normal sexual feelings?*

I tried to act nonchalantly with my dad, but it was impossible. When Dad entered the room, my body flooded with unwanted sexual feelings and a silent panic set in. I did not seem to have any control over my reactions, and I was unable to understand what was happening. *What should I do? What is going on?* My thoughts raced. I desperately needed to hide these feelings, and though I tried to act normally, I was wary as I feared my discomfort showed to everyone. No one, not even Randy, said anything to me so apparently I pulled it off.

In the meantime, Randy was having heated discussions with my brother-in-law, and by the end of our two-day visit, they almost hated one another. These negative feelings would last a lifetime. Fortunately, Diane's three boys and my boys played well together. But the pumpkin pie I made was a failure, completing a dismal get-together.

I was relieved when our visit ended. While Randy drove us home, Abram and Noel watched a miniature TV that had an antenna in the backseat while I wrote a paper for one of my classes. It was a somber drive, and I knew something was deeply wrong with us.

Body memories don't lie. They fester and rumble around deep within our being, deep in our muscle structure, waiting for an opportunity to reveal the truth. The brain remembers everything, beginning at birth. The memories may be hidden, but they are alive and ready to inform us when we can handle it. Body memories do not deceive. The body feels again what has happened.

When I got home, I had to face the truth. I could no longer reject or ignore the suspicion that my father had abused me when I was an infant. Added to the realization of this betrayal was the loathsome and excruciating awareness that for my entire life, I had missed out on having normal, sensual, and loving sexuality. I was robbed. Randy too. My gut ripped open again as if I had had surgery in my gut without the benefit of Oxycodone.

I took two days off from teaching. After everyone left the house, I collapsed on the floor in our walk-in closet where I wailed, moaned, and cried out to God. I felt like a tractor had rolled over me. My mind and body were in discord and struggled to accept that the sexual attraction I was supposed to have toward my husband was instead directed toward my dad. So, this is why I've been plagued with that knife-like pain all my life. I vomited to expel from my body this new reality, but the truth slowly seeped into my psyche. Distraught does not describe the depth of my grief. Through my crying and wailing, I purged enough of the pain that I could get dressed and be Mom when the kids came home. Two days lying on the closet floor had to be enough. I forced myself to function and get back to my teaching job.

Randy was aware of my distress and insisted I tell him what was wrong. We argued. "It's private," I said. He hounded me for hours over several days, and I gave up. Mustering the courage to explain, I coughed up, "When we were at Diane's house, I had a weird thing happen. Every time I walked into the room where Dad was, I was turned-on."

From all our discussions about sex, and about my parents, Randy immediately understood what this meant. Both of us remembered the night my Dad said to Randy's friends, "I always thought it was a good idea to masturbate your baby."

In my despair, I wanted to melt into Randy's arms for comfort, but there was no melting or comfort. I was alone with shame. He was furious, visibly distraught, and mortified knowing that our suspicions of my abuse were confirmed. Each of us carried our heartbreak alone. The *us* we always longed for was not going to happen.

We had had years together, but the dysfunction in our relationship damaged what 'might have been.' I did not know if Randy would choose to live with me anymore now that we knew the truth.

After Thanksgiving, there were three more weeks of classes at the university. I turned in my papers and took my tests. Abram and Noel had two weeks of Christmas vacation, and I had five weeks off before returning to classes at CSU Chico. I was looking forward to spending time with my family, and after finals, I bounced in the front door, "Hi everyone, I'm home. It's Christmas vacation!" The kids were glued to the TV, and Randy, who was fixing dinner, glanced at me but said nothing. My heart and hopes sank; my presence at home seemed invisible. *I make no difference.* If I'd been in a stronger frame of mind, I might have insisted on hugs, but I was in a familiar self-defeating belief that *nobody cares.* I wondered: what does a little support and friendship feel like?

Christmas day arrived, and Randy's family came to our house. We opened presents, enjoyed the traditional turkey dinner that I alone made. Afterwards we sat in the living room together while I rocked Kris's baby. I was tired and happened to doze off in the chair. *Uh-oh!* I woke and

Randy's eyes met mine. He was angry because I had drifted off. I was the only one who could read his face. I married a man who embodied my Mom's disgust and my dad's irrational irritation.

On December 26th, Randy blurted out, "I finally found the woman I've been waiting for. I have been looking for her for eight years. I'm going to marry her!" *There it is: eight years.* I was so despondent by this time that I had no response. He told me that the woman had been a student in his psychology classes for two semesters and she met weekly with him for 'counseling' sessions at school.

Four weeks later Randy moved out while I was working. I returned home to find all his clothes gone, as well as other mutual belongings. There was no discussion about who would take what; he justified taking whatever he wanted because he had given the house and furnishing to me.

In fact, my mother's inheritance paid for most of the down payment on our house. Now I had a two-income home to support, and my low-paying intern teaching position didn't come close to making up for the loss of Randy's income. Three weeks later Randy appeared at my door. He stood with open arms, and I let myself melt into his familiarity. I hoped this might be an overture toward reconciliation. However, an hour-and-a-half later he zipped up his pants and walked out the door, this time for good.

During our marriage, I had given him information about my past, hoping that he would be compassionate, but instead he chided me and then blamed me for his decision to leave the marriage, telling me, with my kids in earshot, "You are impossible to live with." My sharing, trusting, and willingness to be vulnerable with him backfired. There was no safe place in this marriage, and feelings of devastation are mild words for the chaos in my heart.

What happened to me as a child was not my fault. "You are damaged, and you will never recover," Randy yelled. No matter how hard I worked, no matter what I learned or how fiercely I tried, Randy showed no compassion or interest in me and little respect for my efforts to heal. He hadn't been seriously interested in trying to make our relationship work for eight long years. I tried too hard and stayed too long, and my prayer for our love to be renewed, for reconciliation, was impossible, even for God. Our marriage was over, right on time, just as God had informed me in my prayer in Wisconsin.

So many of my prayers to God had been miraculously answered. *Save us from being hit by that truck. Save us from a fire in this faulty wired house. Help us find a better place to live where we can raise our boys, and oh, could you send us a Toyota Van?* I was confused: why didn't God answer my prayers for us to heal and stay married? We did love each other once upon a time, why didn't God help us?

When people from church found out we were splitting up, they spouted the familiar Christian jargon, "If God let this happen, it must be for the best." That just made me want to puke. I began blaming myself, repeating the mantra: *I am never good enough, and neither are my prayers.*

My worst thought was that *I shouldn't be on this planet.* On and on around the merry-go-round. My self-mocking voice alerted me that I was in serious trouble. I figured if I stayed with these messy thoughts too long it would endanger me and my boys' recovery and healing, so I spent some of my inheritance money on counseling. I learned it was not my responsibility to make Randy happy. The divorce was not my fault; I did my fair share. I learned that God does not cross a person's free will, so our divorce certainly was not God's fault or a lack of caring about me. Once I let myself off the guilt trip, my thinking cleared, and I felt better. My marriage was blasted to smithereens; my dreams splintered. The beast could not or would not be soothed by Beauty's attempts at love. It was time to stop placating him; I wasn't Belle in *Beauty and the Beast*. I needed to pick up the pieces and trust God  for a new beginning. *I've been blessed with two sons. Their emotional and mental health in this madness is most important. I will deal with my sorrow with a smile on my face and create harmony in our home. I will work to set aside my anger and depression.*

Depression is catching, like a virus, and I did not want to infect my children. I had faith that with time, we would all heal.

*Oh LORD, I call to you; come quickly to me.*
*Hear my voice when I call to you.*
*May my prayer be set before you like incense.*
*May the lifting of my hands be like the evening sacrifice.*
Psalm 141 1-2 (a David Psalm)

CHAPTER 21

# The Fallout—1991

*You may not always have a comfortable life, and you may not be able to solve all the world's problems at once, but don't ever underestimate the importance you can have because history has shown us that courage can be contagious and hope can take on a life of its own.*

MICHELLE OBAMA

In my last conversation with Randy that had any substance, I said, "Randy, I'm sorry I couldn't give you the love you needed, the right kind of love."

He looked bewildered and said frankly, "Oh, I knew you loved me!" *Why then a divorce?* Tina Turner's songs popped into my head, songs about love being powerless to make a relationship work. Perhaps compatibility is more important, and love will follow.

As he indifferently ambled away, I called to him, "Randy, after all these years can you say just one nice thing about me?"

Turning his head over his shoulder he replied, "You were a good mother." Then he walked out of my life. It was a small comfort to hear one positive sentence from his mouth, especially after all the criticism I'd endured about my motherhood over the years.

Randy's self-centeredness prohibited him from thinking let alone understanding the emotional fallout that would occur after our divorce. He justified his decision to leave me by blaming me. *Nothing new here.* He didn't consider how his slanders would affect my ability to be head of the household, to take authority and finish raising Abram and Noel.

The boys had different emotional responses to their dad's absence. They knew not of their dad's improprieties. I had never told them. Abram saw me as the problem and never recognized Randy's angry or critical behavior toward me as inappropriate or unkind. Noel, ever the peacemaker, was too quiet, but I knew he was emotionally distraught.

Now as a single parent, I needed to become the authority figure in their lives. Since Randy had undermined me and disrespected me, I was aware of the challenge ahead.

At fifteen, Abram's anguish about his father's leaving was beyond his ability to cope. One evening Abram and I were in the kitchen, and Abram was raging. He opened a kitchen drawer, pulled out a large carving knife, and pointed it toward his stomach. I thought about grabbing the knife but knew that wouldn't work. *Stand here with him. Stay calm.* I stood there feeling panicky, and said softly, "You're holding that knife to tell yourself how sharp your pain is inside. You are hurting from our divorce, and your dad is not here. The pain is as sharp as the knife."

Abram dropped the knife. Then he ran into the room with the pool table, with me right behind him. He grabbed a ball off the table and drew his hand back. I hoped he wasn't aiming at me. Banking on my own experience with rage and emotional pain, with gentle authority, I said, "That's another sign to tell yourself what you'd like to do to the world that has hurt you so much. You feel that you can hardly bear it." He dropped the ball on the table, his face fell into his hands, and he started crying uncontrollably. He stumbled to the nearby couch and cried himself to sleep. I sat beside him for an hour. I didn't know what else to do but pray for my son. When he woke up, we said no more, and he silently walked to his room. Nothing like this ever happened again.

In the meantime, Noel, now eleven, became chronically depressed, and every day became more despondent. I waited for some measure of healing. He came home from school and laid on his bed and cried. I sat beside him, rubbing his back, trying to comfort him, and praying silently to God: *what should I do?*

Day after day, his sadness, lack of hope, and inability to cope deepened. One day there was a knock at my door, and there stood a woman I recognized from church. Handing me a little pink book, she spoke matter-of-factly, "The Lord told me that you needed this book, so I brought it to you." I looked at the book while she continued, "That's all. I'm just supposed to deliver this book to you, and I don't know why." She scurried off so quickly I didn't get a 'thank you' out of my mouth. I never saw her again.

I figured that if God sent me a book, I'd better read it. The author's premise is that positive reinforcement is essential in changing a person's feelings. This can be accomplished by using simple, but powerful, touch. When a person is touched, connections in the brain fire and unconscious associations are made. Safe touch creates positive emotions that are the connector to knowing ourselves. When our emotions are in sync our responses and motivations are affected.

If anyone could understand this it would be me, a touch-deprived child. When a person is feeling sad, touch reinforces the downhearted emotion; when a person is feeling happier, as in reading or playing, touch reinforces a warmer, pleasant feeling.

Encouraging good feelings with safe touch became my goal. (I loaned this book to a friend: I apologize to the author that I cannot give her credit.)

Aha! I felt like God had given me a plan of action. I was intentional in finding meaningful touch to help Noel and Abram feel more cheerful. I knew what to do to create a positive environment and warm feelings for my children. I paid close attention to their demeanor and on the occasions when they seemed happy or lighter, I consciously touched them by smiling and hugging, tousling their hair, brushing my hand on their backs as I walked by, or gently caressing the nape of their necks. I stayed alert to their needs and was faithful to my program of creating associations with new positive feelings.

One night I argued with my boys, trying to assert my authority to get them to brush their teeth. They seemed to enjoy getting my ire up as I tried to enforce this simple request. If I wanted the kids to brush their teeth, I needed to find a way to create a pleasant experience. It drove me crazy but I waited three days for them to spontaneously decide to brush their teeth, which they did together. At that moment, I zipped into the bathroom and gently stroked their backs and had a short conversation. I repeated this morning and night for twenty-one days, the recommended amount of time it takes to change the brain's patterns and learn something new.

*Hmm…will this work. Will they continue to brush their teeth without my prodding them?* Sure enough! After breakfast and at bedtime, I no longer had to say a word to them. My touching strokes had made positive feelings and associations. *Viola!* Making beds, doing dishes, vacuuming! Yay!

Abram still had many angry outbursts. Sometimes we fought with each other, and he challenged my authority. Since this argumentative style was what he grew up watching, it wasn't out of the norm. I thought Abram and I should see a counselor, but when I went to interview a counselor who told me that it wasn't Abram who needed counseling; it was me. "When you get your act together, Abram will follow suit."

One afternoon in the kitchen, Abram started yelling, and instead of reacting, I listened and responded. He began to list my shortcomings, exhibiting much emotion. I stated softly, "Abram, I'm so sorry God didn't give you the mother you needed," I stated softly. He kept on and so did I, "Abram, I can see you needed something I couldn't give you. I'm so sorry." He walked out.

Several days later, this same conversation began again. I stopped what I was doing and listened intently. The list of my inadequacies as a mother continued. He had spent time remembering things he was angry about. "Abram," I continued, "I am so sorry I wasn't the mother you were hoping for."

He relaxed. "Oh Mom! You weren't that bad!"

However, a lot was still brooding in Abram's mind. He sought me out, in the kitchen of course, to tell me how I failed Randy and caused him to leave. "And Mom! You stomped on my favorite toy and broke it!"

*Oh my gosh! I forgot all about that!* When Abram was three, and I was pregnant with Noel, Randy and I were fighting in the kitchen. Abram's little self-propelled toy train crossed my path, and in my rage, I stomped it to pieces. Abram screamed and dissolved into tears. Randy stopped attacking me and gathered Abram in his arms. He comforted him and then said, "You know your mother is a little crazy." I felt terrible that I allowed my rage to destroy Abram's favorite toy.

Abram had been carrying this deep offense against me for thirteen years. "I'm so sorry that happened, Abram. When your dad and I fought, I was often enraged. When I saw the train go by, on impulse I stomped it. I didn't mean to hurt you. I never should have smashed your precious toy. Will you forgive me?" He turned and walked away. We had this same discussion two more times. After listening the third time, I said again, "Honey, I was wrong. Please forgive me." Abram threw his arms up in the air as if he'd decided, "Of course I forgive you, Mom!" And that was the end of that!

My intention was to give Abram the opportunity to forgive and allow him to let go of his anger. In the process, I was released from my guilt. People often do not want to forgive or release another from guilt because they feel the person who offended them does not deserve to be free from remorse. Refusing to forgive is a strategy to power-over, which is a kind of manipulation.

However, Abram and I valued our relationship, and each of us decided it was better not to defend ourselves or accuse the other, and in this instance, we chose forgiveness.

My takeaway from these lessons? It is our solemn and sacred responsibility to thoughtfully interact with everyone and join with the Creator in fostering healthy, wholesome responses. In the process, we are continuously in the flow of learning the power of forgiveness. My intention with my children was to mitigate our losses, learn to honestly cope with our feelings of rejection, and boost our family's internal functioning. In our new three-person family, I challenged myself to be the catalyst for healing our beliefs that we were of little value to Randy. Abram, Noel, and I muddled through the best we could. I discovered strategies that contributed toward the shaping of a positive stream of feelings for the children and me. I had good results at school as I learned to gently put my hand on a child's shoulder to reinforce positive effort and work habits in the classroom. This small gesture kept them engaged with their task.

The directions from a little pink book, mysteriously delivered to my door, became a cornerstone of my success in my home  life and teaching career.

*Even youth grow tired and weary, and young men stumble and fall, but those who hope in the Lord will renew their strength. They will soar on wings like an eagle; they will run and not be weary, they will walk and not faint.* Isaiah 40: 30-31

*Even if I knew that tomorrow the world would go to pieces, I would still plant the apple tree.*

Dr. Martin Luther King, Jr.

## CHAPTER 22

# Beauty Among the Embers—1995

*(God)… will provide for those who grieve… bestow on them a crown of beauty instead of ashes… the oil of gladness instead of mourning…*

ISAIAH 61:3

Out of the hundreds of sermons I've heard, one of the basic premises is that we can be honest with God. After all, God can handle our emotions, whatever they are, and God already knows our feelings anyway. Better to be honest with ourselves as well.

The third night after Randy moved out, I had it out with God. I crossed my legs and sat on the floor of my bedroom. *Okay, God!* I challenged God in a loud whisper, so as not to wake up my boys. *I'm never getting up, going to bed, eating, working, or doing anything again until you tell me why this divorce is happening! I'm going to sit here, for days if I must, until you answer me.* Job, a well-known character in the Bible who challenged God, wanted an answer to his travails and fasted, pleading to God for an answer. I figured I was in good company.

I said my piece and stubbornly sat. All was silent in my dark bedroom, and after forty-five minutes, which seemed like hours, I heard a voice inside my head, "Here I am. I am protecting you."

Not in umpteen years could I have come up with that idea! I knew it was a God thought. I jumped up, and did I ever have a conversation with God as I stomped through the house, screaming in whispers. *You call this protection? What? My kids' dad ran off with another woman. Not enough money! A house to take care of I personally can't afford! Are you kidding me? This is not protection!* Oh, I was insolent. I knew emphatically that the voice, the message, was not from within me. And though I did not understand what it meant, I was exhausted and went to bed. God had answered my prayer even though I didn't like the answer. What can be more comforting than that?

The next four months I slept only three or four hours a night. Being awakened with pain reminded me of when I was fifteen and had intense pain due to a broken tailbone. What kept me awake now was accepting the losses and ramifications of divorce for my boys and for me. My stomach churned and I couldn't keep food down. Frozen yogurt was all I ate for three months. I lost fifteen pounds. Friends said I looked emaciated and encouraged me to start eating nutritious food. I slowly learned to eat again.

I had a symbolic dream:

*I was dressed for work in familiar teaching clothes, which at that time were calf-length skirts and button-down blouses. Noel was six in the dream and Abram was ten. I held Noel's hand and looked at Randy. Abram stood next to him. Randy and I looked at each other with goodbyes in our eyes, and then I turned and walked into an elevator with Noel. I looked over my shoulder to see Randy and Abram standing together. The doors closed and Noel and I went up several flights. I thought, where will I land?" When the door opened, I saw a desert before me. I took a hard look at what lay ahead, grasped Noel's hand and walked out, leading us into an unknown future.*

My dream revealed what lay ahead, the endurance I would need, and the spiritual nutrition vital to sustain me as I journeyed through the desert's scorching heat and changing sands. And *who knows for how long?*

The failure of my marriage intensified the knife-twisting pain in my gut. The dream expressed a combination of my childhood trauma, a hurtful marriage, and the responsibility I felt for my children. My unwavering faith strengthened me though, as I turned to God to lead me and my children into the future. My go-to was Jesus. Jesus' disciples were caught in a violent storm on the Sea of Galilee. They cried out for help, "Master, Master! We are going to drown!' Jesus stood and rebuked the wind and raging waters; the storm subsided, and all was calm. "Where is your faith?"

He asked his disciples. In fear and amazement, they asked one another, 'Who is this?

He commands even the winds and the water, and they obey him.'" (Luke 8: 24, 25)

I believed Jesus would one day come to me in my "boat" and calm my storms in whatever my circumstances. *God didn't bring me this far just to drop me and forget about me. No, not at all. God's love is certain, and I know God cares about me.* By this time, I trusted in the character and vision of the Man who split time. Then I had this favorite dream:

*I sat on a jetty watching the ocean waves. I was alone, forlorn—nearly comatose. As I sat in my inconsolable sorrow, I felt an arm around my shoulder. I looked up and Jesus was holding me. My pain drifted away, and I felt my heart flood with God's compassion. As comfort enfolded me, I knew I would never be alone.*

This God experience in my dream assured me. *Jesus knows what I'm going through. He cares and has compassion for me. He will be there beside me.* The Man who split time came to me in my deepest sorrow. God is love. (1 John 4:8)

For six weeks after Randy left, I drove like a maniac, nearly causing some accidents. One day when driving ninety miles per hour, I saw the red light flashing in my rear-view mirror and was pulled over for speeding. I got a ticket, but that didn't stop me. Rage was in charge of my mind and body. Two weeks later, while driving through the rice fields, an egret flew up in front of my van and glanced off. *Oh God, look what I've done. I killed a beautiful bird. I don't want to kill any more birds, or people either!* The egret's death forced me to acknowledge how dangerous my irresponsible driving was. God sacrificed one of his creatures to jar me into reality, to reach my disoriented brain, to protect me from myself.

Shortly after this incident, I turned on the radio and "happened" to hear a quick explanation of how people kill themselves. The calm voice explained that men kill themselves with a knife or a gun, or by hanging themselves, and women often kill themselves by driving too fast. *Is that what I'm doing? Am I trying to kill myself? Well now, wouldn't that make Randy happy! He'd get great satisfaction knowing that I needed him so much that I had to kill myself! No! No! No!*

I was not going to give Randy any inkling that I was distressed because of him. Besides, abandoning my boys was never an option. I loved them with all my heart and being there to watch their lives unfold was my purpose and joy. I treasured my life more than I was angry at Randy. That five-minute blip on the radio stopped my insanity.

Even after nine months of being apart, Randy called on my birthday, and I thought he'd called in friendliness to wish me a happy birthday. But no, he said, "I didn't call to talk to you, I called to talk to the kids." I felt he was purposely mean. My heart crushed and started pounding, and by the end of the day I was in a fury.

That night Abram and Noel made me a two-layer birthday cake, but I couldn't eat a bite of it. I didn't even hug them or say thank you. I hurt their feelings, and consequently, they didn't plan anything for my birthday for years. To this day I regret I treated them this way after they made such a sweet effort to make me feel loved. My anger caused me to completely miss the opportunity to make a good memory for the three of us.

That night, I stared at the cane rocking chair that Randy had given me. *He gave me that ugly, cheap rocker instead of what I really needed, a good comfortable rocker for me and my sons.* The kids were asleep, and I was free to vent my anger. I stomped on it, bashing it with my legs and feet, and jumped on it until it was torn. The adrenaline rushing through my veins gave me the strength to smash the back of it and rip off the flimsily attached arms. I ravaged that rocking chair. *Take that, Randy! I'm done with you!* I took it out and threw it into a dumpster before my kids woke up. A few days later when my boys noticed it was gone, I nonchalantly said, "Oh, I didn't want it anymore."

I tried to suppress how hurt, angry, and sad I truly was. One night, sobbing alone in my bed, I heard a knock on the door. It was my friend

Annella, who said, "I was driving around, and God told me, 'Gaynelle needs you.'" She came into the bedroom, laid on the bed with me and put her hand on my shoulder. She spoke in a low soothing voice, "You will get through this with time. I know it seems impossible now, but I will be here and help you through it. It will get better, I promise." She calmed me enough that I could quit crying. She continued, "I had help through everything in my divorce, and I will help you. You are not alone, and God will be there for us."

I decided: *I will learn to live what I believe, walk in faith through this nightmare. "In everything, give thanks to God…"* (Philippians 4:6) This scripture does not say give thanks for everything that happens, but in everything. I became aware of every negative, hurtful thought and with awareness tried Paul's challenge: "Finally, my brothers and sisters, whatever is true, whatever is noble, whatever is right, whatever is pure, whatever is lovely, whatever is admirable—if anything is excellent or praiseworthy—think about such things. (Philippians 4:8) I learned to pay close attention to my thoughts. The first thing I did was practice blocking out memories of Randy. However, he, Abram and Noel, were paired in my mind, so in my memories of fun with the boys, Randy's face was always in the picture. Before I realized what was happening, I had blocked out almost all precious memories of my children's childhood experiences to avoid thoughts of Randy.

A German friend told me about his mother who liked to swim outdoors in the winter. My home had a pool that was about 45°F, so I decided to try swimming in hopes it would help me to feel better. For six months, when I first got up in the morning, I put on my swimsuit and dove into the pool. I glided to the other end of the pool while holding my breath, for maybe six to ten seconds. Every nerve ending in my body was stimulated; my arms and legs woke to the cold blast, titillating my brain and jump-starting me into an alive state of being. Then I took a hot shower, got my kids and me ready for school and went off to teach.

One clear spring morning before my dive, I noticed a tiny sliver of a silver moon. I felt as if the Lord was saying, "You see, everything will be alright." A sweet calmness flowed through me and remained for several days. I was relieved; I no longer had to deal with Randy's disdain or fear of his angry outbursts. My psyche was calming. I gained confidence in my teaching abilities, managing daily responsibilities, doing my best to parent and provide for my boys.

When I arrived at my classroom in the morning, one of my Special Education kids greeted me at the door, "Good morning Mrs. A., I love you." Without knowing it, this special child gave me the kind words I needed to hear to help heal my pulverized heart. I received many blessings from teaching these innocent children.

When we divorced, my personal social life and support community barely existed. Fortunately, I had made two friends the year before Randy and I split up. I met Libby, who was in the same class at the university. Annella and I became friends because we were in the same carpool. Both Libby and Annella had suffered divorce and betrayal by their husbands. They mentored and encouraged me—they put up with my dysfunctional behaviors. *If they made it through, I will too!*

One day I sat on the floor again and asked God to take away my pain. I was weary. Within a few minutes, I felt it lift, and the pain seemed to stay at bay for a while. I was amazed that yet again, my simple prayer yielded relief.

During the summers I took classes, and in the fall, I completed my student teaching and other requirements for my Special Education credential. Having no job for six months while I finished my student teaching had drained my bank account. I was hired at a psychiatric hospital as a teacher for kids ages three to seventeen.

The pay wasn't particularly good, but it was mid-year and impossible to get hired in a school district. This was clearly a different position than the school setting. The psychiatrists wanted the children to act out so they could see their behavioral problems in real life. I wasn't allowed to help fix any troublesome behaviors as I had been trained to do. Since I was stressed, I was relieved I was not responsible for helping change a child's behavior. When a child was out of control, I called the psychiatrist, and he came with a team of helpers to deal with the situation.

My empathy for these unfortunate abused children overwhelmed me. I was reminded of my childhood and many times found myself crying as I drove the fifty minutes home after work. I was at a loss. Jesus, *I need some help down here. Please!*

George was a retired pastor at our church and Arleen was my good friend. I was part of their prayer group. I told George of my distress and about the children I 'taught.' He took my hand in his and looked at me directly, "When someone gives you a birthday present, do you give it back?" I answered no. "Give these children to God on your drive home, and don't take back the gift!" I started praying for each one of these children every day on my way home. I imagined each child placed in God's caring hands and was relieved that I was not responsible for carrying or helping to heal their pain. I trusted God with their lives and practiced what George had taught me. As I did so, I had the clarity to focus on stabilizing my life.

Later that summer, George and Arleen encouraged me to attend a one- week family church camp, known as Camp Farthest Out. I took a week off from working in the hospital and went to a camp located near Mt. Shasta. Part of the program was participation in a prayer group. As I sat in the center of the prayer circle, the people around me laid their hands on my head and shoulders and prayed for a teaching position to come my way. "God, provide a job that will support Gaynelle's family and use her new skills. Send a good job, one where she has friends and can do the work that you have for her to do!" Imagine how stunned I was when a job came to me within a week after camp. It would be by far the best teaching job I ever had.

I attended several more summers at Camp Farthest Out where I learned more about my prayer, and my faith grew deeper in understanding God's love. *God, help me to let go of my worries. I want to focus less on me and open my heart to what you have for my future.* The more I practiced this, the more Jesus took a place inside my soul. "Love the Lord your God with all your heart, with all your mind, and with all your soul." (Matthew 22:37) Randy encouraged Noel to move in with him when he was in the eighth grade. Randy lived forty-five minutes south of me and I was afraid I wouldn't see Noel very often. From the beginning, Noel was good about coming to see me nearly every weekend during his high school years. I felt loved and honored. This weekend arrangement gave me more quality time with him because I wasn't working and doing my lesson planning at night, and he did not have homework. Noel spoke frankly to me about how heartbreaking it was living in two households and making plans to leave every weekend to see me. When talking with relatives about our difficulties adjusting to the divorce, Noel reminded us, "God didn't promise us a rose garden, just that God would be with us."

I needed to sell our house for financial reasons. I couldn't take my dog to an apartment and so took Samantha to a shelter for adoption. They informed me, "She can only stay two weeks before being euthanized." My heart sank. I prayed and prayed for a home for her. On the last day, she had not been adopted and I'd been unable to find a home for her. *Well God, there is only so much you can do.*

That day, I walked into my classroom. "Hi Jeremiah, how are you this morning?" "Oh, I'm good," he said. I'm just sad because my Mom has been looking for a dog and she can't find one. She wants a big dog cause she's alone a lot of the time."

My eyes popped. I called Jeremiah's Mom immediately, and she confirmed that what he said was true. I said, "I have a wonderful dog. I had to give it up when I sold the house. Would you like to have her?" When she immediately agreed, I called the shelter. After school, I got Samantha and took her over to Jeremiah's house. Just like that, Samantha had a family to love her. Thank you, God, for saving Samantha's life and giving her a caring home. You do amazing things, and in our human time frames too! How did You do this? They loved her and said she was the best dog they ever had. We became good friends and have stayed in contact with each other for thirty years.

I made a significant effort toward renewing my relationship with my sisters, and they were supportive and welcoming in return. Slowly, I reconnected with my dad, thinking that when Jesus said to forgive seventy-times-seven, he wasn't kidding. I had to come face-to-face with him, remembering that my dad had suffered serious abuse and tragedy in his childhood and had also gone through two divorces. He didn't have the benefit of the twenty years of counseling that I had. I wanted to forgive him and have him feel my forgiveness before he died. On some of our visits I could manage this, and other times I needed to leave sooner than planned. Over the next thirty-two years, we seemed to have forgiven one another for whatever hurt we remembered, leading us to a genuine relationship, even if it was dysfunctional.

One late night, I had to drive two hours through the coastal mountains to a friend's home for the night. I had an unfamiliar feeling. My heart raced and my hands were sweaty. I sensed a presence in the passenger seat, and I trembled slightly. A kind of awe-fear enveloped me, yet I felt excited at the same time. I thought it might be an angel, or the spirit of my grandfather asking for forgiveness, or perhaps even my Mom. The Presence was from another realm, meant no harm, and comforted and calmed me as I drove the curvy mountain roads. I felt empowered. When I got to my friend's home I delayed going to bed, fearing that this rare peace of mind and heart would be gone in the morning.

*Am I being protected?* When I remember the feelings of the Presence of God, it helps me focus on God's strength. *My faith in God is my hope and security. I've been visited by a messenger of God!*

Our church women's group had a retreat at the same church camp in the mountains that I had attended with George and Arleen at Camp Farthest Out. One late afternoon, while sitting alone in the back seat of my car, the pastor's wife opened the door and sat next to me. "What are you doing, sitting here?"

"Oh, I'm just waiting for my depression to go away."

"Well, that's no good. Get out of the car and come with me." I dutifully complied.

In a matter of moments, a group of women surrounded me in the forest. They began singing songs and delighted in calling upon God's promises to help his people. Strangely, my knees buckled, my legs gave way, and I began to fall backward.

"A deliverance!" Someone called out, much to my surprise. I had no choice but to trust, as a group of women, my friends, gathered around me and started to pray. My knees gave way, and I started to collapse, but was caught and laid on a blanket prepared for me. A few minutes later one of my friends put a Bible on my stomach. She laid her hands on it and prayed with the others that all God's promises written in the Bible would be my deliverance. When I looked up through the trees at the sky, I saw, or imagined, these little black things twisting upward toward the trees. I wondered, *did those things come out of me?* I didn't know what to think. These women, in their faith, continued praying and singing to God for hours as I writhed on the ground crying out loud. I have no idea what I might have said.

I remembered the faith healer, Kathryn Kuhlman, and wondered if this was what she was artificially trying to achieve. But when my knees gave way at the retreat, it was not from someone forcing them to buckle and pulling me down. These prayer healings cannot be contrived.

Prayers return to us from God with some kind of fulfillment. God's promise is that prayer "will not return empty but …will achieve the purpose for which God sent it." (Isaiah 55:11) Prayers offered to God rise to heaven as does the smoke from incense. In the Book of Revelations, an angel receives the sacrificial offering of incense and prayers to God. The prayers rise on the floating incense, and an angel reaches out and catches the prayer in its hands and then molds the prayers into a ball of fire in his hands. The angel hurls them back to earth, empowered by the fire of the Holy Spirit and God's love. (My paraphrases from Revelations 8:3-5)

The teachings I absorbed about God, Jesus and the Holy Spirit were on a continuum toward healing and becoming freer as I experienced the power of prayer. I had been part of a church since I was twenty-five, but I had never experienced such willingness, faithfulness, and sacrifice in those caring for or about me. Impressed upon my consciousness was their belief in God's reliable answers to their prayers. This encouraged me as I grew and experienced more healing. A great sense of release followed this experience in the mountains, and I began to faithfully correct my self-critical mind, trusting in God as I relaxed into Jesus' love.

To keep myself focused and stable during the years after my divorce, I silently recited my version of Psalm 23 hundreds of times.

*The LORD is my shepherd, I have everything I need. He takes me*
*to mountain streams; he restores my soul and guides me to do right.*
*Even though I walk through tough times, You comfort me. You*
*prepare a table before me in the presence of my foes and my cup*
*will overflow. Your goodness and mercy will follow me all the days*
*of my life and I will dwell in the house of the Lord forever.*

My first year of teaching special education at an elementary school went very well with one exception—an over-critical principal. Several parents, who expressed gratitude for my curriculum, made comments that boosted my confidence, "My child has a better attitude toward school and is doing better at home. He is beginning to read." *I am a good teacher.* At the end of the year, the parents planned a patio party in my honor. What a wonderful boost to my sense of self-worth. God's ancient truth was made manifest in the modern world from a well-known prayer, Psalm 23.

As my sons got to know Randy's new family, I heard about the shenanigans going on in his second marriage. I understood from them that he was treating his new wife as poorly as he had treated me. I felt vindicated. *How lucky I am, God, to be set free from a marriage to a man who didn't love me, who was cruel and unfaithful.* I was, for the first time, genuinely thankful God let this divorce happen. God saved me from even more pain and loneliness. "I am protecting you," God had told me when I sat on the floor of my bedroom twelve years prior.

When Noel was twenty-one and ready to graduate from college, we sat together on cliffs overlooking the ocean waves. "Mom, I just realized that our family is never going to be together again." Tears dropped from his eyes, rolling down his handsome young cheeks. When I stood up, he followed my lead, and I put my arms around him.

I said softly in his ear, "I'm so sorry, son. I'm sorry for your pain and hurt over our divorce. It has been so much pain. I feel bad about this for you. Please forgive me." We embraced for a few minutes and cried together. When we let go of each other, something deep inside me felt complete and my heart sang a song. I was forgiven by Abram, and now Noel, and God's love was affirmed. Our lives went forward, and we never discussed it again.

When Abram was thirty, Randy yet again created mayhem within his church, similar to his earlier infidelities. As Abram and Noel watched the results from their father's behavior, they were able to comprehend the reality of their dad's dysfunction and his series of betrayals. What I suffered from the actions of their father became evident to them. It was emotionally devastating for them as they realized how Randy had sabotaged their relationship with me. Abram told Noel, "Who would have thought that Mom was the stable one?"

A year later Abram shared his grief as he realized that Randy had damaged our mother/son relationship. "Mom, I can't believe how Dad poisoned our opportunities to develop love and trust." We'd both lost time together and we knew what the "might-have-been" meant to each of us.

Since that time, we have made every effort to reconcile ourselves, and we are grateful we enjoy a healthy, flourishing relationship.

*When my spirit grows faint within me, it is you who watch over my way.* Psalm 142:3

I've walked the desert sands, trudged through the mud, and sprinted in the soft grass along the mountain streams. None can thrive in life's journey toward Heaven without those who come alongside us. Family, friends, mentors, counselors, prayer partners, and my church community all contributed to my step-by-step faith walk. With the principles in mind I learned from Jesus, the Man who split time, I was able to make some good decisions along the way. He calmed the storms, renewed my mind with new thinking patterns, guided my path, and even sent dogs to unconditionally love me, and angels to protect me and keep me from stumbling. (Psalm 91:11-12)

All the days of my life from the Christmas songs of my early childhood to the present time, I have been blessed with the varying melodies and rhythms that have aided in healing my heart, mind, and soul. God is playing the music of my tears.

*"Give your life to God. God can do more with it than you can."*

Anonymous

*The LORD is my strength and my shield; my heart trusts in him... and he helps me.*
*.... My heart leaps for joy, and with my song I praise (thank) him.*
Psalm 28:7

## The Journey Thus Far

*Ransomed. Rescued.*
*Refuged when I had no willpower*
*To take the next step on the path ahead.*
*Present as I walked through my dreary girlhood,*
*Watched over and guided by God's unseen Spirit.*
*Protected beneath an umbrella of His compassion,*
*Forgiven by the Man, the Man who split time.*
*Jesus allowed me the time I needed to*
*Search, trust, and find myself, and*
*Feel power from God's Spirit.*
*Remembered. Redeemed.*
*Feeling the Holy Spirit,*
*Joining in the joy.*
*Alive to Life.*
*Peace.*

GAYNELLE

## CHAPTER 23

# The Interim Years
# —1997-2019

Six years after my divorce, a friend played matchmaker and introduced me to a man whom I eventually married. Like Randy, he was a pastor, and like Randy, he was troubled. *Déjà vu*. This marriage was chaotic, and by the second year I had moved out twice. Unfortunately, both times I allowed myself to be charmed back into the house to give it another try. In my constant distress, I leaned on family and friends for support. On one of my many distraught retreats to Abram's house, he said, "Mom, how long do you think Noel, our family, Libby and I can put up with you like this?"

I felt discombobulated. I discovered that my husband had moved the money I'd deposited in our joint account to his personal savings account, to which I had no access. I opened my own account. Shortly afterwards I saw him holding hands with another woman. That was the end. Finished! Abram had made it clear that if I stayed in the marriage, I was risking losing my support system and the healthy relationships I had developed since my first divorce. Fear that my family and friends could scatter like seeds in the wind, motivated me to move out a third and final time.

Easter came and I dressed but went alone to a different church. As the congregation began singing the traditional Easter music, forlornness overpowered my grieving heart. The familiar chants, "He is risen. He has risen indeed," turned my sorrow into a river of tears. Embarrassed, I hurried out the door, went home and changed into my blue jeans. Tears morphed into rage; I went for a walk down a long dirt road between rice fields. Not a soul was around. I kicked up dirt, ran until I collapsed on the road, and had it out with God. Adrenaline powered my feet as I booted any stone that dared to cross my path. *"God, I'm done! I don't want to live like this any longer. You've got to help me change my life. I have been trying, but here I am in the same badger hole again. I do not know how this happened to me and I'm mad as hell. You promised to help me. You must do something!"* I walked and shouted until my voice gave out and I was exhausted.

My sacrificial love for this second husband produced no positive results. This was predictable. *How had I allowed myself to be seduced into repeating my past?* Thankfully, I had a counselor to guide me. At my next session he asked, "Gaynelle, why do you think you stayed with two men who were unabashed about being mean to you?"

"Well, everyone needs someone to love and care about them. Just because they can't love me, does that mean they don't deserve to be loved? I want to show them what love is. This is how I serve Jesus, because Jesus said, 'Love one another as I have loved you. As I have loved you, so must you love one another.' Jesus sacrificed himself, so I'm supposed to sacrifice like he did." *Was I still trying to earn love?*

My counselor spoke firmly, "Gaynelle, to sacrifice for the sake of the Lord means a person has a vision for a positive outcome. The purpose of your sacrifice in your first marriage was that you stayed for the good of your children, though it's debatable if it really was good for them. And here you are again, suffering, but for what reason? There is no principle here you are defending, and you are not standing up for your faith as a witness. Jesus sacrificed for a purpose. Your sacrifice devalues your life, and what others see is that you don't love or value yourself. You give love with nothing in return. That is a kind of martyrdom. Jesus doesn't ask this of his followers. The purpose of sacrifice is to advance the Kingdom of God." *Is my interpretation of Jesus' teaching that inaccurate?* "Gaynelle, Jesus had a *self* to sacrifice. You don't. First, you must find your *self*." *What does this counselor mean? Is it that I don't have a self to sacrifice?*

"And Gaynelle, be careful you do not squander your relationship with Jesus, your time with Jesus – with God. Give yourself time to understand and heal." His words were a knock-out punch. I was glad our time was up, and I stood up, ready to leave. "Oh! And don't date any men for at least six years; if you don't take time to heal you will make the same mistakes." As I headed for the door, he added with force, "Run, Gaynelle, run! And don't go back!" *Yikes! Better listen up. I cannot stand to do this to myself again.* My counselor gave me honest and direct counsel. I listened. I ran. I got a divorce and moved to Monterey. I didn't trust my brain to be consistently rational and in charge; I'd known for years that something deep inside of me could take over my feelings and spontaneous reactions. Apparently it was obvious to those who knew me that I didn't understand the edges and fringes of healthy boundaries. Friends gave me books on boundaries which I read, but I still hadn't a clue what a 'boundary' meant. *Did the painful and violent abuse in my childhood cause my psyche to splinter the self I was supposed to know? When my abusers crossed my physical and emotional boundaries and harmed me, did I lose the sense of my natural self?*

It occurred to me that my sacrifice to love was my automatic behavior pattern that moved me around the world without vision or intention. I was not connected to my decisions or feelings; I was a person without a clear sense of *self*. This is why, in my second pregnancy, I believed that my baby belonged to my mother. I was devoid of *self*. I stayed with Randy, despite the turmoil, and then married a second man just like him. I needed to find me, the me that God knew and loved. *God wants me to know and love myself.*

God's love and presence has sustained me. I prayed for guidance and determined my vision and command was to continue healing my true *self*. I would have no more guilt that I was being selfish. I did my part and released myself from blame. Becoming *whole*, whatever that meant, was my intent. I stayed away from men, carefully observing my actions to make sure I did not squander my precious relationship with God. On weekends I read books and studied, and I took three satellite graduate classes from Fuller Seminary. Delving into deeper study of Jesus' teachings helped me identify the glitches in my interpretations of New Testament passages. I was particularly impressed by a professor who interpreted the Greek Bible, reading it in Greek and translating it to English. I was stunned at how profound the original Greek is compared to our English translations.

When I moved to Monterey, I found a new hairstylist. "Just don't cut my hair short," I directed. Without conversation, she lifted a huge swath of hair on the crown of my head and cut it to one inch long. The only word she heard was 'short.' I had a counseling appointment that day and walked in embarrassed and teary. He comforted me, "Your hair is not you!" He said. News to me. *Really?* We had similar conversations, and he helped me sift out my unhealthy thinking patterns.

As I walked the ocean shorelines after my long teaching day, breathing the salty air and  praying, I sensed *myself,* slowly but surely, beginning to integrate back into me.

Primarily, the Man who split time, Jesus, found me. My faith and knowledge of God reminded me to be "… *confident of this, that he who began a good work in you will carry it on to completion.*" (Philippians 1:6)

On my wall hangs a calligraphy, "*Don't be frightened by the size of the task. Be strong, courageous. Get to work, for the Lord God is with you. He will not forsake you. He will see to it that everything is finished correctly.*" (1 Chronicles 28:20) I counted on God's promises.

*The work began years ago…and God is not done helping me through life.*

I met Jerry in 2008, and we married in 2012. My husband is the man I needed, sent to me by God to complete my healing. When I get into a perfectionist mode or become self-critical, he gently hugs me and says, "Now don't you go disparaging, my Sweetheart. I won't have it." There is a Power that thrusts me forward in seeking a life worth living, something vastly different from survival.

My relationship with Jerry is the most sense my life has ever made. My gift of love found a warm heart to land in. God's vision for comfort and rejuvenation is transcending my past. I am myself with a man I adore. It took both of us the good part of a lifetime to find and receive this gift of mutual love and respect. "Life should be fun!" Says my Jerry, and we are having a blast! God is making up for lost time.

# Relapse—2020

When Peggy and I went to visit Dad in the last weeks of his life he was comatose in his recliner. Our conversations threw me back into a time warp that revived childhood memories, and a few days later I became distressed. I thought I would overcome my anger and sadness, but weeks passed, then six months, and my unresolved depression grew significantly worse. I feared I would no longer be able to successfully fake it and then my deep anger and sadness would affect my blooming relationship with Jerry. Feeling lost and alone, I tried my go-to strategies, but they failed me.

I engaged in working hard, visiting those in need, lots of exercise and other habits that I had developed to keep the pain unseen. But these are dangerous schemes and I dare not ignore, overstep, or stuff what I was feeling. I began taking low doses of antidepressants, which lowered my anxiety and reduced the intensity of my depression.

Nevertheless, I was in a downward spiral. There is a price for suppressing my memories and psychic suffering. My experiences warned me that the price was too high. I could no longer hide my terrifying memories from myself. It wasn't new to me that I was forced to remember and deal with something unpleasant. I started therapy with a new counselor trained in EMDR therapy (Eye Movement Desensitization and Reprocessing) which is a strategy used for PTSD (posttraumatic stress disorder).

During our first session, the discussion began with the usual: "What brings you in today?"

"It was a conversation I had with my older sister, Peggy," I answered quickly. "Talking with her brought up buried memories. These memories have flooded my consciousness. Since then, I have felt sick to my stomach, I'm depressed and anxious.

"I'm angry beyond my ability to cope. I can't digest what happened to us! I am so disgusted that even a thought about my parents drives me to near insanity. I'm scared of what I might do. I'm in a tailspin and I'm afraid I'll crash."

And so…. The story continues, yet it begins anew.

## CHAPTER 24

# Tailspin—2020

*He who learns must suffer,*
*And even in our sleep*
*Pain that cannot forget*
*Falls drop by drop upon the heart.*
*And in our own despair, against our will,*
*Comes wisdom to us*
*By the awful grace of God.*

AESCHYLUS, ABOUT 500 B.C.E., GREECE

I wasn't motherless in this world because God gave me my older sister. Peggy, my surrogate Mom, taught me various strategies to survive my childhood. Her loving mannerisms and kind, soft voice became my 'go to' model. I knew very little about her early childhood because she is seven years older than I am. I had known she lived with Dad's parents while he was overseas during WWII, and that in that house was a mean and evil man, my Dad's father. Mom was gone every day, working as a secretary, so there was no one to protect Peggy from our Dad's father who severely abused her.

On one visit we sat on the couch in her living room and began catching up on the family news and chatting. As we got more comfortable with each other, she related this story: "Grandpa came into my room whenever he wanted and did awful things to me. No one came to help me. Granny was the only adult around and she couldn't do anything to protect me. When Mom came home, I was so happy to see her. Before bed, she played with me for an hour. I knew she loved me, and she saved me during that time."

Peggy continued with intensity. "When I went to Kindergarten, I'd never even seen another child. *(I can't imagine a child never having seen another child until five years of age).* I didn't know what they were doing or talking about. I kept my head hung down. When I did my rocking thing, the kids said, 'Uh-oh, Peggy's rocking again.' I heard them, which stopped me for a little while, but I never knew when it would start, and I had no control over stopping it. It would just start and stop. Rocking put me in a different zone. I think I did it to survive. I rocked in school until I was fourteen. The teachers got used to it and left me alone. I was so shy I didn't even talk in school until fifth grade. On one of my report cards a teacher wrote, Peggy appears to be mentally disturbed. This always bothered me."

My mind flashed back to Peggy at thirteen years old, rocking back and forth in the back seat of the car, her eyes closed, and sucking her thumb. Peggy quietly continued, "When I was a toddler and little girl, Grandpa *(he doesn't deserve such a kind name)*, sent me to my room whenever I rocked." The message was clear, *get out of my sight, do not bother me*. Her tears revealed the residue of pain that still plagues her.

I tried to comfort her, "Peggy, rocking is self-soothing and a clear sign of abuse in a person's life. It is a sign of a serious violation of our bodies, our minds, and souls. Our bodies are always talking to us. Swaying to-and-fro was a way for you to soothe your tender and hurt emotions." I embraced her and we cried in each other's arms. "You and I have post-traumatic stress disorder. Any child who suffered abuse as we did, has symptoms. Peggy, we are no exception. Our bodies and brains want to find ways to heal us. You were trying to heal yourself. So, you see, we are normal!" I smiled at my sister, and she returned a faint smile of acknowledgment.

In 2019, several years after that conversation, Peggy and I drove to visit Dad for two days at the assisted living home. Dad was 102, and this was within the last few weeks of his life. He slept a lot, and Peggy and I sat in the room with him and filled the hours conversing about our crazy childhood. Each of us had years of counseling and various therapies behind us, and this was an unusual opportunity for us to share.

Tears rolled down our cheeks as we shared our stories.

Peggy asked me, "Why did you and Mom have such a difficult relationship? Why didn't you get along? I never understood that. I always counted on Mom."

I made this as brief as possible, skipping over the inconvenient details of my mother's disgust with me due to her childhood sexual shame. I told Peggy, "Mom and I missed each other because Dad undermined our relationship. Dad criticized us and we never had a chance to develop a trusting relationship. While Dad was having a two-year affair with the escrow officer in the bank, he blamed me for Mom's unhappiness, saying things like, 'What did you do to make your mother cry?' I now know it was Dad's betrayal of Mom, and nothing that I did that caused her tearful distress. But at the time, I didn't know about his affair. I thought, 'I'm just in the way, I make everyone unhappy just by being here.' I internalized the blame. He was an expert at shifting blame. Nothing was ever his fault."

After so many years of trouble between Mom and me, I was thankful that I got the opportunity to say goodbye to her before she died. I know Mom was glad we had some moments to apologize to each other too. Peggy accepted my abbreviated explanation of my relationship with Mom.

We accomplished a lifetime of catch-up in those six hours during which time Dad was comatose. Peggy's voice quivered, "Horrible things happened to me in the house in San Bernardino. Grandpa (my father's father) would come into the bedroom and shut the door. I cried as loud as I could, but Mom and Dad didn't do anything to help me. I begged them to put a lock on my bedroom door when grandpa came over, but they wouldn't do it."

Suddenly there was no oxygen in the room and I froze as her words jolted my mind. When Peggy was thirteen and I was six, Dad's parents were there. This was the same grandfather who flushed my fish down the toilet (and molested her when she was a toddler and as a little girl, something I couldn't have known when I was six). I remember sitting on the carpet in the living room, coloring contentedly. I heard Peggy screaming—the sound was coming from my parents' bedroom. I sped to my father, "Daddy! Peggy's crying! Help her!" I looked at Mom who held Diane's tiny hand tightly. Then Dad snatched my wrist, and I was held motionless in my Dad's strong grip. We stood in a row, silently listening to Peggy's high-pitched screams. "Daddy, Peggy is crying!" I repeated. No movement. No words. My parents were statues. Peggy was desperate for rescue, and I knew it, but I was helpless to run to her and see what was happening.

Finally, the bedroom door opened, and I was released and ran to my sister. My grandfather walked out with a smile on his face that made me feel like throwing up. I watched him zip up his pants and buckle his belt. Peggy flew past me, head down, her eyes red and swollen as she ran to her room and slammed the bedroom door. I ran after her with the desire to comfort her. "Leave her alone now," my Dad's firm voice commanded. At this early age, I didn't understand what had happened, but I knew that something was badly amiss. I felt miserable.

Until this conversation with Peggy, the memory was irretrievable. But suddenly, it came rushing back—the motion picture playing in my mind felt like it was happening in real time. Anger pulsed through my veins. The memories, once locked in the recesses of my mind, were now burning in my brain. I was so shocked—so furious with my parents—I couldn't offer my beloved sister comfort. I couldn't even hug her.

In that burst of photographic memory, I understood Peggy's childhood trauma. When Dad's father came to visit, he was allowed to '*prowl around like a roaring lion looking for someone to devour.*' (1 Peter 5:8) He marked his territory, stalking his prey within our home. I will never call him a 'grandfather'—that devil lion who devoured my sister from ages two through fourteen.

My parents knew what was happening and did nothing! I knew the intensity of this fire burning deep within me could be ruinous to my life – or someone else's. My rage might explode at any moment. I tried to harness the havoc of my feelings, as one might round up and corral a wild bronco. The problem was that to keep my anger and fear under control, I had to hobble myself. Internally, pain and grief enveloped me. My strategies of denial, or distracting myself by being over-busy, or even praying, were not helping me to overcome this. I could barely put on a presentable face. *My sister, a sweet helpless toddler, a child, and a teenager.* I was nauseated and wanted to vomit up the scene that tormented me. I was desperate to expel my grief.

After Dad's death, the tailspin of emotions spun out of control. I spent time gardening, taking long walks and praying. I thought the pain in my gut would ease, but instead, my chronic depression deepened. I lamented for the tragedies each member of our family had suffered. I worried my distress might affect my marriage, so I returned to antidepressants and counseling.

Provider my Dad was, and worker bee my Mom was, but protectors they were not. How does a person forgive parents who betrayed their God-given duty to protect their children? *How do I forgive the loss of all that could have been in Peggy's and my life? How do I forgive Mom and Dad's blatant refusal to defend Peggy?* In the mayhem, and during the isolation of the Covid pandemic, I lost my sense of a healthy identity.

My anger festered; my mind became disconnected and numb. *God, I don't know how to heal this sorrow. How will I? Is it possible to find a path to help me let go and forgive? Help me God!*

*Trust in the LORD with all your heart and lean not on your own understanding; in all your ways acknowledge him, and he will make your paths straight.* Proverbs 3:5-6

## CHAPTER 25

# Finding Why—2020-2022

*Like a lonely Beacon marking the edges of a treacherous coastline
on the darkest nights, the human Spirit can be sustained,
focused, and directed by the smallest glimmer of hope.*

PATRICK J. AND CLAUDETTE M. MCDONALD

In Greco-Roman mythology, Psyche is a beautiful maiden who personifies the soul. She is loved by the god of desire, Eros. The term psyche means the distinct mental and spiritual entity that coexists within the body but is also independent of it. Dr. Carl Jung received his medical degree in 1902 and worked at the University of Zurich psychiatric clinic. Jung studied spirituality and the unconscious. In his book, *The Undiscovered Self*, he wrote that the psyche is a unique characteristic of the human species that a person "cannot know himself and therefore remains a mystery to himself." The psyche remains an "unsolvable puzzle" and an incomprehensible wonder. (But) .... We still have hope of making more discoveries and finding answers to the most difficult questions (1957)."[10] The psyche holds the phenomenon of consciousness.[11]

Approximately one-third of America's population is traumatized and functionally compromised. Abused and traumatized children often grow up and abuse and traumatize their children. Our human situation is indeed an unsolvable conundrum, and no one walks through life unscathed. The good news is that new understandings and methods for healing trauma are coming to the forefront. This involves further study in counseling practices, brain scanning research, and knowledge about ways that the brain and the body interact.

My therapist recommended books to help me understand my brain. I am grateful to the authors of *The Body Keeps the Score* by Dr. Bessel A. van der Kolk;[12] *The Mindful Way Workbook* by John Teasdale, Mark Williams, and Zindel Segal; *The Self-Compassion Workbook* by Kristin Neff, PhD and Christopher Germer, PhD; and *Adult Children of Alcoholics* by Janet Geringer Woititz, ED. In addition, a book by Dr. Leonard Matherson, *Your Faithful Brain, Designed for So Much More*, validated the power of my Christian faith in healing my brain.[13] Dr. Gabor Maté's books, *When the Body Says No* and *The Myth of Normal* gave me further insights.[14]

No matter the type of abuse, the brain logs any threats to one's personhood. This, in turn, becomes hardwired into the memory bank of the brain. The primary function of the brain is to ensure our survival. It will not ignore or deny perceived or real danger. Our brain can keep the alarm bells ringing for a lifetime. It is not a surprise, then, that people who have experienced terror have difficulty tolerating their memories of tragedy or abuse. Sometimes the reality is too much to bear.

Peggy and I sought to thrive, not just survive; we needed help in making sense of our experiences. This process inevitably involved remembering what happened and processing hurtful, unwanted, information.

We practiced and learned to find self-compassion and forgiveness. Today, we no longer endure days of grieving or concern about what is wrong with us. In other words, we have normal brains.

*I'm a normal person.* I have flaws and misperceptions. I make mistakes. Normal stuff for any person. Knowing I'm not crazy or stupid has helped my emotional brain become better synchronized with my reasoning mind.[15]
[16 17 18 19 20 21 22 23 24 25 26 27 28 29 30 31]

**Note:** *The Glossary in the back of the book has a partial list of terms commonly used to describe the functions of the brain. These terms are frequently used in the following chapters, so I encourage the reader to become familiar with them.*

# Chapter 26:
# Trauma: Awareness and Understanding

*There is a Twilight Zone in our heart that we ourselves cannot see.*
*Even when we know quite a lot about ourselves—our gifts and*
*weaknesses, our ambitions and aspirations, our motives and our drives—*
*large parts of ourselves will remain in the shadow of consciousness.*

FRED ROGERS

According to van der Kolk, in *The Body Keeps the Score,* "The essence of trauma is that it is overwhelming, unbelievable, and unbearable."[32] The entire body responds to trauma with visceral reactions that can affect the chest, lungs, heart, or other parts of the body.[33] "Trauma results in a fundamental reorganization of the way the mind and brain manage perceptions. It changes not only how we think and what we think about, but also our very capacity to think."[34] A traumatized person lives in a dual reality. One reality is a secure and predictable present. The other reality is that of a ruinous past. The two realities live side-by-side and rob a person of a sense of empowerment over his/her self.[35] Trauma leads to ignoring gut feelings and becoming numb to sensory awareness.

Traumatized people "learn to hide from themselves; this often leaves them bewildered, confused, ashamed…they develop anxiety and are afraid of their own irrational fears."[36]

In a microsecond, the brain determines whether we are safe or in danger in any given situation. Since danger and safety are opposites and cannot exist together, the perception in the brain is one or the other.[37] Steven W. Porges, director of the Kinsey Institute Research Traumatic Stress Consortium, states that we experience three levels of safety. The first level of safety encompasses meaningful social engagement where a person understands that they are helped, supported, and comforted. However, if the social system is dysfunctional or broken, the DANGER signal flashes, and the second level, fight or flight, ignites. The third level kicks in when an individual or animal senses it is helpless or trapped. This response is known as freeze or collapse.[38] We have sayings in our culture that describe this phenomenon: "I was frozen in space," or "I was like a deer caught in the headlights."

A physical example of collapse happened when I was walking in the park, and a friend happened to see me and decided to surprise me. "Boo!" I froze and fell to the ground.

The freeze or collapse response causes the traumatized individual to disengage from the conscious mind. As a child, I remember leaving my body when my grandfather abused me. My body went limp, and although I knew what was happening, I no longer felt part of it. Peggy said she had the same experiences, "When grandpa came into my room, I went into another zone. I saw what he was doing and knew it was me, but I didn't have to feel it." This is how a helpless person reacts. Our brains are hardwired to protect us, to make sure we survive.

My third level of the safety response, freeze/collapse, I knew were firmly in place. I could feel my self tense up in social situations, I often froze on the inside, held my breath, and remained voiceless.

Now I realize that my uncontrolled responses don't mean there's something wrong with me. For much of my life I experienced daily life as full of danger, whether it was real or not. My second level of safety, fight or flight was ready to respond at a moment's notice. I didn't know why I jumped when I heard loud sounds: the annoying ding-dong signaling someone coming into a store or the sudden crash of a glass breaking in a restaurant. When I'm working or alone in a room and my husband walks in behind me and says something, my body jumps. "It's just me!" He says, a little hurt and surprised. When these responses happened, people often thought I was a nutcase.

Trauma is nearly always attached to a memory in which the person is helpless or has the perception of helplessness. When the situation is perceived as life-threatening, the cerebral cortex's ability to reason diminishes as the threat increases. When threats occur, the limbic brain takes over because it responds at a faster speed than the cortex, instantly signaling us to run, fight, or freeze. The need to survive overrides the more rational approach of "thinking it through." The cerebral cortex and the limbic brain do not communicate well with one another.

I was at the gym, and a man behind me dropped a heavy weight on the floor which caused a thunderous sound to reverberate throughout the room. My hands jumped off the handles of the stair master, and my heart left its place in my chest. That response is the activation of the vagal nervous system. I noticed the woman next to me also startled at the same moment, her hands jumped off the handles at the same time. We smiled at each other, and I asked, "Did you have a difficult childhood?" She nodded.

In his book, *The Body Keeps the Score*, Dr. van der Kolk describes this phenomenon as *hijacking*. Hijacking happens when a part of the brain, the cerebral cortex, becomes powerless. Because the nerves in the limbic brain fire at the speed of light, the limbic system supersedes the cortex (the rational brain). The limbic nerve system, called the vagus nerve, signals the heart to pump faster, the sweat glands to activate, and the breath rate to increase. When the limbic brain perceives there is no escape route through fighting or fleeing, the choice for survival is collapse, numbness, and/or total shut-down.[39]

**Vagal Complex:** A nerve system located in the reptilian brain which serves as the last resort, the ultimate emergency system where the body signals defeat and withdrawal, then collapse. It sends motor messages to the heart, lungs, palate, pharynx, larynx, trachea, liver, and GI tract. It sends sensory messages to the heart, lungs, trachea, bronchi, larynx, pharynx, GI tract, and external ear.

*(See Glossary Page 286)*

# Vagus Nerve Illustration:

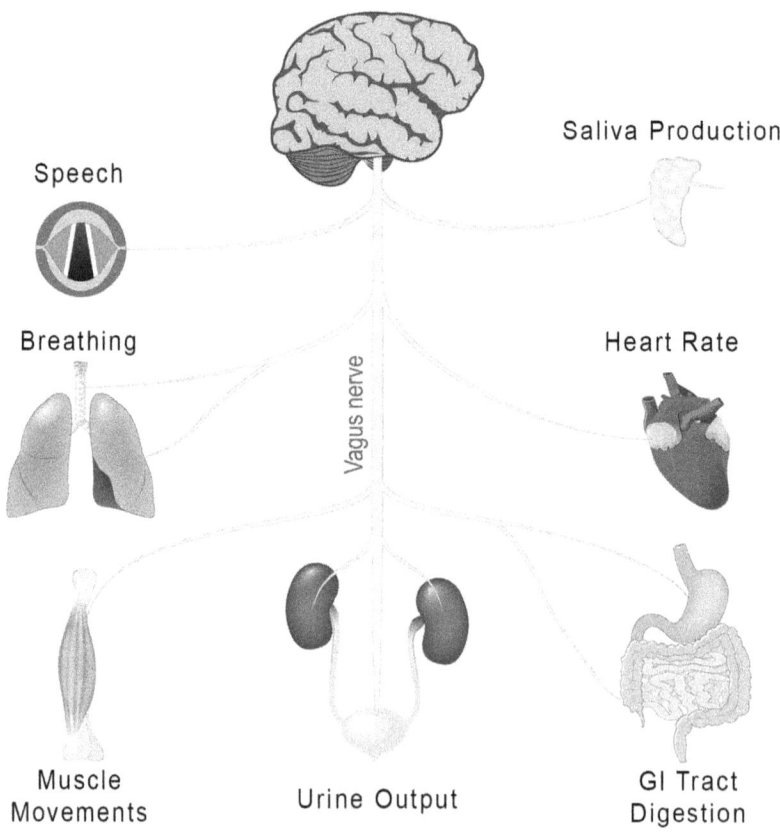

*The drawing shows the vagus nerve system which has its origins in the limbic brain. These nerves are part of the vagal complex (see definition above).*

*Image © 2025 Designua / Shutterstock. All rights reserved."*

In situations when people perceive danger, their limbic brain will take charge.[40] Their rational thinking will be left in the lurch, taking second place. They will be hijacked by their *vagus* nervous system

As a young woman, I stood in a faith healing circle and accomplices forced me to the floor at a Kathryn Kuhlman meeting. A feeling of helplessness and betrayal flooded my body and triggered me into an intense four-hour crying jag. I felt tricked and in the grip of something sinister. My limbic brain perceived that my survival was in jeopardy and curtailed any ability to reason out the situation. This experience reminded me of my terror and helplessness at being held down—as when my grandfather pinned me down and molested me. I was unable to regulate my feelings. I was embarrassed and ashamed—common emotions for a person who has no ability to cope and control their own reactions. My limbic brain interpreted this situation as life threatening, and its duty is to facilitate survival.

When a person's brain is triggered, as mine was in this situation, the brain becomes hypervigilant in maintaining its 'on-guard' mode, so much so that a person loses the ability to enjoy the simple pleasures in life. This can even cause the brain to miss real danger signs and, thus lose the ability to defend.[41] "The price is that one becomes unable to detect what is truly harmful or what is safe and nourishing,"[42] states Dr. van der Kolk.

I always had a desire for my parents to see me, to acknowledge my presence in the family. But at the same time, I needed to keep myself out of trouble and my mouth shut. My first memory at two was standing in the backyard thinking, *I wish Dad wouldn't come home*. At two years old, I was already in a level two safety level, my fear keeping me in fight or flight safety mode. A child of that age cannot fight very well, but they can figure out ways to be invisible and out of harm's way. At night, I learned to tiptoe as silently as possible to the bathroom and leave the door slightly open to assure I wouldn't wake my dad.

The heaviness for me is that I believed to the core that I didn't matter to anyone else, and that I didn't deserve to matter even to myself. Traumatized people chronically feel unsafe inside their own bodies: the past is alive in the form of gnawing interior discomfort.[43] The knife-twisting pain in my gut sometimes turned into uncontrollable rage. My anger was sometimes preferable to shutting down or becoming numb to daily life. Periodically I exploded, which scared not only me but everyone in the family. Peggy reminded me, "You fought with Dad, something I never would have done. I thought you were so brave. But then you ran into the bathroom and kicked the shower door, and it broke. I remember Mom crying in the kitchen, 'I just don't know what to do with her.'" My initial reaction was to fight, and my second reaction was to run away, (flight). I was chronically on edge because nothing ever relieved the pain.

I asked my counselor, "Why does my brain argue with itself? How is that possible? Why would that be? It is one brain, but it feels like the little cartoon of the devil talking in one ear and the angel whispering in the other. It's crazy making." The positive affirmations I had spoken to quiet my degrading self-talk seemed of little avail. I remained my most severe critic.

Since the emotional brain and the cognitive brain are sometimes in conflict and do not communicate very well, the result is a kind of tug of war between the brains,[44] each wanting control. My emotional limbic brain and rational cortex brain were parts of me that were in a sparring match, each taking turns trying to dominate the other. According to Dr. van der Kolk, "Usually the tug of war is played out in visceral feelings which are manifested in the gut, heart, or lungs. This will lead to physical discomfort and psychological misery."[45] I used to hyperventilate when anxiety suddenly hit me, or had panic attacks. I knew when I vomited, I was trying to eject the memories of what happened to or around me.

I was obedient and studied to get good grades, despite my severe emotional pain. In a world that is set up for the attentive and stable, I endeavored to function normally. With great effort and stress, I complied, and I paid a price. The visceral emotional sensations were like a dagger in my stomach. After Randy and I moved in together, we argued and the fear coursing through my veins sparked my instinct to run. I was often gone for several hours at a time. This worried Randy, so instead of running away, I threw myself under a blanket on the couch and stayed there for hours. When I could bear to look at the world again, I crawled out and was assaulted by guilt. I'd wasted Randy's and my precious time together. It puzzled me as to why I acted in ways I knew to be irrational. Now I can connect the dots: trauma during a child's developmental years gets hardwired in the brain. Running away or hiding are part of the body's way of handling overwhelming feelings. So, my irrational, quirky brain is like any other brain that had my kind of experiences.

Reason and emotion are not opposed to one another. When reason and emotion are in balance, we are attuned, we feel in touch with ourselves. However, when the two systems are out of balance, and survival is at stake, they operate independently.[46] That is why it was difficult for me to trust my body: I never knew how I would show up. *Will I be numb and unable to think? Will my emotions remain stable?* I suffered with constant anxiety because I did not know when my ability to think would suddenly be absent, hijacked by my limbic brain. My systems were out of balance, and this left me floundering.

Randy was in turmoil much the same way. We moved twenty-four times during our marriage. His father used cruel punishments for benign things such as forgetting to take out the trash or feeding the dog too late. His father gave him severe spankings until he was fifteen. Randy had to bend over, grab his ankles, and receive three hard blows on his buttocks. I recall his words: "They were so painful I could barely stand it." Now I understand how demeaning this must have been for him – standing with his head hanging between his legs. Such a humiliating position. How could he believe that he mattered? Randy was powerless to defend himself. He was a traumatized child too. His *self* was damaged just as mine had been.

I wish at the time I'd had more compassion for him and that I had known then what is known now about how trauma upends our brains.

After our divorce, I conjured up ways to end my life. I thought about drowning myself in freezing water. I considered diving into the ocean waves at night. Or I could drive off a bridge or into a tree. Such dire imaginings frightened me. I wanted to live a functional life, and not a life that might put me in a wheelchair because of acting stupid. It terrified me to think that my children could end up finding me dead as the nine-year-old boy in my class in Tiny Town had found his mother. I so wanted to be a good mom to my sons.

My will to live won out; *Somehow, I will find relief from my overwhelming pain*. My dad used alcohol to ease his torment, and I decided I would never complicate my life with alcohol or drugs. *I will endure this suffering no matter how severe*. As a child, I believed, *I'll grow up and move away and I would be fine*. 'Fine' didn't happen because my damaged child always came with me.

When one of my therapists asked me to remember a happy time in my life, I couldn't remember a single joyful moment. I had my babies and should have been filled with awe, but at that time I was too scared to let myself feel anything fully. When good things happened, I unconsciously heard my dad's voice, "What do you think you're so happy about?" The message was: Don't be happy. Other times, seeing my sadness, he'd say, "Why do you have a frown on your face? Put a smile on your face!" Life was a teeter-totter, tipping between anxiety and non-feeling numbness. But the goal was to look normal no matter what my body was telling me.

I believed there had to be a way to get through the suffering and find the other side, whatever that was. I often wondered if Jesus was the answer, and if so, why didn't things change when I prayed? It turns out that Jesus is not a magician. Matthew Kelly says, "The history of God's relationship with Humanity has always displayed his preference for collaboration over intervention. God will not snap his fingers and bring about the type of transformation we are talking about. He desires dynamic collaboration with each of us. He wants us to do our part."[47] I did my best to collaborate with God by studying the Bible and asking for help. I felt guided toward becoming a Special Education Teacher and went back to school to get a second credential. I attended church, and when I needed guidance in raising my family, I dutifully read the book God mysteriously delivered to my door by a woman from my church. I did my part.

The conundrum was/is that our bodies use very effective mechanisms to survive. Those life-supporting systems of fight, flight, or freeze/collapse, discouraged me, causing me to feel out-of-sync and unbalanced no matter how intensely I tried to manage these responses.

The great news is that our bodies and brains want to heal themselves. When in sync, the three brains cooperate. (The third brain – the brain stem, or the reptilian brain, hasn't been discussed because its functions do not affect emotions and decision making).

My brain was continually healing. I was able to stay alive and engage in this highly technical and demanding society, raise my children, and become a teacher in a specialized field. These accomplishments were more than minor miracles to me. I prayed my way through, and my petitions to God, and the answers to my prayers, kept me moving forward. God's guidance kept flowing through me. Jesus changing my limbic brain system wasn't part of an equation for healing. But Jesus said to his followers that even greater things were to happen than the miracles he performed (John: 14:12).

We can cognitively understand how our brain works, but that is poor consolation for continued suffering. When the brain on trauma is tuned out, a person has difficulty remembering, feeling, or making sense of his/her circumstances. My personal story was distorted and didn't follow a logical pattern.

The brain needs to catalog experiences and make meaning of them for further application in a person's life. Talk therapy with a counselor was supposed to be the answer to correcting this, but I learned that for people who have been traumatized, "conventional talk therapy was virtually useless."[48] Although years of talk therapy and Cognitive Behavioral Therapy helped me, this process did not change my internal brain map. Cognition and understanding were not the complete answer for me.

When people expected a rational or analytical response from me, and my response was inappropriate, I recognized that people judged me. Their reactions prompted negative thoughts of my own, such as: *maybe there really is something wrong with me.*

Now I am compassionate with myself: I have learned that my rational brain never got the chance to mature socially. My unsophisticated responses came from my limbic brain, which was and is my defender, and will always be in charge. Remember, when there is a conflict or perceived danger, the limbic brain overrides the analytical cortex. One of the consequences is that, until people get to know me, their initial perceptions of me are often misguided. Sometimes I sense others think of me as unintelligent. Other times I'm discounted, excluded in conversations, or my comments are disregarded as if I had not spoken. In the past I have felt afraid in social situations because I wasn't sure how to respond and I feared that my emotional limbic system would hijack me. The fallout from this was an overriding anxiety.

After trauma, one perceives their world with an altered sense of risk and safety. Porges coined the word 'neuroception' to describe the brain's capacity "to evaluate relative danger and safety in one's environment."[49] These pathways and connections remain for a lifetime. A factual understanding of the workings of the brain has helped me to grasp and accept my difficulties.

I live in a dual reality where both danger and safety exist. Even when I'm secure and safe, there are times when my limbic brain hijacks my cerebral cortex. When this happens, I think, *I've been stung again.* Thankfully, I'm learning to adjust to what happens in my nervous system. My self-dialogue has improved, and I am no longer governed by internal criticism. I have compassion for myself. *This is not my fault. This happens sometimes,* I say to myself. I pause…take some deep breaths and refocus. *Look at what's happening in real-time…the now. These are emotions from the past and are not needed. I'm just feeling them right now. Once upon a time, I needed them to survive, and it's okay.*

The autonomic nervous system is shaped by early childhood experiences and reshaped with ongoing experiences. Habitual response patterns can be interrupted, and new patterns developed.[50] Retraining the brain and making new connections have helped me create feelings of safety. I'm thankful that every day I'm improving.

*Be on your guard; stand firm in the faith; be of courage; be strong. Do everything in love.* 1 Corinthians 16:21

CHAPTER 27

# Damaged Parents; Damaged Children

*Every human being comes from the hand of God, and*
*we all know something of God's love for us.*
*Whatever our religion, we know that if we really want to*
*love, we must first learn to forgive before anything else.*

MOTHER TERESA

What a pair. Did you happen to have parents whom you thought should not be together? Or wonder if they should not have been parents?

After my divorce I took a four-day seminar on self-awareness. Participants provided the facilitator with information about our jobs. In this exercise, we met in a large room and the leader announced, "There are one hundred people in this room, and for every person in our group there is another person who performs the same job as you do. You are to find your like-minded individual. The only rule is that you may not say what your job is. You have ten minutes. Find your match." He set his stopwatch and yelled: "Go! Mingle."

"Stop! Is there anyone in the room who did not find someone with a matching job?" No hands went up. Yes, in ten minutes I had found my special education teacher match, and my lawyer friend found hers!

"Here's what I want you to know," explained the facilitator. "Think how fast each of you found your person. Realize how much you know at the intuitive and emotional levels. Listen to your still small voice, your deeper knowledge. Listen. Your awareness will serve you well."

Shortly after the seminar I met Libby, who would become my lifelong friend and mentor. We were both taking special education classes and when I saw her, I had a warm, visceral feeling. This time I did not ignore these guiding feelings and send them away as I had in the past. Instead, I initiated our friendship and today we are two peas in a pod.

When my parents met, their unconscious brains and deep intuitions recognized the trauma of sexual childhood abuse. There was a feeling of familiarity between them. Both my parents had fathers who had abused them. This abuse continued to my generation; my parents allowed their fathers to abuse Peggy and me.

My poor mother. She was damaged in heart, mind, body, and soul. She had a deviant and sordid father, which I knew first-hand from my own experience. My Mom's disgust with sex came from the abuse by her father. Her core fears surrounding sex caused her disdainful reactions toward me.

My mother told me, "Your dad was a much better father than his dad. His father went into his room at night and ransacked his belongings. He never knew what would happen at night." My dad's evil father did more than that. My dad's younger sister, Holly, hated her father, and she suffered serious life-long health and mental problems. His older sister, Lucile, had serious dysfunctions as well. Lucile's daughter told me that when she was in tenth grade, her Mom punished her by refusing to speak to her for a full year!

When my Aunt Lucile was ninety-four, in one of our living room conversations, she admitted that her father sexually abused her when she was a child. That kind of unthinkable trauma is what Peggy suffered from our grandfather.

At seventy-five, Dad told Peggy, "When I was nine years old, I was raped by our pastor. That's when I stopped going to church." I've wondered if the pastor intuitively sensed that my father had already been abused, and he sensed he could get away with further abusing a child. Dad's nightmarish childhood and unaddressed trauma fast-forwarded into the lives of his daughters. Now it made sense to me why Dad had a vendetta against religion.

When Mom was 66, she learned she had melanoma in her eye; her eye needed to be removed. I recall wrestling with this thought: *Did she have to suffer losing an eye because she turned a blind eye to terrible things done to Peggy and me?* The doctors thought they got all the cancer, but two years later the cancer had moved to her liver. I was forty when my Mom was diagnosed with malignant melanoma in her liver. I had expected her to live well into her eighties and nineties, as her parents did, but she died four months after her diagnosis.

My mother wanted a Hospice death at home and medication to alleviate the pain. I visited her several weekends in those last three months. She and I were a bit wary, but during that time we gained a degree of trust, trust that we did love each other. Before she morphed into a ten-day drug-induced coma, we had a brief exchange, though she was clearly in extreme pain. I crawled up on her bed and lay quietly next to her. "Mom," I whispered. "I want you to know I've always loved you. I'm sorry for any way I may have hurt you. I didn't mean to. I love you, Mom."

Stammering out a response, she moaned, "What matters is that we found each other. You were always such an interesting child." Within ten seconds she was asleep; those were the last words we said to each other. I was grateful that before her death, she felt that we had 'found each other,' something that I believed to be true as well. It was a brief exchange. It had to be enough.

Mom didn't say she loved me, instead she said I was interesting. *What in the world does that mean?* Thirty years later, I asked my dad, "Do you know what Mom meant when she said I was always such an interesting child?" He thought for a minute and replied, "Well, we just never knew what you would do or what you were thinking."

Perhaps Dad was remembering times when I was young how my impulsivity took charge. When I was four years old, I scrambled up a big rock in Joshua Tree National Park. Enjoying my view and feeling proud, I noticed it was a long way back to earth. "Daddy, Daddy!" I yelled from the top of the rock. He came closer, and looking up at me said with a half laugh, "What are you doing up there? How are you going to get down?"

"You have to get me down, Daddy." He shook his head side-to-side, but sure enough, he found a ladder at the campground, climbed up, and somehow grabbed me in his arms, and got me back to earth.

Still looking for clues as to why my Mom said to me in her last days that I was an 'interesting' child, I asked Aunt Georgia, my Mom's older sister, what my Mom might have been thinking.

"Oh, you were so disobedient," she said, "You did not listen, you didn't hear us or care what anyone told you. You did whatever you wanted." This was an enlightening interpretation since I knew, then and now, that I had attempted to comply and earn their love. I was most likely distracted, so my mind was too busy to pay attention. I was not intentionally disobedient.

When I was twelve, a woman stood next to me in the grocery store. My mother directed me to get some carrots, and as I reached over the woman's arm, I bumped into her. "Gaynelle didn't you see that person next to you?" Mom snapped. "You bumped right into her." Then Mom turned to the woman and apologized, which confused me. *I didn't know I bumped into her!* I really didn't even know she was there. I was oblivious to other people around me.

Before Mom died, Aunt Georgia asked her if she had any regrets. I hoped my aunt would tell me that Mom always wished she'd had a better relationship with me. Tears welled in my eyes. *Did Mom think I was a selfish daughter? Did I hurt her by staying away? Did she hope for or want a relationship with me as much as I did with her?*

Aunt Georgia said matter-of-factly, "Your Mom said that she wished she'd been able to be a golf club champion."

*Well,* I mused, *guess I don't need to cry or feel guilty!*

Unknown and unspoken emotional recognition brought my parents together. Two lost souls were seeking a life partner. Their insidious familiarity took them down the path of unhealthy, dysfunctional family relationships. My parents' boundaries were skewed, and they lacked the ability to say 'No.' Their limbic nervous systems were in charge and made them unable to make good decisions. Like me, they were disconnected from themselves, their feelings, and from good reasoning. Violent trauma had left them confused, and unable to feel or create love between themselves or with their children.

They did not protect us when we needed protection. At the campground in Oceanside, Dad left me alone in the car at night. They left Diane and me visible to the world as nightfall came to our new curtainless house. They stood frozen in the living room, Mom holding Diane's hand, and Dad clenching mine. They ignored Peggy's frantic cries. Their fear of acting was rooted in their trauma, and this kept them from acting decisively to care for us and protect us.

My father was mentally unstable, sexually deviant, irrational, and quick to anger, all common symptoms of sexual abuse. My dad took me to Las Vegas for my twenty-first birthday to give me the thrill of watching a strip-tease dance show! Later in life, he bragged to Randy and me about his promiscuity. My Mom endured this marriage mayhem, and this gave me a great deal of compassion for what she had to live with.

Early in my parents' marriage, Mom's symptoms pointed to her childhood sexual abuse. Her symptoms were displayed in shame, disgust, and a rigidness toward my dad. "Don't tell anyone I told you this, but your Mom was frigid," Dad once told me.

The only time my mother explained sex to me, she made a fist and thrust her arm upward. "The man sticks it into you," she said emphatically. Her actions and voice were violent. I was mortified to learn what I would have to endure if I wanted to be a mother.

My Mom's grandparents were born in the 1890's. Dad was born in 1916 and my Mom in 1920. At the time, women had just won voting rights. Even in the 1950s the culture dictated that women stay home when they were 'with child.' Women were trained to be quiet, compliant and to basically put up with anything, and I mean anything.

Women were systematically blamed for the misbehavior of their husbands, no matter if the man beat them up or went out on the town drinking, or…Women were told, "If you were a better wife, those things would not have happened." At that time there were few defenders for the rights of women and children. Granny was present when my parents allowed my older sister to be molested by our grandfather. Poor Granny, married to a devil of a man. She endured a lifetime witnessing her husband's sexual, verbal, and physical abuse of her children, her daughter-in-law, and her granddaughters. What terrible pain and suffering for her. Who knows how my grandfather treated her?

Granny was sweet and read to me tirelessly when she visited. She was a loving mother and served the devil-man as a dutiful wife. She carried her pain privately. Men like my grandfather seek others to serve their needs, and he found such a woman in my thoughtful Granny.

Aunt Lucile shared some of Granny's poems with me and this one speaks volumes:

*I've seen the violets in the spring,*
*The shiny satin of a blackbird's wing,*
*And white clouds driven by the breeze,*
*Tall chapels of majestic trees.*
*But I could wish for more than this,*
*The lovely ecstasy and bliss,*
*Of being safe within your arms,*
*Serenely sheltered from all harm.*
*So I will take the gift of love,*
*Knowing it must come from above.*
*And keep it ever bright and pure,*
*A gem to treasure which endures.*
*For I have lived, and loved, and learned,*
*Each thing of value must be earned.*
*And willingly I pay the price,*
*Of joy, tears, and sacrifice.*

Mable Clare

There were no informed counselors or self-help books to help my parents. In my Dad's mind, if God were real, God would have prevented the sins committed against him and the atrocities that happened in WWII. The sins against my father were many and evil. Knowing and understanding this is where the first smidgen of compassion for my father began. Nevertheless, when I asked my father's sister, Aunt Lucile, if she felt sorry for him, she replied without hesitation, "Only when I'm not with him."

My Mom and Dad were not evil. They were sincere in their motivation to give positive things to their daughters. My Dad's first job was as a Realtor, but he discovered there was more money to be made as an escrow officer. Then in the 1950s, he became a contractor/developer for small affordable homes. By 1960, the booming economy rocketed him to a position as a 25% owner and president of a savings and loan bank. He was then elected to the California State Board of Savings and Loans where he served for four years.

To my father's credit, it was his desire to give his daughters a diverse and fulfilling life. He taught us to fish and golf, took us to the beach and boating on weekends, and we enjoyed numerous trailer trips to national and state parks. My functional habits came from my dad, who felt a deep responsibility to teach us practical survival skills.

When I needed a new kitchen table, I went to Goodwill and spotted an inexpensive veneer table in good condition. *How will I get this home? I have no one to help me. It won't fit in my sedan. Hmm...*I heard my dad's voice, "Where there is a will, there is a way. Just think it through, Daughter. Think about it all the way through. What could go wrong, what will happen if you do this?" There I was, thinking through a solution, and I produced a plan. I paid for the table and told the people I would be back within the hour to pick it up. I went home and got an old blanket and rope from the garage. I returned to Goodwill and I put the blanket on top of the car. A man helped me carry the table to the car and turn it upside-down on the blanket.

He looked at the arrangement, "You can't drive that home like that, lady."

"I've got it figured out, don't worry." He shrugged his shoulders and walked back into the building. I took the rope and tied it to the table with a knot I had learned from Dad during our fishing days. I strung the rope through the open windows, tied the rope to the four table legs and back through the windows, then tied it off. This arrangement tied the car doors shut, but I handily climbed through the open driver's window and drove home. *How did I think this up? My dad.* "Make things work with what you already have. Save money when you can, and remember, everything you own is an asset, so take care of your belongings and treat other people's property as if it is your own."

The work ethic training from my dad included long hours of cleaning the pool and the patio around it. "You are lucky to live in this house, so you need to help take care of it." Added to these duties were the chores Mom gave me to do in the house. I spent my teenage years alone on Saturdays, working while my parents played golf with friends. I thought every kid worked seven hours on the weekends. There was no time for social activities. So as far as knowing what to do in social situations or how to make friends, I lacked the normal practice when growing up, so I was adrift in this area.

I am more attuned to my intuition. Counseling, studying, writing, and meditation have helped me to become more calm. Each day when I wake, I focus on God's Presence and believe that the day will reveal itself. Like the waves that pound the shores, the sphere of God's grace and forgiveness is constant. *I couldn't count on my parents, but I can count on God.*

I believe that there are human tragedies that break God's heart. I searched and found God's amazing grace, mercy and compassion. Traumatized people need understanding, compassion, and forgiveness. Jesus knows me and he is compassionate and forgiving toward me. That sounds like love, and love was exactly what I needed if I was going to find a way to forgive my parents.

> *So I say to you; ask and it will be given to you; seek and you will find; knock and the door will be opened to you. For everyone who asks receives; he who seeks finds; and to him who knocks the door will be opened.* Luke 11:9-10.

CHAPTER 28

# Consequences of Trauma

*Success is going from failure to failure to failure*
*without losing your enthusiasm.*

ABRAHAM LINCOLN

Various symptoms affect a person who has been traumatized. Part of piecing the puzzle of my psyche came from learning known principles in brain science and psychology. The following concepts have helped me to understand myself, my grandmother, my parents, and yes, my friends.

## Lack of Agency

*Keep your eyes on the stars, but your feet on the ground.*

THEODORE ROOSEVELT

Agency is a person's ability to stand up for what is right, to speak or ask for what one needs, and to have a sense of confidence to protect oneself. Agency refers to a person's ability to actively exert personal power and to provide a sense of *selfhood*. It starts in infancy and develops from trusting relationships "created in our most intimate minute-to-minute exchanges with our caregivers."[51] This is crucial for a person's sense of well-being and personhood throughout life.

One's inability to find a *no* can last for a lifetime. My parents had no sense of agency. My Mom could not say *No* to her dad, and Dad could not stop his father with a firm *No*. My parents could not exert the personal power called agency.

When my Mom was in her early sixties, she apologized to me, "I wish that I had protected you. It was wrong of me to let my father molest you." I felt Mom's sincerity, but I wanted to know why she'd failed us. In the 1980s, information about the damage of sexual abuse surfaced in the culture and this led me to imagine the guilt my mother must have felt. Herself a traumatized child, she did not know how to defend her children.

Everyone knows not to get between a mother bear and her cubs, but my traumatized mother had lost her basic instinct to defend herself, much less her children.

Agency is confidence in one's ability to express one's needs and desires. The ability to defend oneself by saying *No* is an important self-knowledge skill. Infants and small children need to be encouraged, heard, and understood. Children know they are helpless and vulnerable.

When kids start saying *No*, we call it the 'terrible twos,' but this is a misnomer. Learning to say *No* is a developmental stage from which a sense of agency advances. Children need to experiment with this behavior, and it is best if parents do not perceive this as unacceptable. Children's caregivers need to provide a safety net for them to experiment in verbalizing their specific needs and wants. Children at this age have not developed cognitive abilities, so their emotional brain is in charge. When overwhelmed, a young child needs help sorting out their upsets. Usually, when a child is held tightly, as when in the womb, the child feels the safety and comfort he/she needs. The life-long belief in one's agency is developed in the first two years of life, and these early patterns can continue for a lifetime. If we allow children to set boundaries and defend their rights, they gain confidence in themselves, which allows them to keep themselves safe as they grow up.

When a sense of agency is thwarted or warped, it causes confusion about when or how to stand up for oneself. This part of my personality was weak, and other people could sense it. Even though I tried to act and look confident, at some unconscious level, I could not disguise my lack of agency. It took me well into my adulthood to understand these concepts and develop my own sense of agency.

During my career as a special education teacher, I encountered several principals and school psychologists who sniffed out opportunities to criticize my personality and teaching abilities. At a parent-teacher conference with the principal present, a mother smiled at me and said, "My boy is so much happier when he comes home from school. He's learning to read at long last. He really likes coming to your class, Mrs. G." *Surely this is a good report for me.*

The principal shot back, "I don't think it's so much about Mrs. G. I'm thinking it's most likely his regular teacher." Not knowing how to respond, I sat there, voiceless. I could have talked about the child's despondency when he initially arrived in my class, and the wonderful progress he'd made since he first started with me, but I didn't.

I complained to my good friend, Libby, of these humiliations from my principal. "Why don't you push back on the principal a little?" I hadn't a clue what she meant. "Push back!" She reiterated.

"What?" I drew a blank.

"Push back!" Libby recognized my dismay. She walked over and gave me a nudge on my shoulder. "Now, push me!"

*Are you kidding? I don't do that. No way. Not allowed.*

"Come on. If you don't stand up for yourself, you'll be overrun. You need to find a way to speak up, to defend yourself! Now try it. Push me!"

*Is that what push back means?* I thought. "I can't!" I told her.

"Yes, you can!" She gave a harder shove on my arm. Still, I stood there, not frozen but confused. "You can say something good about your teaching. Come on, you're a good teacher and you know it! Tell your principal what you've accomplished. Now push back!" *No.* In frustration, she thrust her arms against my chest and shoulders which caused me to step backwards to catch my balance. That did it! We started a push/shove dance. "Good! Do it again. Harder!" I was surprised but I sensed her support and encouragement, so it was a safe experiment with a trusted friend. She pushed me and I pushed back! It felt good, liberating. "See?" We laughed.

This was the first time I'd understood 'push back,' so I started experimenting with my push back. My friendship dance with Libby empowered me.

I believed I was secure in the loving arms of the Savior. I envisioned sitting on Jesus' lap enfolded in his safe arms. Jesus proclaimed, "Let the little children come to me, and do not hinder them, for the kingdom of heaven belongs to such as these." (Matthew 19:14) God knew I needed a Savior. I was learning about the meaning of Christianity both for my personal life and for the world.

> *I tell you the truth, anyone who will not receive the kingdom of God like a little child will never enter it.* Luke 18:17

# Dissociation

*The body is emotion.*
*All emotion is stored in the body.*

MICHAEL TONETTI

One day in sunny Southern California, at the age of 23, I sat visiting with my friend, Evy. During our lunch conversation on her porch, I casually mentioned, "I feel as though my arms are floating up in the air somewhere and my legs feel as though they're not part of me. It seems like they don't belong to me." Although it was a good description of what I frequently experienced, that statement cut short her interest in our friendship.

Dr. van der Kolk writes, "I was amazed to discover how many of my patients told me they could not feel whole areas of their bodies." People who've experienced trauma often feel disconnected not only from their bodies but from people or events happening around them. These experiences can result in a loss of self-regulation.[52]

Self-regulation is one's ability to react to situations, knowing that the responses will be consistently appropriate. It's a developed sense of what is expected in social settings and one's sense of knowing that he/she can be present and react in acceptable ways. A self-regulated person carries an intuitive confidence that they can stand up for themselves and take care of their personal needs. In dissociative personalities, this sense of agency is missing.

Without knowing it, what I had described to Evy was that my body was out of touch with relevant associations or connections needed to function well. My emotions and reasoning brain were not paired and this disconnection, or mismatch, played out in my body's feeling of wholeness. Although I was coordinated athletically, I would often trip or misjudge my spatial surroundings. Sometimes, when walking through a door, I bumped my shoulder on the door jam or hit my hip on the doorknob. In essence, I was disconnected from my physical self. In psychology, this is the disorder of dissociation.

I was never sure how I would react or how I would appear to others. When I walked into a room of people, I feared that I would somehow fail, knowing that I didn't know how to react as people anticipated. When a child develops normally, self-regulation becomes automatic. However, the opportunity in my family structure to develop socially was limited. Knowing how to respond appropriately has been a steep learning curve.

Usually, an image and an emotion pair to form a memory and a person can readily recall something that had happened. However, if an experience is traumatic or painful, the brain records the emotions in one part of the brain, but the thoughts, sounds, and images that would normally pair with the emotions are split off, which causes the memory to become fragmented.[53] If the experience is overwhelming and traumatic, messages to the brain are not fully comprehended and the information flowing into the brain is like a "jumbled cloud."[54] I called it scrambled brain; nothing seemed to make sense.

When normal associations are lost to the brain, and emotions and events do not make normal connections, the result is that one's personal life story or self-narrative does not develop properly. The needed patterns to make associations do not integrate well.[55] Without continuity of memories, a person is unable to develop his/her sense of self.

When a person experiences an emotion without a memory attached, the person has a dissociation. In South Dakota when I was twenty-three, Randy and I were traveling and decided to sleep the night in the car. Irrational fears emerged stemming from a memory that had been lost to me, I felt trapped and helpless.

I needed to think back to the trailer park when I was six and my dad forced me to sleep in the car without parental protection. This event and my terrified emotions were not paired and thus there was no reliable association. So as an adult, I was frightened by having to sleep in the car. I was so upset that I started kicking the window. I screamed, "Let me out of here." I was out of control and felt like I was a crazy person. Once the memory became clear, I understood the impetus of my fear, and my panic attack subsided.

"Dissociation prevents the trauma from becoming integrated with the conglomerate, ever-shifting stories in autobiographical memory, in essence creating a dual memory system."[56] Lost to the person is the continuous flow of associations which make a story one can count on. During trauma, emotions become dissociated. The "…sensations and emotions of trauma can be stored separately as frozen, barely comprehensible fragments."[57]

Stephen Segaller and Merrill Berger in their book, *The Wisdom of the Dream, The World of C.G. Jung*, explain the power of our dreams. Jung taught that our dreams are part of the psyche, and we should honor and pay attention to them. "The dream is uncontaminated by conscious thinking. The dream itself is pure memory."[58] Carl Jung wrote, "The reality of the psyche is what we feel and think at the deepest part of the unconscious dimension, which is active and dynamic."[59] The dream very often expresses a truth and opens the conscious mind to a consideration of an alternative point of view.... "If you have a dream which tells the truth, it is an experience of your soul. It is like listening to your inner, knowledgeable voice."[60]

This dream was a picture of how disconnected I was from my own self, a clear example of dissociation:

*I was in bed with Randy, and we were getting ready to have sex together. I looked over and standing nearby was a seven-year- old girl. I gazed at her and wondered who she was. Then it dawned on me that she was me. She was looking meekly at me, begging, "I want to come too!"*

*I retorted angrily, "You are too little. Only adults have sex together, not little girls. You stay there." She disappeared.*

The little girl, me, split away from me. When I woke up, I shared my dream with Randy, and he intrinsically knew what the dream meant; that sex was not a holistic experience for me. This recognition inflamed his frustration with me, "You are damaged goods!"

*People toss out damaged goods. But I'm not goods! I'm a person.* Randy started threatening me with the D word.

A part of me split off from myself when I was a child. As an adult, I felt sorry for this part of me who felt like she belonged nowhere. I named her Little Gaynelle, and I talked to her as if she were a separate person, *I love you. You are dear to me. I know you did your best to help and comfort me. I appreciate all that you did for me.* I wanted to comfort the part of me that my parents had never seen nor consoled.

I began speaking out loud to that little child in my dream. *I love you.* I repeated it thousands of times. But my little Gaynelle shouted back at me, "No you don't! I don't believe you!" I could read her face and feelings, and she seemed to me like she was a real child in the here and now. *I love you. I love you.* "No, you don't love me," she shot back. It took months, but finally my overtures of love to my split-off little girl trusted that we could love and care for each other. I knew I could keep her safe as I had done for my children. My little Gaynelle began to believe me. We merged as one person, because of course in my psyche, the *we* I perceived was always one person. This was the beginning of experiencing wholeness, agency, and homeostasis.

My dreams informed me about what happened to me. Even if my rational brain, the cerebral cortex, couldn't understand it, my body and limbic brain did.

Unraveling the past is a deep and challenging effort. In doing this gut-wrenching work, I started to put together a life story that gave purpose and meaning to my life. As my memories moved into my consciousness, I pieced together my life's narrative so that my experiences came together in a story that made sense.

> *...those who hope in the LORD will renew their strength. They will soar on wings like eagles; they will run and not grow weary, they will walk and not be faint.* Isaiah 40: 3

# Depersonalization

*You desire to know the art of living, my friend?*
*It is contained in one phrase: make use of suffering.*

HENRI FREDERIC AMIEL

According to van der Kolk, "Depersonalization is one symptom of the massive dissociation created by trauma." Massive dissociation for me meant that my sensations and emotions were disjointed. My brain stored memories in various parts of my brain, and they were locked up. I was not able to retrieve them except through distress and prayer. Hidden though my memories were, they could come roaring back in the here and now.[61] Understanding myself came partly through the interpretation of my dreams. The following two dreams revealed how severe my dissociation was. On multiple occasions, I awoke crying—it was hard to accept that this was the core of my being.

*I was standing on a large oval field at a traveling carnival, and an oval track carried coaches going around it, each coach seating four persons. I waited my turn for a ride. It looked simple enough. When one person got off all I had to do was jump on and sit down. When I finally got on, someone on the inner seat immediately wanted to get off and this pushed me toward the middle so someone could get on. Then the people on the in-side got off the ride, and with the three new riders I found myself smashed against the inside edge. The ride suddenly sped up and as the centrifugal force increased, I felt trapped. I could not get out and felt helpless, I was scrunched in so tightly I couldn't move.*

The same night I had this subsequent dream:

*My car was stolen from the garage. The police came to my door and said they had found my car. I went outside and they pointed to a bike. I needed to get to work so I hopped on the bike which then turned into a trike, and I tried to pedal, but my knees bumped into the handlebars. I couldn't get to work. I hung my head over the handlebars, defeated.*

When I told my counselor about these back-to-back dreams, he said, "Gaynelle, you feel like you don't deserve to have the necessities of life. You chose a trike, as though your personhood is that small, and you go round and round, on the track of life, helpless and squished and unable to get off this ride. This is what you think your life is. This is the person you see yourself as being." *Oh my, I've made so many decisions with this wounded psyche of mine.*

Dr. James Pennebaker learned that when his patients talked about in-timate or difficult issues, as their emotional state altered it was reflected in their vocal tone, pitch, and style of speech, and alterations of their facial expression, body movement, and handwriting. In clinical practice, this is called "switching."[62] Yes, "switching," much as when I was hijacked by a "flipped switch," which happened after I had not seen my Mom and Dad for several years.

Depersonalization is one step beyond dissociation and is more severe, and more massive. It differs from dissociation in that the brain is even more scrambled, fearful, and disoriented. Round and round on the track of life. Without an escape, I felt empty. Invisible. *Erase me.*

Years passed. I worried I would always be confused and hurt. Would I ever find my *self?*

In my reasoning brain, I knew that Jesus loved me, and that God wanted me to stay alive, and I did so desire to live. But survival is not the same as thriving. The deeper part of myself cried out to God, the great I Am: *Deep calls to deep* (Psalm 42:7).

When I left home, I'd promised myself that I would be okay, that I'd thrive, but that didn't happen. The shadow of my past was sewn into my psyche much as Wendy had sown Peter Pan's shadow onto his moccasins. Peter Pan wanted his shadow, but I desperately wished mine would disappear.

When I was a young woman, insight into the workings of my brain was unavailable. It would have helped to know that I wasn't alone in the world of trauma, that I was programmed normally like the rest of humanity. The recovery strategies and hope for healing finally appeared. Jesus said, "The truth will set you free." *Will I ever be free? I am seeking the truth, God, but I don't feel free.* My heart aches when I recall how much comfort it would have given me as a child to hear the words, "God loves you!

*Look at the birds of the air; they do not sow or reap or store away in barns, yet your heavenly father feeds them. Are you not much more valuable than they?* Matthew 6:26.

# Shame

*No matter how deep and dark the secret, No matter how many times a certain sin has defeated you, God can bring change in your life.*

JIM CYMBALA

The definition of shame is: (noun) a painful emotion caused by contempt, a feeling of conscious shortcoming and guilt, and (verb) to be disgraced.[63] No word could better describe the abyss I lived in concerning my personhood and sexuality.

Dr. van der Kolk writes, "After forty years of doing this work, I still regularly hear myself saying, 'That's unbelievable,' when patients tell me about their childhood. They often are as incredulous as I am – how could parents inflict such torture and terror on their own child? All my patients are ashamed about what happened to them, and they blame themselves. On some level, they firmly believe that these terrible things were done to them because they are terrible people."[64]

"Our most intimate sense of self is created in our minute-to-minute exchanges with our caregivers."[65] A secure attachment in the early years of childhood with the primary caregivers is essential for a child to be in sync with the rest of the world. Security is crucial to developing the self and happens in the minute-to-minute interactions with a child's caretakers. In the last five decades, research has proven that a secure attachment "promotes self-reliance and ...makes it possible to become contributing members of the larger social culture."[66] (For more information on attachment, see John Trent, PhD. and Gary Smalley's work, *The Blessing: Giving the Gift of Unconditional Love and Acceptance*.)[67]

We begin to have memories when we learn language and can put thoughts together with words. We can never remember all that happened to us as infants, but the body holds onto the memories. The body never forgets. It always remembers.

Patterns and early memories can give us clues. I was in counseling with a group of sexually abused women. One woman told us she was afraid of knives but didn't know why. She, like me, carried a gnawing, internal pain she couldn't get rid of and had no control over. Our therapist told us that a symptom of childhood vaginal abuse is often a knife twisting pain in the gut and a fear of knives.

Up popped a memory, clear as if it had been happening right then. As if in a movie, I saw myself running from my grandmother when I was three years old. I had walked through the swinging  kitchen door, and when I saw her chopping nuts with a large knife, I turned and ran.

For years I wondered, why I ran like hell at the sight of that knife? I was terrified, but I never could understand why. Now I know it had to do with my limbic brain. The knife and my pain from my father's abuse sent my limbic brain, the defender of survival, into overdrive. In less than a fraction of a second, it decided that flight mode was the best option to survive. So my three year old legs rocketed me toward the front door. My grandmother didn't want me to run out the door and down the street, so she immediately chased after me, but the knife was still in her hand. I opened the door, but she caught up with me and slammed it shut. I stood facing her, sure she was going to hurt me somehow. After this incident, I never felt comfortable with my grandmother again. This episode in my early childhood always baffled me. It saddened me when I was a child, and even now, to think about how my grandmother and I missed out on our relationship. Everyone in my family loved her, and she was puzzled why I was estranged. So was I. An answer at last, with a context that makes sense and helps me feel more normal.

I learned that the fear of knives and an intense gut stabbing pain are related. Through this discovery, I recognized that my current pain is attached to my body's memory of pain my dad inflicted in my sexual organs. I wanted to keep this hidden, this ugly, hurtful thing that happened to me.

The past and present had become one in my mind. My goal is to unpair this association and make new neural pathways in my brain. When the pain shouts at me, I acknowledge it, like when I talked to my inner Gaynelle, "Thank you for alerting me to the pain, but that isn't necessary anymore because the pain isn't from now, it's from the pain a long time ago. It is not related to my present circumstances." Now this seems weird, I admit, and it's a sad example of what we know is valid, "the truth shall set you free." I've only been having this conversion with my psyche a few days, and already I feel some improvement in the intensity of my discomfort.

When I think back to the Day of Thanksgiving at Diane's house, I struggle with the memory of my inappropriate sexual response when I greeted my dad. The memory, as it came into my conscious focus, was so weird I could hardly bear it. My brain unconsciously spoke to me by creating an inappropriate sexual reaction when I stepped into the room where my dad was. This is an example of a 'body memory.' My body had kept the score.[68]

Unconscious memories flooded my body at a visceral level, informing me, against my will, that my suspicions about my dad's abuse were true. The pain from his abuse terrorized me. I know that because I experience feeling afraid every day. I get depressed if I feel alone. I never experienced a secure attachment to my dad or my Mom - crucial for a child to develop a sense of self. "Gaynelle, Jesus had a *self* to give, but you don't!" Said my counselor. Now I know what he meant.

When I was sixteen, I had a similar body memory. The same reaction of sexual heat flared up in my body when, carrying my prom dress, a man on the street flipped me off. When my limbic system saw that finger, it brought back unconscious memories of the finger in my vagina. This bodily reaction was immediate and out of my control. It was as if my body was trying to let me know that indeed, my body knew something my brain could not access. At sixteen, I had no connections or associations to help me make sense of this situation. The image and my emotions must have splintered into different parts of my brain and could not be paired to make associations. All this skittered about in my brain and shame dogged my heels.

As an older child I slept in a fetal position with my fists clenched. My fists were ready for a fight. I thought if my dad stabbed me in the middle of the night, it would be better to be stabbed in my back rather than in my heart or stomach. My rational, reasoning brain knew that my dad could have killed me years before if that had been his intention, so this fear that he might murder me never made sense. He wasn't life-threatening and I understood that my fears were irrational. Since the limbic nervous system is in charge, it never forgot the stabbing pain in my vagina and who caused it. I feared annihilation as I slept.

Fear shows up in my daily life due to a startle response that my limbic brain initiates. This is wearisome, feeling terror when there is none. I imagined my dad hiding behind trees waiting to kill me. I also had a recurring dream: There was a knock at the door. When I opened the door, I saw my dad standing with a gun in his hand ready to shoot me.

The questions I had from my body memories now make sense. I recognized my profound loss of a normal life and the pain I had to endure. I've had great difficulty accepting the fact that my dad had injured me this gravely.

At some level my mother must have known what my father was doing in the middle of the night when he answered my infant cries. My mother told me that he refused to let her tend to my needs. But she had no agency.

Dad damaged me, and Mom shamed me unmercifully. When I was a child, if my Mom knew I'd masturbated, she wouldn't talk to me. As van der Kolk states, "Hostile behavior from a child's mother, and emotional withdrawal by mothers, has a profound and long-lasting impact upon children, lasting well into adulthood."[69] I anesthetized my sexuality and still felt intensely ashamed.[70] When the victim is in the presence of the abuser, the recall of trauma can cause adverse effects, such as digestive problems or migraine headaches.[71] I have digestive complications and, like my sisters, suffered from migraines growing up. Years later, I took migraine medication before visiting Dad to stave off the headaches. Peggy and Diane had the same reactions, and we connected the dots – when we planned to see Dad, we had physical responses that remained out of our conscious control.[72]

Dr. Leonard Matherson in his book, *The Faithful Brain, Designed for So Much More,* describes the human experience of shame. He writes that shame affects our autobiographical story. The hippocampus is the body and brain's stress apparatus. It is responsible for transferring and storing our memories. It receives current information, *and* it also sends recalled memories to the already established neural networks. Since memories are constantly being refreshed, they are never permanent. A recalled shameful memory can be stored in a way that increases the brain's salient emotions with more shame than the memory contained when it was originally formed. "This is the basic problem with many emotional disorders, including anxiety, reaction depression, and post-traumatic stress disorder."[73] My sexual shame generalized to any kind of pleasurable feeling. My brain's filter annulled joy and pleasure from every area of my life. If the core feelings of sexuality were illegal, then I surmised that all feelings of goodness and warmth were illegal. I decided when I was twelve that I didn't deserve to have anything or anybody and I might as well get used to it.

Sexuality is crucial to every person's identity; it is a natural hormonal drive. Shame happens when these basic functions and feelings get distorted. A person's identity, the self, also gets distorted. As I transitioned into an adult, I did what I could to stay sane by putting distance between myself and my parents. I saw my dad four times in twenty years, and my Mom only found me by hiring a private detective. I avoided them for two reasons: 1) I believed my absence from their lives didn't matter to them, and that I was doing them a favor, and 2) Whenever they were involved in my life, I lost what sense of *self* I had worked to retrieve. I was simply unable to self-regulate when I was with my parents. My parents and I were incapable of creating healthy relationships.

*For I am convinced that neither death nor life, neither angels nor demons, neither the present nor the future, nor any powers, neither height nor depth, nor anything in all creation, will be able to separate us from the love of God that is in Christ Jesus our Lord.*
Romans 8: 38-39

## CHAPTER 29

# Recovery—Healing the Brain

*We are weaving a future on the looms of today.*

GRACE DAWSON

Dr. van der Kolk speaks about recovery when he says, "Children have no choice but to organize themselves to survive within the families they have.[74] The brain works to survive, but when our brains erase awareness and cultivate denial, the price is that one loses track of their feelings, doesn't know who to trust, and loses any real sense of self.[75] It is...as if their personality has definitely stopped (developing) at a certain point, and cannot enlarge any more by the addition or assimilation of new elements."[76] Recovering means learning to integrate "the cut-off elements of trauma into the ongoing narrative of life so that the brain can recognize; 'that was then and this is now.'"[77]

The brain can heal. My strategies were to sit on a blanket and zone out for hours; rock in rocking chairs; or exercise so hard that the stress chemicals sweated out of my body. I held my babies, rocked them, and played with them. Love grew inside my heart and continued to help my body calm and aided my healing efforts.

Sleep disorders, digestive problems, and diseases can actually be part of the body and the brain's desire to heal. These symptoms seem like breakdowns, but they are often the impetus for breakthroughs. This is good news. In recent decades research shows that to heal trauma, recircuiting the pathway in the brain creates a new way to perceive the world. "Knowing what we feel is the first step to knowing why we feel that way."[78]

A new perception for me was a simple thought: *sex can be beautiful*. By practicing affirmations and believing that *God isn't finished with me yet*, I recreated a new narrative; I named my intimate relational experiences as beautiful. As my thinking normalized along these lines, the concept of goodness significantly increased for me, and I felt happier.

I had never been able to create forgiveness deep within my soul. After forty years of prayer, reading books, and verbal affirmations, I gave up. *God, I'm worn out and I give in. Deep down I see I haven't accomplished forgiveness. Forty years is enough—I'm weary of trying. I give up. If you don't do it inside me and for me, it won't happen!* I gave over my problem of failing to forgive my parents to Jesus, much as Pastor George had told me to give the hurting children in the hospital to God and leave the responsibility with God. Jesus, *I've prayed seventy times seven to be able to forgive, and we both know it hasn't happened.*

Even so, I was experiencing a deep sense of healing. I was helped by the discovery of many therapies to heal the brain, some of which Dr. van der Kolk and Dr. Matheson have discussed in their books. Uncanny situations led me to the people who became my healers. How could I have found these perfect mentors and healers if I'd had to search them out myself? It was God's guidance and intervention that led me to more healing. I believe that God is at work in every person's life, even when they are unaware of it. I learned to honor my needs. *I am worth the time it takes to do exercises for my emotions and my brain. I will find a path for my life to be fulfilling and joyful.* The emotional brain does not change itself by understanding how the emotional maps in the brain are developed. Instead, the limbic system needs calming, retraining, and recalibrating.[79] It takes time and commitment to rearrange the puzzle pieces into a coherent story and find harmony.

*Then Peter came to Jesus and asked, "Lord, how many times shall I forgive my brother or sister who sins against me? Up to seven times?" Jesus answered, " I tell you, not seven times, but seventy-seven times."*
Matthew 18:21-22

## CHAPTER 30

# Compassion

*Love means to love that which is unlovable, or is no*
*virtue at all– Forgiving means to pardon that which is*
*unpardonable or it is no virtue at all– And hope means*
*hoping when things are hopeless, or it is no virtue at all.*

G.K. CHESTERTON

## Randy: November 1949 – July 2013

*A discontented man finds no easy chair.*

BEN FRANKLIN

I loved Randy. One of the reasons I married him was because he'd been involved in the church all his life and I wanted to know more about this Jesus guy. At the time of our marriage, all I knew was that Jesus was "the Man who split time." Indeed, I gleaned a rudimentary knowledge about Jesus when Randy was in seminary, taking classes, reading his papers and listening to his sermons, and Bible study. Randy's theme in his preaching was always about God's love. I will always be thankful to him for his willingness to marry a wandering child in the wilderness who needed to learn her way. Randy remains dear in my heart.

Randy's true personality was kind and loving, but sometimes a person can get disconnected from one's self. Most often this is caused by unresolved childhood issues, which was true for both of us. I internalized the fairy tale, *Beauty and the Beast*. I wasn't Belle, and Randy wasn't a beast. We each suffered from our individual heart aches, and limbic brain hijackings.

This affected our family life; I understand how and why our marriage failed. My part of our failure was due to my problems regarding lack of agency, along with the symptoms of dissociation and, even deeper, depersonalization. In addition, my shame around sex contributed to our failure to thrive as a couple.

One of the symptoms of traumatic abuse is to engage in risky behaviors:. Randy pushed the restrictions imposed on a church minister to abstain from sexual activity outside of marriage. Distorted feelings about sex, and unwarranted anger, are other behavioral manifestations that point to abuse. We suffered through enraged outbursts and had difficulty experiencing positive emotions. We were never able to develop a sense of mutual trust, or we were deprived of it from the beginning when we were babies and toddlers.

At the forefront of Jesus' ministry were his teachings about love and forgiveness. He died on the cross, enduring a depth of pain that we shrink from when forced to remember. Even in his suffering, Jesus thought about those who agonized because of the pain they'd inflicted on others. Jesus asked God to forgive his crucifiers: "Father, forgive them for they do not know what they are doing." (Luke 23:24)

Hudson Trevor teaches that, "Forgiveness overcomes evil. It brings liberation from resentment, release from the bondage of past hurts, deliverance from bitterness, and the freedom to live fully in the present moment."[80] After over forty years of reading, praying and studying the Bible, I stopped praying about forgiving. I needed and wanted to forgive my parents and Randy, but I'd made no serious progress, so it seemed pointless. I was sure I'd given this forgiveness idea all my effort, yet I still carried a burr of resentment underneath the blanket of my soul. I hid there, unable to achieve Jesus' command to forgive.

Although Randy knew the principles taught in the Bible, living what Jesus taught seemed unattainable for him, as it is for all people, probably because our reasoning brains often are not in charge. No amount of religion or knowledge changes the limbic brain systems. Any kind of abuse or trauma that is not recognized or treated with therapy leads to unconscious symptoms that play out in our lives. Sounds philosophical, but, "if only I had known what I know now," maybe our lives together would have played out differently.

Patricia Evans, author of *The Verbally Abusive Relationship, How to Recognize It and How to Respond*, writes "…the most significant and surprising discovery I made was that the verbal abuser and the partner seemed to be living in two different realities. The abuser's orientation was toward control and dominance. The partner's orientation was toward mutuality and cooperation. In many respects they *were* in two different realities."[81] Randy had one goal; I had another.

Jane Stanford was head of Stanford University after her husband died. She erected the Stanford Memorial Church in honor of their son, Leland Stanford, Jr., who died at the age of fifteen. Carved on the interior walls is a collection of inspirational sayings gathered by Mrs. Stanford. This one spoke to me:

> *"There are but few on Earth free from cares, none but carry burdens of sorrow, and if all were asked to make a package of their troubles, and throw this package on a common pile, and then were asked to go and choose a package which they were willing to bear, all would select their own package again. Your heartaches may be great, burdens heavy, but look about you, and with whom would you change?"* [82]

I'm certain I would choose my own package. No one walks through life unscathed. Knowing this, I am grateful for my life as it is, for all I have learned and the ways I've been able to extend solace to others. I've developed compassion for myself and others, including Randy.

*Then Jesus said, Father, forgive them, for they know not what they do.*
Luke: 23:34

# Compassion for My Mom: Nov. 1920 – Feb. 1989

*Not knowing when the dawn will come, I open every door.*

EMILY DICKINSON

My tailspin after remembering my parents' inability to act and protect my sister from sexual abuse brought to the surface an unknown grief. I found myself in a dark depression that I could not hide away. I met with my counselor and asked him, "What does it feel like to know your mother loves you?" Tears welled up in my eyes as he took me through the steps of brain spotting. "Please love me, Mama. Please?" I whispered.

This reminded me of the same longing I had as a young woman. *Now I'm seventy and I still have the same longings.*

In fairness, at nineteen my mother married a man who was on the narcissistic spectrum. This must have caused her depression and to live in shutdown mode. Any sense of equilibrium she may have developed earlier in her life was compromised by her marriage.

I perceived that my existence depended on pleasing my mother. I was already a frightened child, and I feared annihilation if I angered her. I wondered what it felt like to trust my mother, to be loved and comforted by her. When my children were born, I tried to be the mother I wished I'd had.

My counselor led me in an exercise called brain spotting. This therapy is related to Eye Movement Desensitization and Reprocessing (EMDR). "She didn't know how to love me," I said with tears. "She was bereft of any ability to connect with me."

As we continued brain spotting, the therapist encouraged me, "Let the brain have its way. Just let your brain relax. Your brain can do its healing work. We are not trying to make anything happen here. Give your brain some time to find its pathway to healing." The purpose of brain spotting is to allow the cortex thinking part of the brain to veg out so that the limbic system can be acknowledged and instigate healing. The technique of brain spotting was like walking out of the dark woods and finding myself bathed in a cleansing rain.

One day after an intense counseling session with EMDR, my car seemed to drive itself to a nearby department store. I was still thinking about my mother. She enjoyed shopping and buying things and during such excursions, she would often be her genuine self, whom I rarely had the opportunity to see. Shopping became an activity where we could be in the moment, distracted from the dysfunction in the family and home. In this setting, I felt cared for, even if I had to wear the clothes I disliked or that she picked out.

On this day, I decided a benign distraction was what I needed. As I wandered around the store, a small wooden plaque caught my eye: "Always my mother, forever my friend." It seemed like serendipity, or God's leading, so I bought it and set it in a place where I would see it every day. *My mother, my friend?* In my early childhood, my mother must have given me some of the attention a baby needs, some form of love and attachment. It had to be true because, despite my life's mayhem of hurt and rejection, I had done things to further my life. I graduated from college, was a loving mother, and became a successful teacher with an advanced credential. *My mother, my friend? hmm…*

When I got home, I looked at myself in the mirror and stared at my mother. Same height, the same brown eyes, the same color of dyed hair, the same thin lips, and hairstyle. *I still wear some of her clothes.* Even though she was gone, I still sought her love and approval. I wanted to know her. I wanted her to know me. I wondered: *did she wish for a mother-daughter relationship like I did? Was that why she hired a private detective to find me? I'm sure my mother longed to love and care for me, her second daughter.*

*What if I were to create a space within myself to imagine my mother as my loving caretaker?*

My mother is still part of me, and I am part of her. At an attachment level, neither of us can do well without the other. I suffered her shame, and she suffered mine. I wanted her, she wanted me. *Is there a part of me that can see her positive side?*

I had difficulty feeling positive about her. The time I tried to explain to my mother about my gut pain. She rubbed her stomach and nonchalantly declared, "Everyone hurts here. That's just life!" She turned away with no further discussion. I wondered, *Does she carry a knife in her gut like I do?* I had so many questions. *Did she unconsciously feel her own shame because she identified my sexuality as though it was her own? Did Mom shame me into compliance so she could squash her feelings?* Somewhere in her psyche, she carried with her the sense that sexual feelings were forbidden or shameful. When I was twenty-one and unmarried, she discovered I was on the pill because I had gained weight. With disgust that felt like hate, she physically pushed me away and turned from me; the message I got was that she wanted to walk out of my life.

*Mom, I can't ever remember one time being hugged by you.* When I was a teenager, I sat next to Granny with my head on her lap. She gently patted my back and comforted me patiently waiting for my tears to heal my sorrow. To this day, I remember her soothing touch because she was the only person who knew what I needed.

*Mom, did you feel guilty that you could not love me the way you knew a mother was supposed to love her child? It always seemed weird that you would not come to my wedding just because I picked out my wedding dress without you. Why did you always push me away?*

On her deathbed, she believed we had found each other. After she died, I imagined her listening in heaven and forgiving me. *Well, Mom, since you are in heaven and earthly things have dropped away, I am sure you love me and forgive me! Our forgiveness of one another can be the starting point for a deeper healing in me and my longings for you. I have asked you to forgive me and it's time for me to believe this has happened.*

*Mama, I appreciate all that you tried to do for me, despite your limitations. You taught me to sew, cook, and clean. You typed my papers in high school and invited my friends over. Those things have helped me much in life. I know you did the best you could to love me and for that I am grateful. In fact, a mother does these kinds of things because she loves her child. I will receive your love.* I have changed my old narrative and made new neural pathways by saying to myself and others, *"My mother loved and loves me!"* Compassion for her heartaches started the path to help me forgive her.

As I concentrate on loving my Mom, in my mind, we are becoming friends.

"Surely goodness and mercy shall follow me all the days of my life and I will dwell in the house of the LORD forever"— and I will be with my Mom! (Psalm 23)

*Let us not become weary in doing good, for at the proper time we will reap a harvest if we do not give up. Therefore, as we have opportunity, let us do good to all people.* Galatians 6:9

## Compassion for My Dad: October 1916 - June 2019

*Selfishness must always be forgiven, you know, for there is no hope of a cure.*

JANE AUSTEN, *Mansfield Park*

When Dad was ninety-five, I said something to him about doing my best. Oops! Without hesitation he retorted, "Your best is not good enough!" I couldn't let it go, and I challenged him.

"Dad, it's been difficult for me to believe I'm 'good enough' in anything I do in life. Trying to be good enough has plagued me."

Not skipping a beat, he said, "When I applied for my first job in real estate in Los Angeles County, my boss said to me, 'Art, will you sell these lots?' I told him I would do my best. 'That's not good enough! You either will sell them, or you won't. What's your answer?' I told him I would sell them. So, you see, daughter, it's either you will do something, or you won't. No in-between." He looked at me with total confidence at having proved his point. I laughed inside. *I was raised on a business mantra! I doubt if most people would interpret the idea of doing one's best as making a 'yes, or no,' statement.*

Dad's second divorce happened when he was seventy-five and his wife was forty-five. After twenty years of marriage and gallivanting around the world, he ran out of money and his wife left him. Peggy and her husband generously supported him by paying his rent for the next twenty-seven years, with one stipulation: he was not to live in their town, my town, or Diane's. This protected my sisters and me, and for that I am grateful.

My sisters and I were dutiful daughters. Dad lived in Southern California and the three of us lived in Northern California. We took turns flying to see him, taking him to the doctor, getting necessities, and, his favorite, going out to dinner.

In those twenty-seven years, in our face-to-face conversations, some kind of trust developed between us. My sense of agency with our father increased. Once I made an insignificant error and he barked at me, "That was stupid!"

I barked back, "Only I can call what I do stupid! Never, ever, say I'm stupid again!" I figured if he was so mad that he'd never see me, *fine with me.* He dropped his head and shook it sideways, as he did when bewildered. He wanted me in his life, and to my astonishment, he complied and never again called me stupid.

"You know," Dad bleated, "I have more Christianity in my little finger than you had in your entire lifetime."

"I've spent decades of my life trying to understand Christianity," I replied with force in my voice. "It's complex and not simple to grasp. You don't know what you're talking about; never say that to me again." Standing up for myself was getting results, so I became bolder. For the first time I understood what my friend Libby meant when she encouraged me, "Push back!" Pushing back empowered me, and I felt safer in the world. A new sense of agency for me. New thoughts. New narratives. Better results.

I helped him feel loved and cared for in his last years. This was important to me because a love in which he felt a connection was foreign to him. He knew his mother loved him, and he shared fond memories of sitting in the kitchen late at night drinking coffee and visiting. She listened well and gave him advice. My dad financially supported his mother for over twenty years after his father died. I believe she is the reason he was a better father than his dad had been to him and his sisters. But Dad's trauma left him disconnected from us, unable to truly feel love for us and experience the pleasures of being a loving father.

In twenty-five years of visiting Dad, I learned more about our family dynamics. These unexpected insights made the strenuous effort and the expense of travel worth it.

Jesus said, "Love one another. As I have loved you so must you love one another." (John 13:4) Tall order. I felt proud that despite my emotions, I cared for my father. My growth gave me satisfaction and hope. *I've forgiven him*, I reasoned, since I could be with him without being hijacked. I became stronger and I noticed my power to self-regulate was increasing. I began to trust myself and I felt safer in the world. I prayed and stayed grounded in my faith, and I believe God helped me in all my endeavors. It was my sincere desire to love Dad as Jesus loved me.

God's message through Jesus is that we are to forgive the sins of others. This summed up Jesus' teaching, so different from some of the teachings in the Old Testament. He demolished the archaic idea of 'an eye for an eye and a tooth for a tooth.'

Jesus demonstrated love and compassion. Jesus walked his talk. His death on the cross proved the extent he was willing to suffer so that we could learn to forgive not only others but also ourselves. His concern and love for me found its way into my heart. I outgrew my fury and transformed it into the compassion Jesus gave me. On my piano of life, each note had to be tuned and then re-tuned until I began to experience harmony. In mindful living, I walked, stomped, stumbled, and ran. I cried, tripped, tiptoed, and jumped for joy. I trusted in God's abundant love made evident through Jesus' actions and his intentional living. He accepted death and then overcame it. Jesus' love and power endure.

> *For I have learned to be content whatever the circumstances. I know what it is to be in need, and I know what it is to have plenty. I have learned the secret of being content in any and every situation, whether well-fed or hungry, whether living in plenty or in want. I can do everything through him who gives me strength.* Philippians 4:11-13

# CHAPTER 31
# The Music of My Tears

*I live to show his power, who once did bring My*
*joys to weep, and now my griefs to sing.*

GEORGE HERBERT
*Joseph's Coat*

M y dad was self-sufficient into his nineties, but by the time he reached 101 years, it was evident he needed help. My sisters and I planned for him to enter assisted living in Reno, Nevada, closer to our homes in Northern California.

I visited him regularly between October and March; by April it was apparent that he was nearing the end of his life. I went to see him every week at that time. The story of his release from this life was divinely meaningful to me. The small miracles that flowed from the love of God to Dad and me will be in my memory forever. They have become a guiding light, and after all I've been through, my journey toward wholeness makes sense.

## Journal of Dad's Last Days

### April 7-9, 2019

Peggy and I drove from Sacramento to Dad's place in Reno. He was asleep in his recliner chair; when he woke, we were surprised that he seemed to recognize us. Peggy leaned down and spoke gently in his ear and though he mumbled, he was able to respond. "How'd you get in? How did you get here? Is it okay with your husband that you're here?" Then he looked at me. "Is it okay with …" he stumbled, unable to remember Jerry's name. We assured him that our husbands supported us in seeing him, and he seemed satisfied. His lunch was on a hospital table next to his chair; Peggy fed him. To our surprise, he ate it all. Then he looked up and said, "Oh, how I've missed you!" He turned to me with a confused expression, as if he didn't recognize me and said, "Who hired you?"

"You did!" I laughed. He looked puzzled.

After eating, he went back to sleep, and Peggy and I talked. We didn't know if he was sound asleep or sedated, but he seemed comatose, his eyes fluttering now and then and mumbling something unintelligible.

In the first three hours of conversations with Peggy, she described in detail her horrific abuse from our dad's father over the course of her life, beginning as a toddler, then as a young girl, and finally as a teenager. It was intense for me to listen, and Dad was only a few feet away. My mind retrieved memories of my own. I wondered if, at some level, he could hear our conversation.

"Peggy," I whispered. "I think dying people can understand what's being said around them. Dad might hear us, so maybe we should change our conversation."

"I don't think so. Look at him, he's unconscious and can't hear anything." In our second three-hour conversation, I continued to be concerned that Dad could hear us deep in his unconscious mind. In the end, I decided that if he did understand what we said, it wasn't my responsibility to protect him from hearing about our experiences. He didn't deserve to be excluded from his daughters' stories, much of which was his responsibility.

Peggy spoke openly and honestly with me, so I felt safe sharing some of my deep childhood problems with her as well. I knew she would understand without judgment. I talked about my life-long inability to feel joy on our family vacations and how confusing it was to be in such beautiful places and still be unable to experience happiness. I shared about my struggle to believe I didn't deserve to have anything or anybody. And I told her how I'd considered ending my life because it seemed like I wasn't supposed to be around. It was clear that my sister was as sad for me as I was for her.

I continued, "I felt afraid to see beauty and sometimes buried my head in a pillow or covered myself with a blanket to avoid feeling. I loved to swim and once I was invited to go swimming with some friends but decided not to go. For some reason, I refused to let myself have even that little piece of joy." I didn't mention my belief that my baby did not belong to me but to my mother. That was too difficult even for me to comprehend. We found ourselves dismayed as we shared how Mom and Dad failed us in our growing-up years.

Dad woke, but only for three or four minutes. We walked over to him and leaned close enough to hear him mumble, "Sometimes people do the wrong thing, and sometimes they do the right thing." I was flabbergasted. Seconds later he turned his head and looked me squarely in the eyes. He spoke clearly: "Remember, the world was made for you, too!" *Did I hear him right? The man who told me no one could love me.* I looked at Peggy for confirmation.

"Dad, tell me again what you said?"

His eyes gazed intently into mine. "Remember that the world was made for you, too!" His words were for me, and his care about me at that moment allowed me to surrender my misheld fear that I didn't belong on the planet or that I wasn't in sync with this world. *The world was made for me, too. He had heard us talking.* I painted his words on river rocks and placed them in my garden where I can read them often.

With effort, Dad turned his head toward Peggy and then toward me as he enunciated his words so we could understand him, "Sometimes we do the wrong thing, sometimes we do the right thing." Dad's comment was a plea for forgiveness. He said it twice so we could understand through his mumbling. *He did do what right he could do.* After his experiences during the Depression, he vowed his family would never go hungry. He deeply desired to provide a good life for us. He did the best he could under the circumstances he was given. I don't know if I could have done any better if I'd been him. Who in their life's journey does not experience adversity? In his asking for forgiveness, he granted me permission to fully experience life. I was pleased because Dad was standing up for us, encouraging us to finish our lives well.

When he went to bed that night, he was lying comfortably tucked in. Peggy tenderly stroked his head, combing his not-yet-white hair with her fingers. Her genuine gesture of love for Dad expressed compassion for his struggles in life. I was touched as I sensed her forgiveness toward him. I adored my strong, loving sister. "Thank you, girls, for taking such good care of me. Thank you, and… thank you," and he drifted off, comatose for the night.

Peggy and I had spent twenty-five years apart, but we had traveled together. We marveled that each had found healing using many of the same recovery strategies. While Dad was asleep, Peggy spoke softly, "I always wonder what my life might have been like if I hadn't had all this pain and sorrow to deal with."

"I've wondered the same thing, too, Peggy. But this is our life, our journey. It's what was given to us, and I've learned to accept that this is my path." We embraced one another for long moments, receiving sisterly love and a deeper connection.

## April 11-12, 2019

I drove back to Reno. Dad was eating lunch downstairs. He was re-markably lucid and recognized me. After lunch he took a nap; I talked to him because I now knew he would hear me. "Dad, I want you to know that Peggy, Diane, and I forgive you.

Whatever went wrong, it doesn't matter because we love you. We have always loved you and we always will." Then I read two chapters from the book of John to him.

I stayed two nights and three days. When it was time for me to leave, tears formed in Dad's eyes as he pleaded, "I wish you could stay. Can you stay?"

"Dad, I can't stay." Tears rolled down my cheeks.

"Why not? You're my daughter. Oh, I wish you could stay." After twenty-seven years of living alone, I can only imagine the depth of his loneliness. "It's not right that we should be parted." His grandmothers lived with his family when he was a boy, and he fully expected that in old age he would live with his daughters. I knew some families did things differently than we were able to do. I agreed: *We shouldn't be parted at this precious and precarious time in life.*

My psyche has a limit as to how much time I can spend with my dad without losing my sense of well-being, but still, I wished I could stay. Coming back home and being with friends and family grounded me. I explained my conflict with a Christian friend who reassured me, "You are doing the best you can. It requires a lot to drive over to Reno and back again. This is your time to help your father die, something you only get to do once. And you're doing well to have spent as much time as you have."

### April 21, 2019

Ten days later, I felt compelled to return. He mumbled, and what I could understand made no sense. He knew he was dependent, something that must have been difficult to accept for such a determined man. I'd never seen him submit to anyone, but that day he said to his caregiver, "What do you want me to do? I'll do anything you tell me to do."

I spent the day with him, sitting close by and reading out loud while he slept. When he woke up momentarily, I greeted him and fed him a bit of food. That afternoon, while he slept, I sat next to him again. I held his hand and stroked it, admiring the wrinkles and bulging veins from a long lifetime of service and many difficulties. My thoughts gently wandered as I beheld this poor, sick, dying man who was my father. I could feel my genuine compassion was leading me to a deeper forgiveness. I was in awe of what God was doing in me and my thoughts morphed into personal revelations. *God, I couldn't forgive him on my own. It's you. Your power is working through me to forgive him, and now I ask you: please forgive my dad through me.* A well-known scripture finally made sense to me: "If you forgive anyone's sins, their sins are forgiven; if you do not forgive them, they are not forgiven. (John 20:23) *God, you are completing something in me. Keep working. Work your forgiveness in me, through me to my dad and my family.*

Over the last forty years of faith-based living, my petitions to Jesus were for wholeness and healing. I doubted not Jesus' intervention and participation in my life. On earth, Jesus demonstrated his care for the sick, mentally ill, impoverished, and marginalized people. *Jesus cares about me. And Jesus loves my dad, too!*

God's compassion held me in deep reverence for some time. Gazing lovingly at my dad as he lay in his recliner, a silent whisper drifted through my mind. I saw a window open with a yellow frame, and the whisper wafted to me on a breeze. A current coursed through my body—my body from his seed. *God is in me. Jesus abides in me.* In awe, I recited Acts 17:28, "For in him we live and move and have our being." *Through me, God has forgiven Dad! The forgiveness work is complete.* This revelation transfixed me. I sat in stillness, the dawning of peace came from an other-worldly presence and brought my mind and body into harmony, homeostasis. *Joy.* I breathed deeply. The Holy Spirit moved through me. Love lifted me, and in one dawning moment, the whole of my life's journey made sense. *The wrong shall fail, the right prevail, with peace on earth, goodwill toward men. O God! You came to me. Even my dad, with his faults of selfishness, anguish, and anger, is forgiven. Even my dad, who rejected Your overtures of love. You know the things that happened to him to make him the way he is. God. I am so grateful for your forgiveness.* "Taste and see that the Lord is good, blessed is the one who takes refuge in him." (Psalm 36:8)

Eternity came to me, touched me, and in that moment I remembered the good I had done in Dad's life. *Take him home, Lord God, and let me see him again in heaven.* A few moments later, I heard a voice say, "Gaynelle, all is forgiven."

*All? Ahhh…Mom, Dad, me. All is forgiven. Any hurt I've caused and guilt I've carried, my worries. All of it: Forgiven. Believing I wasn't good enough to receive Your love? Forgiven. Tearing my hair out, risking others' lives by driving out-of-control: Forgiven. Randy's and my dysfunctions and quarreling: Forgiven. All is forgiven.*

When I left on Saturday, Dad tried to drink through a straw, but he couldn't manage it. He had no sucking power, so he started chewing on it. I held out a glass of water and after he'd had a sip, I kissed him goodbye. I told him he was loved and forgiven. Then, knowing this would be my last time with him on earth, I employed all my strength, much as I had when I'd said goodbye to my Mom, and turned to walk away. I didn't look back—I couldn't. On the way home, my wailing reverberated inside the car. I reflected on Jesus hanging from the Cross, saying, "Father, forgive them, for they do not know what they are doing." (Luke 23:34)

The commandment: Forgive. God forgave the tattered men who drove the nails into Jesus' hands and feet. Even them.

Four years later, I reflected on this time with Dad. *Hey, there was no window with a yellow frame in Dad's room.* The memory was so clear that when I tell this story of God's action in my life, I see that open, yellow-framed window in my mind, feel the breeze coming through it, and I would testify that it was real.

### May 31, 2019

It's been seven weeks since I last saw Dad. I am in Ashland, Oregon, with Jerry. We attended the Shakespeare play, *As You Like It.* "O the splendor of death that waits for us all. The meek inherit the earth and the earth inherits us all."

This quote was one of my dad's favorites. He strutted around the house, repeating this, and crowing, "All the world's a stage, And all the men and women merely players. They have their exits and their entrances, And one man in his time plays many parts, His acts being seven ages." *How is it, God, that you would use Shakespeare on this night to soothe me?* I had been struggling with a bit of guilt about not being with Dad to hold his hand when he was on the brink of death. But here, in Ashland, was my dad's voice speaking to me through the words of the play. *I am where I am supposed to be, with my husband, not with Dad.* Over the years, Peggy, Diane, and I had worked together to meet Dad's needs, and we covered for each other when one of us was unable to help out. Peggy and I had plans we couldn't change, but I trusted Diane and her husband would come through for us. *No one wants to die alone God. Please give my father the gift of family beside him. Please.*

## June 1, 2019

The next morning, Diane called to say she was with Dad and that the hospice nurse wondered why he could not let go. "She asked me to call everyone," Diane said. "I've already called my boys, and Peggy and her kids too. The nurse said it would give Dad comfort to hear our voices and help him let go. She said it didn't matter that he is comatose. He can hear us." Diane held the phone up to his ear and I spoke loudly, "Dad, this is Gaynelle. I love you so much. All is forgiven, Dad." I paused. "Look for your sisters, Lucile, and Holly. Do you see them? Do you see your Mom bidding you to come to her and waiting to greet you? Look for Granny, Dad. All her life, and in heaven too, she prayed for you because she loves you so much. She is there waiting for you to come to her. We are all fine and taken care of. Dad, we are glad for your life and that you were our father. But now it's time to let go. You're safe now and you can go home to your family."

Ten minutes later, Diane's call came in. "Dad passed." Her voice was full of joy. "What was extraordinary was that Dad's door was open, and down the hall in the lobby, a gospel choir was singing hymns! It uplifted us. I felt close to Jesus. I knew God was speaking to me and helping me. It was just what I needed. We were blessed! God is so good!

Dad's last days and his death felt miraculous. God's grace and mercy showed up in real-time. From death came a new life, and this new life began for me with the freedom of forgiveness, not the forgiveness I tried to create, but a deeper soul stretch, Deep calling to Deep. "You shall know the truth and the truth will set you free." (John 8:32) *The truth, the truth of the power of forgiveness, set me free. "All is Forgiven."* My guilt, fear, and anxiety, cleansed. I carry these moments in my heart, these feelings, this knowing, every day of my life. The future shines brightly before me, beckoning me forward in joy. God is playing the music of my tears, tears of healing, tears of forgiveness, tears of joy.

*Jesus said, "…so I have loved you. Now remain in my love I have told you this that my joy may be in you and that your joy may be complete. …You are my friends, … This is my command: Love each other."* John 15: 9-17

## CHAPTER 32

# Radical Compassion

*Compassion is that singular quality of heart that has the
power to transform resentment into forgiveness, hatred
into friendliness, anger into loving kindness.*

CHRISTIANA FELDMAN AND JACK KORNFIELD

I've been brought to a place of peace and harmony where my heart, mind, and soul are integrated and I feel whole. I am forgiven and I go forth in freedom and singing, *Spirit, open my heart, to the joy and pain of living, as You love may I love, in receiving and in giving.*[83] Forgiveness and mercy are God's grace put on full display.

I may be poised to sail my boat, but unless the sail fills with wind, the breath of the Holy Spirit, I am dead in the water. I love the ocean. I can count on the fact that I can walk out on the beach and witness the ebb and flow of waves thrust upon the shore by a great power we know is there but cannot be seen. So is it with God.

The ever-present seas have lulls, and I bobble around, waiting. Other times, waves rock my tiny boat, or the white caps wash over the bow. The Lord comes and calms the storms, then fills my sails. The gentle salty breeze caresses my face and tussles my hair. Eventually, I glide through safe waters and make land. Life, our great teacher, holds me still alive as I sail under God's constant watch. I have grown to know *myself*, and as this happens, I continue to make peace with my past.

*Dear God, be good to me. The sea is so wide and my boat is so small.*
The Brenten Fisherman's Prayer

# Epilogue

Perhaps you know someone who has experienced trauma or has had difficulties coping with a life-threatening trauma, whether those circumstances were perceived or real. Someone you know or love may be dealing with aggression, addiction, depression, post-traumatic stress disorder (PTSD), or suicidal thoughts. They may be concerned about issues that are affecting them in unhealthy or unproductive ways. Perhaps that person is you.

I prayed for help and help came. God helps those who ask. "You do not have because you do not ask God." (James 4:2) Despite the popular slogan, 'God helps those who help themselves,' there is nothing in the Bible to support this idea. I asked for help because I was lost. I had nowhere else to turn. I found One who offered me healing and understanding.

My college roommate was diagnosed with Multiple Sclerosis when she was twenty-one. As she grew older her pain became more intense. When I asked her what her pain felt like, she answered, "It's like a thousand spiders crawling all over me, and every time they take a step, they shock me." Of the people with MS, she was one of three percent that had that variety of the disease. Still, she always said, "I'm so glad I got MS, or I never would have known the Lord. He is worth whatever I needed to find him. I am healed." Every day I see someone less fortunate than I am. No one has a perfect life, and no one gets it all. *So it's ok, God, that I feel whatever I feel in the moment.* In accepting my feelings, whatever they are, I appreciate who I am, who I have become. I love life and myself.

Diane and I developed a new relationship. Thankfully, she did not suffer from sexual abuse (I protected her when she was very young, and later one grandfather died and other got too old.) However, my parents' obsession with golf and bridge left her feeling disregarded and alone. She married and they had three sons.

After Randy's and my divorce, we had a semi-cordial relationship. Randy remarried twice and died of leukemia in 2013.

Recently Peggy and I spent three days together. We shared and laughed as sisters do, and she told me things I didn't know. "You were so special to me, you were the most adorable little girl. Mom encouraged me to play with you, it made me happy to see you laugh. I dressed you in the clothes that I picked out for you. When I came home from school, you ran into my arms and hugged me and it made me feel so good. Mom and Grandma told me that I would be a wonderful mother. I wouldn't be who I am today without you in my life." Wow! I'm going to carry those words with me for a long time—what a gift!

Peggy also told me that my mother cried at night because she missed me. "She knew she'd done something that kept you away from her. She didn't know what it was and she was sad about it." *So she did want a relationship with me, as much as I did with her. Deep in her heart, she loved me.* I felt sad for her and for me, yet I was so glad to hear she cared. Another gem of truth revealed.

May God bless and keep you, and guide your journey.

With Peace and Love,

*Gaynelle Gooch*

# Acknowledgments

IT TAKES A TEAM. *Thank you everyone!*

I am grateful for the support and comfort I have received over the years from counselors, relatives, friends, and the whole of the church. They have participated in my healing in a variety of ways.

I am especially touched and grateful for my kind and generous husband, Jerry, who has taken an active interest in this project, which is to say, interest in me. Because of his unwavering support and encouragement, I walk a little taller and express loving smiles more often. His thoughtfulness and kind deeds pulled me through some rough surf. He coordinates the business part of this project. My heart is full of appreciation for his constant positive outlook and warm hugs.

Libby Knight, my editor in chief and life long friend, spent countless hours visiting with me and rehashing my childhood memories. My book began with jumbled, rambling stories. She asked me questions and we delved into the meanings of the stories we chose to include. We cobbled them into a context to make sense to the reader. Without her expertise, my writing would not have the power and meaning that the two of us developed. Her patience and friendship, understanding and compassion fills me with gratitude and amazement. Her valuable knowledge as to the flow of a story is immeasurable.

Lauren Mesa found time to read the story aloud with me and gave me valuable feedback. She showed me how to include details that made a difference in the context of the story. Lauren is a devoted Christian who understood what I wanted to communicate.

Michael Tonetti is a friend, professional massage therapist, and author of the book, *The Tonetti Method*. There was a lot of trauma stored in the muscles in my body, and for thirty years he has been healing my psyche, my self, my pain, through deep tissue massage. He encouraged me to have faith in my book and to keep working until I was truly satisfied with the manuscript. His healing touch kept me free of knots and pains so I could keep writing.

When I started writing out memories, my older sister, Peggy, offered me her cabin where I could be alone and write. In the quiet of the woods, I found a safe space to start writing. In her sisterly thoughtfulness, I felt the same light I felt when we were kids. My life is filled with gratitude.

My friends, Marva Knox, Laura Coe, Annella Beattie, Trudi Stettler, Pam Scott, and Sharon Barnhard selflessly gave of their time to read sections of the manuscript. Their insights helped me refine the text and find direction.

I wish to thank Shannon Coon, a pastor and mentor in Presbyterian churches, currently serving at St. Andrew's Presbyterian Church in Newport Beach, CA. She is genuine, compassionate, and an excellent teacher. She is currently working on her PhD at Fuller Seminary in Pasadena. During her ministry at Bidwell Presbyterian in Chico, she became a trusted confidant and friend. I deeply appreciate Shannon's outreach, her insights and encouragement.

Thank you to Greg Cootsona, PhD, a published author of nine books, for reading my book and believing in its value. Our conversations were enlightening and his suggestions and encouragement for publishing were helpful.

Thanks to Leonard Matheson, PhD, a neurorehabilitation psychologist, and founder of *Your Faithful Brain Institute*, for verifying my understanding of the terminology used in brain science and psychology. Frequently people use these words casually, and I wanted to convey accurate vocabulary in layman's terms. His expertise and counsel kept me working on this project.

Many thanks to Jody Colvard, my publicist at *FMG Press*, who guided me through to the completion and publication of this book.

I give thanks to my parents: my life was woven with theirs. In a parallel and mutual journey, we learned the power of compassion and forgiveness.

And, Thanks be to God, The Man Who Split Time, and the Holy Spirit.

# Suggested Reading

Gabor Maté, M.D. *When the Body Says NO, Exploring the Stress-Disease Connection.*

Gabor Maté, MD. *The Myth of Normal: Trauma, Illness, and Healing in a Toxic Culture.*

Brene Brown, PhD., L.M.S.W. *The Gifts of Imperfection, Let Go of who You Think You're Supposed to Be and Embrace Who You Are, Your Guide to a Wholehearted Life.*

Brene Brown, PhD., L.M.S.W. *The Power of Vulnerability, Teachings of Authenticity, Connection, and Courage.*

Janet Geringer Woititz, Ed.D. *Adult Children of Alcoholics, Expanded Edition.*

Lysa Terkeurst. *Good Boundaries and Goodbyes, Loving others without Losing the Best of Who you Are.*

David E. Clark, PhD, with William G. Clark, MA. *Enough is Enough, A Step-by-Step Plan to Leave an Abusive Relationship with God's Help.*

Anne Lamott. *Help! Wow! Thanks! The Three Essential Prayers.*

Stephen Segaller and Merrill Berger. *The Wisdom of the Dream, The World of C.G. Jung.*

Ronald, J Frederick, PhD. *Loving Like you Mean It; Use the Power of Emotional Mindfulness to Transform your Relationships.*

L J Saylors, #DELETE, *Navigating the Narcissist WEB, Recover Your Hard Drive After Narcissistic Abuse.*

Bruce D. Perry, M.D., Ph.D., and Oprah Winfrey. *What Happened to You? Conversations on Trauma, Resilience, and Healing.*

Patricia Evans, *The Verbally Abusive Relationship, how to recognize it and how to respond*, expanded edition.

Kristin Neff, PhD, and Christopher Germer, PhD. *The Mindful Self-Compassion Workbook, A Proven Way to Accept Yourself, Build Inner Strength, and Thrive.*

John Teasdale, Mark Williams, and Sindel Segal. *The Mindful Way Workbook, an 8-Week Program to Free yourself from Depression and Emotional Distress.*

Leonard Matheson, PhD. *Your faithful Brain, Designed for So Much More!*

Thomas Moore, Mother Teresa, *No Greater Love*. The Most Accessible and Inspirational Collection of Her Teachings Ever Published.

John Trent, PhD, and Gary Smalley. *The Blessing, Giving the Gift of Unconditional Love and Acceptance.*

Wallace J. Nichols. *Blue Mind, the Surprising Science That Shows How Being near, in, on, or under Water Can Make You Happier, Healthier, More Connected, and Better at What You Do.*

Greg Cootsona. *Say Yes to No, Using the Power of NO to Create the Best Life, Work, Love.*

Bessel van der Kolk, M.D., *The Body Keeps Score, Brain, Mind, and Body in the Healing of Trauma.*

Elizabeth Kubler Ross, On Death and Dying, *What the dying have to teach doctors, nurses, clergy, and their own family.*

Matthew Kelly, *Rediscover Jesus, An Invitation.*

Bessel van der Kolk, *The Body Keeps Score.*

Tim Madigan, *I'm Proud of You, Life Lessons from My Friend Fred Rogers.*

# Glossary Basic Vocabulary in Brain Science

**Agency:** A technical term for the feeling of overseeing one's life and knowing where you stand, that you have a say in what happens to you, and that you have some ability to shape your circumstances. [12]

**Amygdala:** Closely related to the thalamus and hippocampus, which are part of the limbic system of the brain. The amygdala is one of the first brain structures to develop in infancy, providing babies with sensory information and emotions. [13]

**Attunement:** The ability to find harmony and understanding within the context of one's being. For an attuned individual, feelings are attached to thoughts. Attunement means memories are "strong enough to retrieve the images, emotions, sounds, tastes, and smells." [14] These sensory experiences intertwine and make associations in the brain that make sense to an individual.

**Autonomic Nervous System:** The part of the vertebrate parasympathetic and sympathetic nervous system that stimulates and arouses actions that are more or less automatic (body secretions, constriction of blood vessels to increase blood pressure, swallowing, blinking, heart rate). [15]

**Cortex:** The analytical, thinking and reasoning part of the brain is located at the front part of the brain; which contains the gray matter and neurons that control many of our cognitive processes. The neocortex is the largest part of the cortex, having many functions and patterns of connections. [16]

**Dissociation:** A phenomenon "which is manifested in feeling lost, overwhelmed, abandoned and disconnected from the world and seeing oneself as unloved, empty, helpless, trapped, and weighed down." [17]

Dissociation often results in a "loss of self- regulation."[18]

**Emotional Brain:** The heart of the central nervous system. The emotional brain is composed of the reptilian brain and the limbic system. The emotional brain causes sensations that have a huge influence on the small and large decisions we make throughout our lives. It initiates pre-programmed escape plans like the fight or flight responses.[19]

**EMDR:** Eye Movement Desensitization and Reprocessing: a process therapists use to facilitate their clients' communications to calm an overactive limbic system (fight, flight, or freeze responses).

**Hippocampus:** New information is temporarily stored here before emotional salient memories are transferred to long-term memory. The hippocampus is the doorway to your autobiographical brain that describes you to yourself.[20] "It's one of the few brain structures to grow throughout adulthood, regenerating itself constantly."[21]

**Homeostasis:** A complex set of automatic processes that constantly monitor and adjust systems in your brain and body to maintain physiologic stability and to support emotional balance.[22]

**Hypothalamus:** Modulates the body and brain's complex stress reactions and affects the immune system. It responds to the autonomic nervous system as it sends stress chemicals throughout the entire organism. It signals energy and psychological information that affects interpersonal relationships and one's relationship to self.

**Limbic System:** Also known as the mammalian brain because all animals that live in groups and nurture their young possess one. It is located above the reptilian brain.

Development of this part of the brain takes off after a baby is born. It is the seat of emotions, the monitor of danger, the judge of what is pleasurable or scary, the arbitrator of what is or is not important for survival purposes. It is also a Central Command Post for coping with the challenges of living within our complex social networks.[23]

**Neuroplasticity:** The ability of the brain to become rewired. If a part of the brain is damaged, and the damage results in a failed ability or function, the linkages among the neurons in the brain can sometimes be trained to take over the failed function.[24]

**PTSD:** Post-Traumatic Stress Disorder: A result of a fundamental reorganization of the central nervous system based on having experienced an actual threat of annihilation (or seeing someone else being annihilated, which the brain recognizes as self-experience). In PTSD, the central nervous system interprets trauma as a reality that applies to every situation and happening and sees the entire world as a dangerous place. [25]

**Reptilian Brain, Brain Stem:** The most primitive part of the brain – the ancient animal brain that develops in the womb, is in the brainstem which is located just above the place where the spinal cord enters the skull. The reptilian brain is responsible for all the things that newborn babies can do consciously: eat, sleep, wake, cry, breathe; feel their temperature, wetness, and pain. The reptilian brain rids the body of toxins by urinating and defecating. The brainstem and hypothalamus (which sits directly above it), control the body's energy levels. It maintains the life-sustaining systems. [26]

**Synch (cync):** An attunement to oneself and others requiring "the integration of our body-based senses: vision, hearing, touch, and balance."[27] Sync refers to a connection with others that gives feedback helping us to create an autobiographical story for everyone.

**Thalamus:** The central relay station for most of a person's sensory data. Everything the body senses, other than smell, is routed through the thalamus and transmitted elsewhere.[28]

**Trauma:** A psychological or emotional stress or blow that may produce disordered feelings or behavior; an inescapable state or condition of mental or emotional shock produced by stress or physical injury. [29] [30]

**Vagal Complex:** A nerve system located in the reptilian brain which serves as the last resort, the ultimate emergency system where the body signals defeat and withdrawal, then collapse.[31] It sends motor messages to the heart, lungs, palate, pharynx, larynx, trachea, liver, and GI tract. It sends sensory messages to the heart, lungs, trachea, bronchi, larynx, pharynx, GI tract, and external ear.

**Visceral:** A gut or core physical reaction that runs through the blood and bones of one's body. It is felt in the body and is noticeable in the gut, chest, lungs, heart, throat, and other parts of the body.

# Resource List

## CHAPTER ONE

**1**  p. 10 Lucado, Max. Grace for the Moment, Volume II. J Countryman, A Division of Thomas Nelson, Inc.,Nashville, T,. 2006. p.39.

## CHAPTER TWO

**2**  p. 20 Morgan, Robert J., 300 of the World's Greatest Hymn Stories, Then Sings My Soul, Nelson Reference and Electronic, 2006, pp. 248-249.

**3**  p. 20 Ibid., The Psalm referenced in this song, God Rest Ye Merry Gentlemen is Psalm 121:4 Behold, He who keeps Israel shall neither slumber nor sleep

**4**  p. 21 Webster's Third New International Dictionary, Vol. II. G. & C. Merriam Co. 1971, p. 1414.

## CHAPTER ELEVEN

**5**  p. 79 King, Martin Luther. Jr., PhD., Strength to Love, Beacon Press, Boston, MA,1963 198. p. 19.
**6**  p. 79 Ibid., Morgan, Robert J., p. 248-9.
**7**  p. 80 Andersen, Noel. Sermon, 2011

## CHAPTER THIRTEEN

**8**  p. 89 Peck, Morgan. Scientific American Mind. "Pain Lessens Guilt, Physical Discomfort Can Alleviate Mental Suffering.". No.3. May 2011, p. 22.

## CHAPTER TWENTY

**9**  p. 166 Deirdre Barrett. "Answers in your Dreams." Scientific American Mind. November/December 2011, pp. 27-29.

## CHAPTER TWENTY-FIVE

**10**  p. 209 Jung, Carl. The Undiscovered Self, Routledge, New York, NY, p. 32.
**11**  p. 209 Ibid., p. 33.
**12**  p. 210 van der Kolk, Bessel, M.D. The Body Keeps the Score, Brain, Mind, and Body in the Healing of Trauma. Penguin, New York, NY, 2015, p.97.
*See Glossary Entry, "Agency".*
**13**  p. 210 Matheson, Leonard, M.D. Your Faithful Brain, Designed for So Much More. Westbow Press (A Division of Thomas Nelson and Zondervan), Bloomington, IN, 2018, p. 95.
*See Glossary Entry, "Amygdala".*
**14**  p. 210 Ibid, pp. 58,71.
*See Glossary Entry, "Attunement".*

15  p. 210 Webster's Third International Dictionary Vol. I.,
G. & C. Merriam Co., 1971 pp.148,1165, 1166.
*See Glossary Entry, "Autonomic Nervous System".*
16  p. 210 Ibid., Matheson, p.196.
*See Glossary Entry, "Cortex".*
17  p. 210 Ibid., van der Kolk, p. 182.
*See Glossary Entry, "Dissociation".*
18  p. 210 Ibid., p. 195.
*See Glossary Entry, "Dissociation".*
19  p. 210 Ibid., p. 57.
*See Glossary Entry, "Emotional Brain".*
20  p. 210 Ibid., p. 46.
*See Glossary Entry, "Hippocampus".*
21  p. 210 Ibid., Matherson, p. 95.
*See Glossary Entry, "Hippocampus".*
22  p. 210 Ibid., p. 94.
*See Glossary Entry, "Homeostasis".*
23  p. 210 Ibid., p.56.
*See Glossary Entry, "Limbic System".*
24  p. 210 Ibid., p.81.
*See Glossary Entry, "Neuroplasticity".*
25  p. 210 Ibid. van der Kolk, p. 258.
*See Glossary Entry, "PTSD".*
26  p. 210 Ibid., p. 56.
*See Glossary Entry, "Reptilian Brain, Brain Stem".*
27  p. 210 Ibid., p.124.
*See Glossary Entry, "Synch (cync)".*
28  p. 210 Ibid., Matherson, p. 95.
*See Glossary Entry, "Thalamus".*
29  p. 210 Ibid., Webster's Vol III, p. 2432.
*See Glossary Entry, "Trauma".*
30  p. 210 Ibid., van der Kolk, p. 29.
*See Glossary Entry, "Trauma".*
31  p. 210 Ibid., p. 85.
*See Glossary Entry, "Vagal Complex".*

## CHAPTER TWENTY-SIX

32  p. 211 Ibid., p. 197.
33  p. 211 Ibid., p. 11.
34  p. 211 Ibid., p. 21.
35  p. 211 Ibid., p. 205.
36  p. 211 Ibid., p. 65.
37  p. 211 Dana, Deb. Polyvagal Exercises for Safety and Connection. W. W. Norton & Company. Inc. New
York, N.Y., 2020. p.23.
38  p. 212 Ibid., van der Kolk, pp.80-82
39  p. 213 Ibid., p.176.
40  p. 215 Ibid. pp. 84-85.
41  p. 215 Ibid.
42  p. 215 Ibid., p. 99.
43  p. 215 Ibid., p. 98.
44  p. 216 Ibid., p. 65. Frightened by someone we depend on, angry with someone we love, often results in
lusting inappropriately.
45  p. 216 Ibid., van der Kolk.
46  p. 217 Ibid., p. 64.
47  p. 219 Kelly, Matthew. Rediscover Jesus, An Invitation. Beacon Publishing, 2015. p.102.
48  p. 220 Ibid., van der Kolk, Ibid., p.72.
49  p. 220 Ibid., p.82.
50  p. 221 Ibid., Dana, Deb. p.xxiii.

## CHAPTER TWENTY-EIGHT

51  p. 233 Ibid., van der Kolk, pp.111, 113.
52  p. 236 Ibid., p. 124.
53  p. 237 Ibid., p.66.
54  p. 237 Ibid., Matheson, p 58.
55  p. 238 Ibid., p. 182.
56  p. 238 Ibid.

**57** p. 238 Ibid., p. 181.
**58** p. 238 Segellar, Stephen, and Berger, Merrill. The Wisdom of the Dream, The World of C.G. Jung. Shambhala Publications, INC., Boston, 1990. p. 26.
**59** p. 238 Ibid., p. 16,17.
**60** p. 239 Ibid., p. 58.
**61** p. 240 Ibid., van der Kolk, p. 72.
**62** p. 241 Ibid., van der Kolk pp. 243, 244
**63** p. 243 Wester's, vol. III, p. 2086
**64** p. 243 Ibid., p. 34.
**65** p. 243 Ibid., p. 111.
**66** p. 243 Ibid., p. 113.
**67** p. 243 Trent, John, PhD., Smalley, Gary. The Blessing; Giving the Gift of Unconditional Love and Acceptance. Thomas Nelson, Nashville, TN, 1986, 1993. Pp. 117-120.
**68** p. 245 Ibid.
**69** p. 246 Ibid., p.67.
**70** p. 246 Ibid.
**71** p. 246 Ibid.
**72** p. 246 Ibid.
**73** p. 247 Ibid., Matheson, p. 40.

## CHAPTER TWENTY-NINE

**74** p. 249 Ibid., van der Kolk., p. 135.
**75** p. 249 Ibid., p. 136.
**76** p. 249 Ibid., p. 182.
**77** p. 249 Ibid., p. 183.
**78** p. 249 Ibid., p. 97, 98.
**79** p. 250 Ibid., p. 124.

## CHAPTER THIRTY

**80** p. 254 Ibid., Hudson, Trevor, p. 119

**81** p. 255 Evans, Patricia. The Verbally Abusive Relationship. How to Recognize It and How to Respond. Expanded Second Edition. Adams Media Corporation, Avon, Massachusetts, 1992. P. 31
**82** p. 255 Jane Stanford's Inscriptions on the Interior Wall of Memorial Church. A Publication of Stanford Memorial Church, p. 5.

## CHAPTER THIRTY-TWO

**83** p. 273 Duck Ruth and Vedak, Alfred V., Spirit, Open My Heart. Morning Star Music Publishers, St Louis, MO. MSM-50-5556.

# Author

Gaynelle Gooch is a seasoned public-school teacher who became a keen observer of behavioral patterns and worked to influence her students to make positive changes.

She grew up in an abusive household, where both of her parents had endured similarly traumatic childhoods. Her first marriage was also marked by abuse, as her husband had faced significant challenges in his own upbringing.

Gaynelle has authored numerous short stories and children's books, with Finding Self being her first full-length work.

Her book is the culmination of a lifetime of experience and six years of dedicated study and writing. Although she does not hold a degree in psychology, she has studied the subject extensively. Gaynelle writes from the heart, drawing on her deep understanding of human behavior.

www.ingramcontent.com/pod-product-compliance
Lightning Source LLC
Chambersburg PA
CBHW051609120626
46551CB00014B/1728